UNDER DISCUSSION

Donald Hall, General Editor

Elizabeth Bishop and Her Art
  Edited by Lloyd Schwartz and Sybil P. Estess

Richard Wilbur's Creation
  Edited and with an Introduction by Wendy Salinger

Reading Adrienne Rich
  Edited by Jane Roberta Cooper

On the Poetry of Allen Ginsberg
  Edited by Lewis Hyde

Robert Bly: When Sleepers Awake
  Edited by Joyce Peseroff

Robert Bly
When Sleepers Awake

Edited by Joyce Peseroff

Ann Arbor
THE UNIVERSITY OF MICHIGAN PRESS

Copyright © by The University of Michigan 1984
All rights reserved
Published in the United States of America by
The University of Michigan Press and simultaneously
in Rexdale, Canada, by John Wiley & Sons Canada, Limited
Manufactured in the United States of America

1987   1986   1985   1984   5   4   3   2   1

Library of Congress Cataloging in Publication Data
Main entry under title

Robert Bly : when sleepers awake.

   (Under discussion)
   Bibliography: p.
   1. Bly, Robert—Criticism and interpretation—Addresses, essays, lectures.
I. Peseroff, Joyce. II. Series.
PS3552.L9Z87   1984   811'.54   84-17234
ISBN 0-472-09354-1
ISBN 0-472-06354-5 (pbk.)

Contents

Introduction   vii

Part One: Essays

Thinking About Robert Bly
   WILLIAM MATTHEWS   3

Inward to the World: The Poetry of Robert Bly
   WILLIAM HEYEN   13

Robert Bly: "Like Those Before, We Move to the
Death We Love"
   RICHARD HOWARD   23

Robert Bly Alive in Darkness
   ANTHONY LIBBY   37

Robert Bly: Watering the Rocks
   JAMES F. MERSMANN   54

Robert Bly
   EKBERT FAAS   101

Varieties of Immanentist Experience: Robert Bly
   CHARLES ALTIERI   125

"Rejoice in the Gathering Dark": The Poetry of
Robert Bly
   CHARLES MOLESWORTH   144

"Of Energy Compacted and Whirling": Robert Bly's
Recent Prose Poems
   RALPH J. MILLS, JR.   179

"Walking Where the Plows Have Been Turning":
Robert Bly and Female Consciousness
   VICTORIA HARRIS   208

Back to the Snowy Fields
   WAYNE DODD   223

Sentences as Measures in Two of Robert Bly's Prose
Poems
   DONALD WESLING   232

"Still the Place Where Creation Does Some Work on
Itself": Robert Bly's Most Recent Work
    WILLIAM V. DAVIS   237

Part Two: Reviews, Conversations, Memoirs, Poems

From the Introduction to *Contemporary American
Poetry*
    DONALD HALL   249

From "The Wesleyan Poets—III: The Experimental
Poets"
    NORMAN FRIEDMAN   251

From *Spinning the Crystal Ball*
    JAMES DICKEY   255

From "Jeremiads at Half-Mast"
    ROBERT MAZZOCCO   258

From *North of Jamaica*
    LOUIS SIMPSON   264

Notes on Robert Bly and *Sleepers Joining Hands*
    DONALD HALL   272

Instruction from Bly
    CYNTHIA MACDONALD   278

From "James Wright: The Art of Poetry XIX"
    PETER STITT   281

Two Poets Translating
    ROBERT BLY AND TOMAS TRANSTRÖMER   284

From "Three Poets"
    HUGH KENNER   298

From "Music to Your Ears"
    ALAN WILLIAMSON   300

From "Dark Volumes"
    PETER STITT   302

News From Robert Bly's Universe: *The Man in the
Black Coat Turns*
    ROBERT PETERS   304

An Interview with Robert Bly
    JOSEPH SHAKARCHI   315

Bibliography   335

Introduction

Seventy or eighty times a year, Robert Bly travels from his native Minnesota to read his poems and to speak on psychology, spirituality, politics, and literature—questions of both the outward and the inward journey. Those who come to hear his poems are just as likely to hear the poems of others, for Bly offers French prose poets and Sufi masters, South Americans and young Americans in generous measure, along with his own work. They will hear not only poems but ideas, for, more than any other of our excellent contemporary poets, Robert Bly has attracted his extensive audience by engaging the great issues of this century—in science, in religion, and in history—through his art.

For three decades Robert Bly has brought energy and vision to American poetry. Thinking about Bly, we must remember his important translations of Neruda and Vallejo, the seminal criticism he wrote and published in his magazine *The Fifties, The Sixties,* and *The Seventies,* and the books he produced for The Sixties and The Seventies, and now, The Eighties, Press. In the 1960s he cofounded Poets Against the Vietnam War, and when he won the National Book Award in 1968 for *The Light Around the Body,* he publicly donated his prize money to The Resistance.

But we must not forget that Robert Bly is first of all a poet of superb gifts who has tried to waken us all to see, with Keats, that "life is not a vale of tears but a vale of soul-making." This collection attempts to consider the nature and variety of those gifts. It is a sample of what critics have written about Robert Bly's poetry since the publication of his first book of poems, *Silence in the Snowy Fields,* in 1962. In the first section I include essays of some length, written between 1969 and 1982, which address themselves to major portions of Bly's work. In the second section, I include more fragmentary pieces—book reviews, conversations, memoirs, and poems—also published between 1962 and 1982, which give historical perspective to Bly's career. In each section I arrange pieces chronologically by year of publication, and previously unpublished material by date of composition. A bibliographical note and a selected bibliography follow the final article.

PART ONE *Essays*

WILLIAM MATTHEWS

Thinking About Robert Bly

For some people *The Light Around the Body* legitimized an incipient Bly backlash. Earlier, they compared Bly (to his disadvantage) to the poets associated with *The Sixties* and his influence. Now they remember with nostalgia the unique force of *Silence in the Snowy Fields*—its remarkable power to evoke emotions almost wholly absent from the American poetry of recent years.

For all his talk of solitude Bly has come to dominate American poetry. Young poets refer to him either with rancor or like Sunday golfers talking about Arnold Palmer. Some magazines are obsessed by him. His influence is apparent in *Tennessee Poetry Journal,* for example, where it is largely salutory. He infuriates H. L. Van Brunt, editor of *The Smith.* Van Brunt has a good idea: reviewing other little magazines in strong language; but he will veer off in any direction to vent his excessive dislike of Bly. And editor William Taylor's odd picture of James Dickey as middle-class bard in *Poetry Florida And . . ./2* is a silly defensive reaction to Bly's attack on Dickey.

Bly's incendiary criticism and crusade for the poetry he admires have annoyed many and threatened not a few. When *The Light Around the Body,* which includes some bad poems, came out, open season was declared on Bly. One young poet who heard I was going to do a piece on Bly said, "Good, it's time somebody got him." He assumed I wouldn't write for any other reason. It is very difficult to think straight about Robert Bly. I'm writing these notes to help me try.

It is nearly impossible to overemphasize the importance of Bly's criticism. John Haines was the first to say in public that there has been nothing so interesting or influential since Ezra Pound began

Tennessee Poetry Journal 2, no. 2 (1969): 49–57. Reprinted with permission.

sending reviews to *Poetry*. Poets who are also critics write not only about other poems but always, in an elaborate code, about their own—both those they have written and those they aspire to write. We can learn a lot about *The Light Around the Body* from Bly's criticism.

In his essay "Prose Vs. Poetry" in *Choice*/2 Bly writes, "The New critics and the Thirties critics urge poets to adopt sociological or cultural prose ideas as the substance of their poems." Too many poems in *The Light Around the Body* contain sociological or cultural prose ideas.

> The coffins of the poor are hibernating in piles of new tires
> ("The Great Society")

and

> We distrust every person on earth with black hair
> ("Hatred of Men with Black Hair")

and

> Men like Rusk are not men:
> They are bombs waiting to be loaded in a darkened hangar
> ("Asian Peace Offers Rejected without Publication")

are all prose ideas. The ideas may be interesting or true (though the lines about Rusk, half-true, are also half-false: a major problem is that men like Rusk *are* men). But, as Bly wrote of a Denise Levertov poem about Eichmann: "We learn much about her sensibility, but less about her secret feelings than we seem to. Her feelings about Eichmann, for example, are too much like other people's feelings to be her own." Obviously Bly doesn't mean that no recognizable idea or concept may be used in a poem. The notion that the poet's feelings can be too much like other people's feelings to be his own helps us think about what prose ideas we are disappointed to see in a poem. When we have predictable feelings about a familiar idea—Eichmann was monstrous, Rusk is dangerous—nothing new has happened; it is as if we were watching Walter Cronkite. The poet has not created a response in the reader (or in himself). He has relied on what he knew was there.

The poems in *The Light Around the Body* are based in a virile mysticism, a secular faith drawn partly from the writings of Jacob Boehme and partly from Rilke's *Letters to a Young Poet*. Like Rilke, Bly relies on the value of solitude as a condition the poet cannot escape; indeed, he cannot prize it too fiercely. From Boehme he draws the idea that there is an inner and an outer world. As Boehme wrote, "Since then we are generated out of both worlds, we speak in two languages, and we must be understood also by two languages." A glow around the body would show that the two worlds have met there.

Some poems in the book stay in the outer world while the poet seethes inside his skin—these are the poems overloaded with prose ideas. Others want to go infinitely inward, like the vanishing perspective of a High Renaissance painting. Look at these lines from "Evolution from the Fish":

> A man goes inside a jewel, and sleeps. Do
> Not hold my hands down! Let me raise them!
> A fire is passing up through the soles of my feet!

and from "Moving Inward at Last":

> When the smoke touches the roof of the cave,
> The green leaves burst into flame,
> The air of night changes to dark water,
> The mountains alter and become the sea.

Compared to the superb poem "Romans Angry about the Inner World," these poems are about longing for the inner world, not about a real relation between the inner and outer worlds.

> What shall the world do with its children?
> There are lives the executives

Know nothing of,
A leaping of the body,
The body rolling—and I have felt it—
And we float
Joyfully on the dark places;
But the executioners
Move toward Drusia. They tie her legs
On the iron horse. "Here is a woman
Who has seen our mother
In the other world!" Next they warm
The hooks. The two Romans had put their trust
In the outer world. Irons glowed
Like teeth. They wanted her
To assure them. She refused. Finally they took burning
Pine sticks, and pushed them
Into her sides. Her breath rose
And she died. The executioners
Rolled her off onto the ground.
A light snow began to fall
And covered the mangled body,
And the executives, astonished, withdrew.
The other world is like a thorn
In the ear of a tiny beast!
The fingers of the executives are too thick
To pull it out!
It is like a jagged stone
Flying toward them out of the darkness.

Bly's belief in the value of solitude enforces his faith in the language of the inner world considered apart from the language of the outer world. We get Robert Bly, solitary saint.

Yet this man is housed in the same body with Robert Bly, fiery preacher, who reminds me of D. H. Lawrence.

Like Lawrence, Bly is interested in the spirit of nature, the dark gods, and in a meaningful secularization of religious energies. These lines are from the important poem, "Turning Away from Lies" (in an early issue of his magazine, Bly quotes Lawrence: "The first freedom is the freedom from lies"):

> Christ did not come to redeem our sins
> The Christ Child was not obedient to his parents
> The Kingdom of Heaven does not mean the next life
> No one in business can be a Christian
> The two worlds are both in this world

Like Lawrence, Bly believes that too much intellection throttles the imagination. And Bly's active encouragement of harsh criticism and literacy feuding sounds like Lawrence advising husbands and wives to fly at each other until no antagonism is hidden.

Living in Zennor, Cornwall, in 1917, Lawrence and his German wife Frieda found themselves the objects of a persecution supported by war hysteria. One night when they were dining with friends police burst in and accused Frieda of signaling to a German submarine they imagined lurking off the coast. The Lawrences were forced to move away from the coast and were under surveillance for the rest of the war. In *Kangaroo* Lawrence has a chapter about his reaction to these incidents. "He had always *believed* so in everything—society, love, friends. This was one of his serious deaths in belief." These lines by Bly show a similar despair:

> That is why these poems are so sad
> The long dead running over the fields
> ("Those Being Eaten by America")

and

> There is a bitter fatigue, adult and sad
> ("Listening to President Kennedy Lie about
> the Cuban Invasion")

and

> . . . one woman climbed
> A high elm above her lawn,
> Opened a box, and swallowed poisonous spiders. . . .
> ("Hurrying Away from the Earth")

7

Kangaroo is a violent novel, attempting to wrench Lawrence free from a bitter despair. *The Light Around the Body* has the same quality; it is Bly's attempt to save himself from the horror of the Asian War without, as no moral man could contemplate, ignoring it.

In his review "Moths in the Light" in *Kayak*/14, Louis Z. Hammer notices many instances when feet and "similar extremities wander off by themselves. Bly," he says, "has made this sort of thing into a cliché." These images are related to many images of disintegration, splitting, explosion. Some are:

> The filaments of the soul slowly separate:
> The spirit breaks, a puff of dust floats up,
> Like a house in Nebraska that suddenly explodes.
> ("Watching Television")

and

Those shredded inner tubes abandoned on the shoulders of thruways,
Black and collapsed bodies that tried and burst
("Come with Me")
and

> One leg walks down the road and leaves
> The other behind, the eyes part
> And fly off in opposite direction.
> ("War and Silence")

Whatever these images suggest in the poems, it is clear to me they are also about Bly, who is violently fighting the tendency of the outer and inner worlds to fly off in opposite directions, each carrying a part of Bly—the saint to the inner world and the preacher to the outer.

The war was brought on in Bly another similarity to Lawrence, a tendency to preach. Some consider this an unbearable breach of decorum, like burping at table; I do not. I am tired of the ironists who sit around protecting themselves with cynicism while men like Bly, Dr. Spock, and Rev. Coffin go out on a limb. I'm glad that poets have begun to write about politics and the tone of national life, which they cannot honestly fail to notice. Furthermore, preaching gives expression to a side of Bly's personality which he has suppressed in his poetry. He obviously enjoys his roles of editor and critic; he enjoys literary correspondence; he enjoys his antiwar activity though he detests that it is appropriate. There are moving poems in *Silence in the Snowy Fields* about drinking with friends, being near friends, driving to town late at night to mail a letter. These themes don't appear in the new book. Friends are no longer people whom one loves no matter what; there are instead those who have made the right moral decisions: "the small colonies of the saved." This is an unhappy by-product of preaching.

Or maybe I should put it this way: Bly has written of the attribute of some Oriental poets, "good will toward the self." *Silence in the Snowy Fields* is filled with it. The Asian War and the stifling of the inner life in America disrupt this hard-won peace. In *The Light Around the Body* there is a more muscular, rhetorical, ambitious style. Its ambition is to hold the saint and the preacher together. Many people talk about the book's style as if it were an excess in manner, like wearing spats to bed. It's clear though that Bly's style has changed for a reason: to cope with and discover new content. There are crucial issues at stake: reading the book, we watch a man trying to deal with them.

Of course there are failed poems in the book. I have named some I didn't like and tried to say why. The title image is richly suggestive. Some poems leap into the outer world in a mixture of fury and compassion; but they bog down in prose ideas and outer-world debate. Others dive inward in despair and an attempt to stay whole. But it is at the meeting point of the two worlds where the whole man wants to be. Never mind that he cannot stay there, that he is always shooting by like a skier who hasn't learned to stop yet. Still, he is always aiming for that balance, though he knows it will not hold. The best poems in *The Light Around the Body* contain the apparent paradox of seeking a balance that will not hold. It is a risky enterprise.

An attractive feature of Bly's Vietnam poems and antiwar activity is the willingness to take risks. The timidity of much recent poetry and of polite political protest is completely absent. Though ironists love to disparage Bly for this, it is an important part of literary life in the 1960s and Bly is greatly responsible for its being in the air. One form it has taken is a willingness to move ahead, to follow one's own instincts in the face even of lavish praise from those whose praise is conventionally considered valuable. The careers of James Wright and W. S. Merwin exemplify this, and the change between *Silence in the Snowy Fields* and *The Light Around the Body* shows Bly's refusal to repeat what he has already learned.

Compare this need to move on to the conventional poet's career. In his youth he is encouraged to "expand his range" rather than write about the subjects and imagery that obsess him. When he has "found his voice" he uses it on everything, like a Swiss Army Knife. It becomes his only achievement and the real subject of all his poems. Poets like Charles Bukowski and Larry Eigner are typical of this pattern.

Important critical pieces by Bly are the "Crunk" essays in *The Sixties* (especially the piece on James Wright in /8; the essay on Gary Snyder in /6 is the only "Crunk" article Bly didn't do), the omnibus review in *Choice*/2 and the essay "A Wrong Turning in American Poetry" in *Choice*/3, and the introductory essay to the Sixties Press book *The Lion's Tail and Eyes*. The best thing I've seen on Bly's earlier poetry is Douglas Collins's letter to the editors in *Lillabulero*/4. The most interesting comments on *The Light Around the Body* are in Hammer's essay, though my interest has generally taken the form of disagreement.

Hammer's piece may reflect the "get Bly" psychology I mentioned earlier. He badly misreads "Opening an Oyster," one of the best poems in the book. He says he is tired of the image of a murdered prince, which Bly has used in only one other poem I know. He calls the book "a disappointing collection" though he says there are ten poems in it that are "unquestionably good." In my opinion that is a low estimate; but, more important, the only other book published in 1967 with more unquestionably good poems in it was Merwin's *The Lice*.

But Hammer has a very interesting idea: he talks about Bly's advertisements for the inner world, which have a tendency "to impose a moral earnestness on the irrational life below the conscious mind." His suggested remedy for Bly is that he "allow himself to be inundated by the world so that the poem can be a torrent and a dance." It is too mystical for me to believe.

I'm not sure Bly needs a remedy. One thing nobody noticed about *Silence in the Snowy Fields* is its moral seriousness. Most people have talked about the book as if its great achievement were the development of a personal formula—a spare syntax bearing rich imagery—for presenting emotions. Clearly, though, the book is concerned with placing man in the universe, seeking a basis for moral judgment, and with the conflict between any person's need for human contact and the poet's special need for solitude and inwardness. And at no time does he pretend he has solved these problems. The book instead moves toward a consistent attitude toward them: one not so firm it will construct a falsely fixed model, but one coherent enough to give a man integrity. I cannot think what problems might be more important to a poet.

The problem, I take it, is that a man must be morally serious; he must want to be honest. Traditionally, moral understanding is grounded in metaphysics; a metaphysical system guarantees that a moral understanding drawn from it is not capricious. But systems are false: as D'Annunzio had it, "Anatomy presupposes a corpse." This is not a new but an enduring problem. So one tries to base an honest life on an understanding of experience that will not fix, systematize, or otherwise falsify experience. Poetry is a very subtle tool—art is subtler than the intellect—for this impossible job.

To put it too simply, Robert Creeley is always talking to and James Wright about himself. Everyone knows they are serious. Because Bly comes at it more obliquely, some readers miss the point and talk about his style.

Of course earnestness alone will not make a reader share that worthy intention. It is important to notice what poems don't mean as much to us as others. Some poems in *The Light Around the Body* flatly fail for me. Because the book attacks crucial problems, problems I recognize because they haunt my own life, I find the book exciting and painful to read. It is not a "lesser" book than the first one. The good poems are wonderful. Only Bly could have written them.

Bly could become too much embroiled in the outer world. He could become like André Breton—self-consciously a leader of a literary movement, a literary figure in radical politics, a man who diffused a great talent (if you doubt that, read *Nadja*) in too public a life.

In reaction to that possibility he could become a mystical believer in a solitude that excises the legitimate pleasures of human contact and seeks, finally, only to uphold itself.

Too, he could write too much criticism, lessening energies and instincts that would otherwise drive his poems.

My guess, though—even the failures in *The Light Around the Body* confirm it—is that he will continue to take risks, to over-reach. He will continue to face important questions in his poems. I imagine his new poems are already moving toward new dilemmas. Bly has tremendous imaginative power. A serious application of it should produce wonderful poems, as it has many times. Because he has been personally overpublicized and because his literary personality is strong and dominating, we need not fail to notice his bad poems, his achievement and power, the new air his poems and essays allow us to breathe, and the pleasure we take in the difficulty of thinking about Robert Bly.

WILLIAM HEYEN

Inward to the World
The Poetry of Robert Bly

I

For several years I disliked what Robert Bly had done in *Silence in the Snowy Fields* (1962). Indeed, I was surprised that the book had even made it into print. His risks, I felt, were all bad ones. And his dust jacket remarks to the effect that "any poetry in the poems . . . is in the white spaces between the stanzas" offended me. I didn't expect these poems. The ones I had happened to read, in magazines and in the first selection of *New Poets of England and America,* were noisier, more ambitious. I thought that his collection was a mistake, a group of journal jottings.

Where was his "heightened speech"? How, if to suggest something is to create it and to state something is to destroy it, could he write lines such as "I have awakened at Missoula, Montana, utterly happy" ("In a Train") and "There is a privacy I love in this snowy night" ("Driving to Town Late to Mail a Letter")? Didn't he know such bare statements were against the rules?

How could he employ the "pathetic fallacy" with such carelessness? I looked on such images as

And I know the sun is sinking down great stairs,
Like an executioner with a great blade walking into a cellar . . .
                ("The Clear Air of October")

as combinations of cliché and absurdity.

The Far Point 3 (1969): 42–50. Reprinted with permission.

Didn't he know enough not to use the word "strange"? Why did he repeat the words "dark" and "darkness" dozens of times? How could he be naive enough to use so many exclamation marks when everyone knows that this shows his language isn't bearing the weight of his emotion? How, in the Age of Eliot, could he write poems that defied serious inquiry and involved explication? What did these poems *mean*? I couldn't surround them, couldn't grip them, couldn't imagine discussing them. What could one say about them?

Silence in the Snowy Fields was like a cluster of gnats. No matter what else I did, I couldn't remain neutral about Bly's poems. It will be impossible for me to discuss my change of mind rationally, but I've come to believe that my reservations about Bly were only nigglings, that measuring the accomplishment of his work against petty objections is something like dismissing *Moby-Dick* because Melville loses track of his point of view. Bly is free from the inhibitions of critical dictates many of us have regarded as truths. He manages, in fact, to write poems that are themselves suspensions of the critical faculty. The poems had to become what they are. They are quiet, unassuming. They are uninsistent, unrhetorical; they depend, often, on one another for total effect. They do not lead to the kind of intellectual pleasure (an antipoetic pleasure) one gets from having traced down all the allusions in *The Waste Land* or from having used the unabridged dictionary to come to terms with "The Comedian as the Letter C."

In the full senses of the words these are—may I attach labels to poems that defeat labels?—"symbolic" and "mystical" poems. Yeats said that "the mind liberated from the pressure of the will is unfolded in symbols." He said that a symbol gives "body to something beyond the senses," that "any one who has any experience of any mystical state of the soul knows how there float up in the mind profound symbols, whose meaning, if indeed they do not delude one into the dream that they are meaningless, one does not perhaps understand for years." The emotional meanings of a symbol, the meanings beyond words, can never be exhausted.

Bly's poems do not wear thin. Our inner lives speak in them, speak out from the silence and solitude of the American Midwest. And there is a profound correspondence between "the man inside the body" ("Silence") and the oceans of air and water and land through which he moves. A car is a "solitude covered with iron" ("Driving Toward the Lac Qui Parle River") and so is the man moving inside his struts of flesh and bone. For years I felt that Bly's poetry pointed at a mysterious and dissatisfying nothingness that was a nonsubject. But he has one subject that speaks out from the spaces between lines, stanzas, and poems and unites them:

II

The Self. But I can only attempt to express this. The most difficult sentence to understand in *Walden* is the one in which Thoreau says that he went to the woods because he wanted "to front only the essential facts of life, and see if I could not learn what it had to teach, and not, when I came to die, discover that I had not lived." My almost every action is a form and a habit. Even as I give lip service to this recognition I realize that my almost every action is a form and a habit. I cannot begin to move inward until I can strike up a dialogue with a tree, with Whitman's leaf of grass, with Blake's grain of sand. Sons of Benjamin Franklin, sons of generations of orthodox mothers, sons driven by the furious ethic that tells us we must keep our hands and heads busy, we have, in effect, despite appearances, moved through the world with a vast disinterestedness. Bly quotes Jacob Boehme: "We are all asleep in the outward man."

The journeys in Bly's poems are journeys to the interior, as Theodore Roethke put it. Bly has stopped somewhere and is waiting for us. He can find no spiritual fathers among politicians, or the rich, or the self-satisfied (hence his increasing social criticism). But the poet still has friends, a few people to share the inexplicable inner life with. When he is with them he writes quiet, almost melancholy lines:

A few friendships, a few dawns, a few glimpses of grass,
A few oars weathered by the snow and the heat,
So we drift toward shore, over cold waters,
No longer caring if we drift or go straight.

The only contest in life worth our while, perhaps, is the one suggested by the title of the poem from which this stanza comes: "After Drinking All Night with a Friend, We Go Out in a Boat at Dawn to See Who Can Write the Best Poem."

And what Bly finds, when he is alone, when he is his own inner man, is joy. He has said that "the fundamental world of poetry is the inward world. We approach it through solitude." No matter the eerie desolation of the landscape. Happiness, a quiet beauty at the heart of things, comes through. "Alive," not asleep in the external man, "We are like a sleak black water beetle / . . . soon to be swallowed / Suddenly from beneath" ("Night"). But, for now, we have the intense pleasure of the journey, sometimes the pleasure of feeling pain, as in "Images Suggested by Medieval Music," a key poem. The hard mystery itself is the joy:

> I have felt this joy before, it is like the harsh grasses
> On lonely beaches, this strange sweetness
> Of medieval music, a hoarse joy,
> Like birds', or the joy of trackless seas. . . .

Here, and frequently in Bly, there is a sense of déjà vu. In 1966 he asked Pablo Neruda: "Do you think you have ever lived before?" Bly's poems are intimations of immortality, for when we shuffle off the coil of habitual response, we feel eternal and no more sad or out of touch with being than a decaying log. Stephen Stepanchev, in *American Poetry Since 1945,* is wrong when he says that Bly speaks with the "irremediable loneliness of man, who can never make contact with the things of the world." Dead wrong. Roethke tells us that a blind man who lifts a curtain knows it is morning. Bly knows that even "the deaf [can hear] through the bones of their heads" ("After Working"). The empty forms of our lives, certainly, lead us to feelings of emptiness and despair; but when we enter the dark caves of grass, we sense the immutability of our internal selves. For the mystic the hair shirt of life is the origin of pleasure, and for Bly

> It is a pleasure, also, to be driving
> Toward Chicago, near dark,

to bomb Los Angeles or Chicago, two things would have been accomplished: if a great many of us were killed our guilt, to some extent, would be assuaged; and we would have a hearty excuse to level Asia and the Asians.

Bly claims that he and the poets he most admires have written the first valid political poems in our history. Now, I'm not sure what he means by this, but if his claim is that he has found a medium which bears the weight of political protest poetically, I'm fully in agreement. I can't think of a poem in *The Light Around the Body,* no matter how stark, which is open to the charge that it is essentially journalistic or propagandistic. What we are experiencing now we have experienced from the beginning. Bly's "deep images" speak a language we know, regardless of our political consciousness. Witness this stanza, at first bordering on abstraction and cliché but breaking toward concrete surprise, from "Turning Away from Lies":

> If we are truly free, and live in a free country,
> When shall I be without this heaviness of mind?
> When shall I have peace? Peace this way and peace that way?
> I have already looked beneath the street
> And there I saw the bitter waters going down,
> The ancient worms eating up the sky.

Or these timeless lines from "At a March Against the Vietnam War":

> But there is something moving in the dark somewhere
> Just beyond
> The edge of our eyes: a boat
> Covered with machine guns
> Moving along under trees
>
> It is black,
> The hand reaches out
> And cannot touch it—
> It is that darkness among pine boughs
> That the Puritans brushed
> As they went out to kill turkeys. . . .

The last section of *The Light Around the Body* consists of ten poems grouped under the subtitle "A Body Not Yet Born." Here, as elsewhere, Bly feels intimations of the self locked inside its "bubble" and wanting out. There are sounds from another room we can almost hear; there are stirrings of another ocean, *the* ocean. Bly's stand, usually, is one of despair. The world is too much with us. We are wasting our lives, our powers. There is an obliquely stated death wish, a longing for the time when "The house fallen, / The gold sticks broken, / Then shall the talkative be silent, / And the dumb shall speak" ("When the Dumb Speak"). This is where Bly, a hard Romantic, leaves us. He leaves us as he does in "Looking into a Face," neither in nor out of this life. He leaves us at the edge of our realization of the inner life. This poem dramatizes a moment of truth. Here,

> I have risen to a body
> Not yet born,
> Existing like a light around the body,
> Through which the body moves like a sliding moon.

RICHARD HOWARD

Robert Bly
"Like Those Before,
We Move to the Death We Love"

Born on the western plains of Minnesota, Robert Bly forty years
later won the 1968 National Book Award, making in the curious
words of its citation "a great leap . . . into a center of resemblances we had not recognized before" and of course mocking that corporate accolade by strong political disavowals which
his very acceptance of such success in polite letters enabled him
to emblazon. But I do not think Bly was belaureled (with whatever wreath of withered sassafras he might press upon his own
brows in preference to Big City bays) for his poems of protest,
his abuse of the Great Society and his abhorrence of the Small
War ("Driving through Minnesota during the Hanoi Bombings," "Watching Television," "Listening to President Kennedy
Lie about the Cuban Invasion"—the present participles in the
titles suggest the journalistic immediacy, the lilt of the bulletin in
these good intentions); any more than I think Bly has become a
certain costive power in contemporary poetry just because of his
intemperate, his downright ill-tempered assessments of contemporary poets, or just because of his tendentious magazine *The
Sixties,* with its peppery offerings of parody, translation and
critique. No, these things are distractions from the genuine
achievement and even from the genuine aspiration as the body
of Bly's work (a phrase employed advisedly) articulates them;
we must not allow the foreground swagger, though expedient
to the point of prize-winning and plausible to the point of

praiseworthiness, to obscure by its mass and noisiness the real burden of this man's enterprise, latent in almost every poem and lovely beyond the measure of mere socializing energy—the burden, literally of a body transfigured by the weight of its own death:

> . . . The wind rises, the water is born,
> Spreading white tomb-clothes on a rocky shore,
> Drawing us up
> From the bed of the land.
>
> We did not come to remain whole.
> We came to lose our leaves like the trees,
> The trees that are broken
> And start again, drawing up from the great roots;
> . . . .
> Men who live out
> A second life.
>
> That we should learn of poverty and rags
> . . . .
> And swim in the sea,
> Not always walking on dry land,
> And, dancing, find in the trees a saviour,
> A home in dark grass,
> And nourishment in death.
>
> ("A Home in Dark Grass")

It is the characteristic Bly contract, a stipulation that in order to escape a living death, i.e., a life which is no more than life in a dying body, the self must renounce its very principle of individuation, must invite death into the body not as a mere nothing at the end but as a positive force throughout, "a saviour, a home," dialectically unified with life; of course, when death and life unite in this inextricable trope, identity must be surrendered—that is what is meant when death is referred to as "the great leveller," not extinction but indistinction: going over to the majority, as the saying goes. And the terms of the contract afford the characteristic Bly music—lagging, irregular, profound, and casting about the image, the image alone, a kind of ontological glamor which leaves unattended so many other kinds of decorum, of propriety, of *keeping* which we may find, or hope to find, in poems; rhetorical splendor, rhyme, a rhythm constructed or at least contested by more than the drawing of breath, wit, elevation, even humor—none of these, but "a poetry in which the image comes forward and much more is said by suggestion . . . a poetry which disregards the conscious and the intellectual structure of the mind entirely and by the use of images, tries to bring forward another reality from *inward* experience." Robert Bly's own account of his undertaking suggests here how much he is willing to give up in order to gain what he must have even without much order, and how—by disregarding the usual congruity of the waking mind—he may even risk spoiling his finest things by an unregarded (or at least unguarded-against) intrusion of factitious material. I have twice used ellipses in the poem just quoted to indicate the omission of a line (not of a verse—Bly does not write verses, with all that the word implies of a return, a commitment to a constant; he writes *lines,* with all that the linear implies of a setting out, a movement in search of a form rather than *within* a form); in each case, the omitted line refers to the kind of specific situation which may have been the genesis of the poem, the grain of grit transcended by the pearl, but which is now irrelevant to the achieved form. In the second stanza, the elided line is "Like mad poets captured by the Moors," and in the third, "That we should taste the weed of Dillinger"—both allusions to the kind of external victimization it is Bly's special grace to refute and exceed by setting all of his poems under the sign—playful, reverent—of Jacob Boehme, who said (and Bly used the saying as the epigraph to his first book in 1962, *Silence in the Snowy Fields*) "we are all asleep in the outward man." Discarding the circumstantial husk, then, it is the inward man Bly is centrally concerned with, though it is not in fact a matter of giving up one thing for another, but rather of permitting reality and circumstance to penetrate each other. Boehme says, "As God plays with the time of this outward world, so also should the inward divine man play with the outward in the revealed wonders of God in this world," and Bly makes what he can of this when he says he "tries to bring forward another reality from inward experience"—that experience where, in an unprovable but not improbable sense, we are all awake. Some weight should be placed upon that "tries," for the "center of resemblances" the National Book Award citation referred to is one which Bly does not always himself recognize or relish or even regard, I believe—how could he? It is an unexplored region he is prospecting, a realm in which there is no such thing as work, sexual differentiation or individuality as we know it in our conscious lives. The "resemblances," then, are not to what we experience—the fall from eternity into time, the vain project of the part to become independent of the whole*— but to what we merely aspire to, what we long for. "I want to be a stream of water falling," Bly begins one of these ventures, though he is so tentative that he must still confuse the issue, which is one of the divine body, with the trappings of the body politic, and he calls his poem—for the most specious reasons— "John F. Kennedy":

I want to be a stream of water falling—
Water falling from high in the mountains, water
That dissolves everything,
And is never drunk, falling from ledge to ledge, from glass to glass
. . . .
I will carry the boulders with me to the valley.
Then ascending I will fall through space again:
. . . .
And when I ascend the third time, I will fall forever,
Missing the earth entirely.

In the same book—his second, *The Light Around the Body,* published in 1967 and whose title shows how urgently Boehme is again invoked for the assurance, the ease of a doctrinal authority: "for according to the outward man, we are in this world, and according to the inward man, we are in the inward world. . . . Since then we are generated out of both worlds, we speak in two

*In "A Man Writes to a Part of Himself" Bly asks, and in his voice there is the despair of many dark nights: "Which of us two then is the worse off? / and how did this separation come about?"

languages, and we must be understood also by two languages"—Bly rewrites the pseudo-Kennedy poem as "The Hermit," evidently having realized its proper nature as a visionary recital rather than a satirical lament, and by the final, obsessive image, to which we shall return, of the open sea (in Minnesota!) the poet reaches rather than merely reaches *for* that area of discourse where all is transformed because all is reborn:

Darkness is falling through darkness,
Falling from ledge
To ledge.
There is a man whose body is perfectly whole
. . . .
Darkness is gathered in folds
About his feet.
He is no one. When we see
Him, we grow calm,
And sail on into the tunnels of joyful death.

There was a fantasy of early Alexandrian philosophy which the heretics of the Renaissance affected to revive and which achieves a more genuine avatar in such poems as Bly's "Hermit"—the supposition that the human race is an incarnation of those angels who, in the revolt of Lucifer, were neither for Jehovah nor for His enemies. The very beings a Dante scorns as unworthy alike of heaven and hell Bly accepts in his own figure, inhabitants (or inhabitant: there is only one person in this little apocalypse, as if all events were to occur inside a single infinite body:

Inside the veins there are navies setting forth,
Tiny explosions at the water lines,
And seagulls weaving in the wind of the salty blood
. . . .

Now we wake, and rise from bed, and eat breakfast!—
Shouts rise from the harbor of the blood,
Mist, and masts rising, the knock of wooden tackle in the sunlight.
Now we sing, and do tiny dances on the kitchen floor.

Our whole body is like a harbor at dawn;
We know that our master has left us for the day.

("Waking from Sleep")

"Our master" being the god that, in Groddeck's phrase, lives us while we sleep, and it is to be noted that Bly casts, or casts off, his apocalyptic metaphor in terms of a harbor scene, an embarkation, a setting out to sea) of a middle world in which life takes no sides and settles no great causes and indeed makes great refusals. There is in the very *façon* of all these poems, in their repetitions and slacknesses, in their organic fatigue that would send them into the ground for repose:

My body hung about me like an old grain elevator,
Useless, clogged, full of blackened wheat.
My body was sour, my life dishonest, and I fell asleep.
. . . .

Now I want to go back among the dark roots;
. . . .
I want to see nothing more than two feet high;
. . . .
I want to go down and rest in the black earth of silence.

("Depression")

—there is here a numbness or torpor, an inertia so new to art, which by its traditional nature is the celebration of energy, of mastery, that Robert Bly himself is not always certain of its accommodation in his utterance; he suffers and thereby celebrates the inertia of a being who would be saved, redeemed, not because he is he, but because he is here, merely present with all the lethargy of a life which contains death—and it is the requisite wonder of Bly's poetry that the physical qualities of his language rehearse and enhance the containment, loyal to their artlessness from the start, unwavering in their oscitance. It is his uncertainty we hear, I think, when he says—as he sourly said in 1960— "our poetry, because of its clinging to things and to the surface of life, has tended to become too barren"; or when he seizes upon the sumptuous negations of a Neruda and renders them in his own embedded accents, tendentiously *taking possession*:

> . . . the extraordinary testimony I bring forward
> with brutal efficiency and written down in the ashes,
> is the form of oblivion that I prefer,
> the name I give to the earth, the value of my dreams,
> the endless abundance which I distribute
> with my wintry eyes, every day this world goes on . . .

On these occasions he is making the gestures of a man possessed to the point of self-suppression by his subject—not waving but drowning, as it were. We must examine what his work betrays but does not parade, what it reveals but does not translate—a sense of the center sufficiently indicated, perhaps, if we say, merely, that all the poems, as we pick them up one after the other, are seen to be *marinating*: they are all at sea.

I have referred to the "real burden" of Bly's poetry, and I have suggested that it coincides with Bly's real body—beyond or beneath the factitious encumbrance of his journalistic protest, though the outrage registered there, the objurgations rehearsed in these snake-dances, torchlight songs and rallying chants are anything but factitious: "We were the ones we intended to bomb!" he gasps, adding a darker outlook to Miss Moore's deep insight that there never was a war which was not inward, when he declares:

> We long to abase ourselves
>
> We have carried around this cup of darkness
> We have longed to pour it over our heads
>
> We make war
> Like a man anointing himself
> ("At a March against the Vietnam War")

—and beyond or above the factual record of those bleak, blatant midwestern landscapes, empty towns and choking farms, the historyless scenery of Wisconsin and Minnesota and Ohio whose reliance, for expression, on a set of declarative aspects ("one thing is also another thing") precludes drama or compression or humor; the real burden, then, of Bly's poetry, the corporal burden which distends language beyond the observation it can accommodate, until it sags into a statement it may no longer bear but merely deliver:

> North of Columbus there is a sort of torpid joy:
> The slow and muddy river,
> The white barns leaning into the ground,
> Cottonwoods with their trunks painted white,
> And houses with small observatories on top,
> As if Ohio were the widow's coast, looking over
> The dangerous Atlantic.*

> Now we drive north past the white cemeteries
> So rich in the morning air!
> All morning I have felt the sense of death;
> I am full of love, and love this torpid land.
> Some day I will go back, and inhabit again
> The sleepy ground where Harding was born.

—the real burden of this poetry ("there is another darkness, / a darkness in the fences of the body") is one qualified throughout as *latent,* and we shall best come to terms with it, I believe— indeed, the terms we shall come to are what Boehme calls Adam's language, a sensual speech free from distortion and illusion, the language man will recover when he recovers paradise—if we dawdle somewhat over the sense of the word itself, in which the Sanskrit word for darkness transpires: when we say a significance is *latent* we mean that it lies, sunk as of its own weight, below the surface, in darkness, brought down by some oppression to that torpor, that inertia which need not show itself

---

*Again, it is worth remarking Bly's discovery of the sea very close to the surface, wherever he is. Dry land is forever jeopardized, and validated, by the encroachment of that old catastrophe, the Flood: "the ground this house is on, / only free of the sea for five or six thousand years."

("the clay is sending her gifts back to the center of the earth")—
and we realize, with Skeat's help, that at least since the Greeks
the word *latent* and the word *lethargy* have had the same root
sense, have grown from the same dark ground. I have already
deliberated a little on the phenomenology of lethargy in Robert
Bly's poems, on the fact that he is the first laureate of "something inside us / like a ghost train in the Rockies / about to be
buried in snow!" But now we can move in on a greater sense of
this conjugation of the hidden and the heavy, the sense given
when we remember that the concealed current, the buried river
carrying all our experience out to sea is precisely the stream the
Greeks called *Lethe:*

> The black water swells up over the new hole.
> The grave moves forward from its ambush . . .
> > ("In Danger from the Outer World")

And just as we must renounce, in order to be reborn to the
divine body, all that we know, all that we remember, by immersion in that water of oblivion, we must also accept a kind of
dying, a dying to ourselves; we must accept, Robert Bly mur-
murs, what is *lethal:*

> There is a joyful night in which we lose
> Everything, and drift
> Like a radish
> Rising and falling, and the ocean
> At last throws us into the ocean,
> And on the water we are sinking
> As if floating on darkness
>
> . . . .
> Then the images appear:
> Images of death,
> Images of the body shaken in the grave,
> And the graves filled with seawater;
>
> . . . .
> Then shall the talkative be silent,
> And the dumb shall speak.
> > ("When the Dumb Speak")

It remains merely (merely!)—relying on Boehme's Fifth Mystical Point that "Imagination is gentle and soft, and resembles water, but desire is harsh and dry, like a hunger that leads the nothing into something"—to trace this buried sea through the inland inertias of Robert Bly's poems, to collect, then, a little garland of kelp from the great plains. We start with the first poems in the first book, the "eleven poems of solitude," where the Ordeal by Water is of course the Trauma of Birth, and the longing to return to the womb is the longing for an introjected, incarnate ocean, as Ferenczi would call it:

> We want to go back, to return to the sea,
> The sea of solitary corridors,
> And halls of wild nights,
> Explosions of grief,
> Diving into the sea of death
>
> . . . .
>
> What shall we find when we return?
> Friends changed, houses moved,
> Trees perhaps, with new leaves.
>
> ("Return to Solitude")

And if the night is naturally construed as an oceanic envelopment, "an asylum of waters," the day too has its transfiguration-by-drowning to offer:

> The new dawn sings of beaches
> Dazzling as sugar and clean as the clouds of Greece,
> Just as the exhausted dusk shall sing
> Of the waves on the western shore.
>
> ("Thinking of Wallace Stevens on the
First Snowy Day in December")

Then, in the title poem of the ensuing section, "Awakening," we endure that process of penetration to sources, to centers and surds required by the epigraph to which I have alluded, Boehme's observation that "we are all asleep in the outward man"; from the long past into the long present we submit ourselves—

As the great wheel turns around, grinding
The living in water.
Washing, continual washing, in water now stained
With blossoms and rotting logs,
Cries, half-muffled, from beneath the earth, the living awakened at
     last like the dead.

—and our past life appears, Bly would say, as a wake behind us:
"I am a ship, skirting a thousand harbors. The voyage goes on.
The joy of sailing and the open sea!" In a poem of this group
called "Unrest" the ship-figure is extended to piracy, of course,
to a buccaneer's raid on the absolute: "This is the last dance, the
wild tossing of Morgan's seas, / The division of spoils," and the
gleeful destruction is echoed and enhanced to its ultimate sense
in "Night":

> I feel a joy, as if I had thought
> Of a pirate ship ploughing through dark flowers.
> . . . .
>
> Alive, we are like a sleek black water beetle,
> Skating across still water in any direction
> We choose, and soon to be swallowed
> Suddenly from beneath.

The triumph of this central group in *Silence in the Snowy Fields*,
however, is not one of Bly's countless committals of the body to
darkness, depth and inertia, to that "silence on the roads" where
"the dark weeds are waiting, as if under water"; it is, rather, a
poem of wakefulness, of inspired consciousness, and the only
poem in all his *oeuvre* not to be devised or derived "Driving
through Ohio" or "Hunting Pheasants in a Cornfield," in that
limitless chthonic expanse which so burdens the vertical self; the
poem is called, exceptionally, "On the Ferry Across Chesapeake
Bay," and because it is the one piece in the canon uttered in the
actual presence of the real sea, of course it is that real sea which is
put aside ("O deep green sea, it is not for you / this smoking
body ploughs toward death"). The waking man, Bly discovers,
cannot *bring forward* the images which will substantiate another

reality; he must listen, rather, to Nietzsche's advice: "you must be a chaos, to give birth to a dancing star":

> On the orchard of the sea, far out are whitecaps,
> Water that answers questions no one has asked,
> Silent speakers of the grave's rejoinders;
> Having accomplished nothing, I am travelling somewhere else
> . . . .
> And the sea gives up its answer as it falls into itself.

The closing poems of the book return to the life and to the death-in-life of that Minnesota mariner so amazingly created out of midwestern elements: "I love to see boards lying on the ground in early spring— / this is the wood one sees on the decks of ocean ships, / wood that carries us far from land . . . / this wood is like a man who has a simple life, / living through the spring and winter on the ship of his own desire . . ." There is nothing taut or wrought about the words, the phrases sink back into silence with all the morose languor of that marooned landscape; yet as Bly insists, in one of the last poems,

> Strange muffled sounds come from the sea,
> Sounds of muffled oarlocks,
> And swampings in lonely bays,
> Surf crashing on unchristened shores,
> And the wash of tiny snail shells in the wandering gravel.
>
> ("Silence")

Like Prospero, Bly *drowns* his book with a final image of renunciation: every hope of distinct and certainly of distinguished life is surrendered for the sake of "the true gift, beneath the pale lakes of Minnesota," the treasure beneath the black water:

> The barn is full of corn, and moving toward us now,
> Like a hulk blown toward us in a storm at sea;
> All the sailors on deck have been blind for many years.
>
> ("Snowfall in the Afternoon")

"We float joyfully on the dark places," Bly exults in the first section of his second book, *The Light Around the Body,* and though the exultation is more than ever endangered by feedback from the public realm ("Romans Angry about the Inner World" as the title of one poem has it), the conviction persists that everywhere, at any time—even "Hearing Men Shout at Night on Macdougall Street"—

> The street is a sea, and mud boils up
> When the anchor is lifted.

The accent lies more heavily, in these later poems, on the death to be assimilated to a life little better than a dark probation: "I have already looked beneath the street / and there I saw the bitter waters going down. . . ." Indeed, in a poem crucially titled "The Fire of Despair Has Been Our Saviour" (no longer may we, "dancing, find in the trees a saviour"), there is none of that jolly submission to the destructive process which gave such a queer nimbus to Bly's discoveries, the sense that "our skin shall see far off, as it does under water," or that "our conversation stiffens the backbone of the sea"; here are rather "images of wasted life, / life lost, imagination mined, / the house fallen, / the gold sticks broken" and an emphasis on the loss rather than on the transfiguration:

> This autumn, I
> Cannot find the road
> That way: the things that we must grasp,
> The signs, are gone, hidden by spring and fall, leaving
> A still sky here, a dusk there,
> A dry cornleaf in a field; where has the road gone? All
> Trace lost, like a ship sinking,
> Where what is left and what goes down both bring despair.
> Not finding a road, we are slowly pulled down.

Yet Bly will not surrender his assurances, granted him by the morality of biology, by the lethargy of a body which must die, by that mortal process in which "the air of night changes to dark water, / the mountains alter and become the sea." The sea is inside him, and the release from selfhood Boehme recognized in Paul's astonishing aphorism: "There can be no male and no female; for ye are all one man in Christ"—and so "this grandson of fishes" as Bly calls himself in "Evolution from the Fish" asserts—though in the unpriestly accents of oblivion, the Lethean language of inertia—a sacramental stature:

> This nephew of snails, six feet long, lies naked on a bed
> With a smiling woman, his head throws off light
> Under marble, he is moving toward his own life
> . . . .
> Serpents rise from the ocean floor with spiral motions,
> A man goes inside a jewel, and sleeps. Do
> Not hold my hands down! Let me raise them!
> A fire is passing up through the soles of my feet!

Nor is it the fire of despair only. "Moving inward at last," as Bly says, "opening the surfs of the body," there is revealed a giant faith in the dismembered flesh of this poetry, the substance of things hoped for and—so far as words can heave them up to the surface of "the vast waters"—the substance of things had:

> I have risen to a body
> Not yet born,
> Existing like a light around the body,
> Through which the body moves like a sliding moon.
>
> ("Looking into a Face")

ANTHONY LIBBY

Robert Bly Alive in Darkness

Often self-consciously, poetry now reassumes its ancient forms. When at Antioch College in the autumn of 1970 Robert Bly began a reading with an American Indian peyote chant, he seemed merely to be accepting a hip convention almost expected by an audience accustomed to Ginsberg and Snyder. Bly chanted for the usual reason, "to lower the consciousness down, until it gets into the stomach and into the chest and farther on." But no such convention had existed in the early fifties, when Bly began to publish his intimations of physical transcendence, poetry of the mystical body, and the conventional mystical terms that have since become so easily available are still inadequate to describe what happens in his unique poetry. To use a characteristic phrase of Bly's, "something important is hidden in there that we don't understand."

Because of the elusively compelling force of its "deep images," Bly's poetry demands interpretation as much as it seems to resist it. When it does not consist of simple deliberately prosy statement, much of it seems obscure, distant, but at the same time it conveys a sense of meaning immediately perceived though seldom paraphrasable in any but its own terms. It is difficult to explain Bly's surrealist poetry, hard to say why some of his imagery moves us so basically and why some appears comparatively contrived, but undeniably his strongest poetry evokes some sort of truth all the more forceful because it exists beneath or beyond any reasoned response. However, what the stomach feels, the mind wants to know. Perhaps the best way to appreciate Bly's irrational evocations is to attempt to explain them logically. If this seems paradoxical, such paradoxes are implicit in the act of analyzing almost all poetry, not merely

Iowa Review 3 (Summer 1972): 78–91. Reprinted with permission.

surrealist poetry, and in any case Bly himself provides ample precedent. Like many mystical poets he writes with large patterns in mind, and behind his explorations into darkness there stands not only a complex poetic theory but also a highly articulated scheme of the psychological development of civilization. This scheme, also like that of other mystical poets (Blake, for instance), is frequently based on logical antithesis suspended in paradox, and only through an understanding of paradoxes simple and profound can we come to terms with Bly's poetry.

He begins with the intention of creating a truly free associationalism, radically opposed to what he considers the calculated and artificially logical associationalism of Eliot and Pound. In an essay called "Looking for Dragon Smoke" he argues that the formalist obsessions of modern American poets (from Eliot to Charles Olson) have obscured the true psychic bases of poetry. "Our task is not to invent and encourage jargon about 'open form' and breath patterns, but to continue to open new corridors into the psyche by association." His associative and implicitly irrationalist poetry depends not on form but on imagery, primarily on the conception of the "subjective image" developed by Bly and such friends of his as William Duffy and James Wright. The successful subjective image (or "deep image") strikes us with the force of a newly discovered archetype, minor or major, coming from the depths of the poet's subjectivity with a paradoxically universal force, his private revelation made ours. In Bly's "Depression," for instance, the poet describes his psychic state in images which despite their novelty seem more discovered than made.

> I dreamt that men came toward me, carrying thin wires;
> I felt the wires pass in, like fire; they were old Tibetans,
> Dressed in padded clothes, to keep out cold;
> Then three work gloves, lying fingers to fingers,
> In a circle, came toward me, and I awoke.

Like these, Bly's images are almost invariably marked by a surrealist concreteness; not only are psychological or spiritual states felt in material form, but all substances seem to seek greater density. In various poems in *Silence in the Snowy Fields,* air frequently becomes water ("the quiet waters of the night"), darkness "drifts down like snow," snow becomes "jewels," moonlight becomes "the sound of the deaf hearing through the bones of their heads," etc. Even when this metaphorical transposition of substances could be interpreted as moving in the opposite direction, toward a reduction of density ("Waterfalls of stone deep in mountains, / Or a wing flying alone beneath the earth") still we feel a pervasive sense of heaviness, a downward drift.

This imagery suggests the constant preoccupation of *Silence*; the metaphorical flow into greater concreteness reflects the spiritual movement enacted or wished for in most of the poems, a sinking into things, into the earth, usually into darkness, finally into death. Often, as Richard Howard explains in *Alone with America,* spiritual immersion becomes a literal immersion in water. Howard's intelligent though rhetorically somewhat convoluted introduction to Bly centers on the "latent" waters of "that Minnesota mariner," which Howard connects with "the stream the Greeks called *Lethe*." As Bly writes in "Return to Solitude,"

> We want to go back, to return to the sea,
> The sea of solitary corridors,
> And halls of wild nights,
> Explosions of grief,
> Diving into the sea of death,
> Like the stars of the wheeling Bear.

But though transcendent death by water suggests ancient mystic patterns, Bly's vision of the death which feeds life is neither exactly traditional nor really transcendental. Another main current of imagery in *Silence* suggests interpenetration of body and world. Animism ("The dawn stood there with a quiet gaze; / Our eyes met through the top leaves of the young ash") is complemented by a sort of bodily surrealism ("Inside me there is a confusion of swallows"). As the psyche is crowded with arcane corporeal images, so the body contains the objects of the world. In the past, for instance in Thoreau, such body-world parallelism and interpenetration has been used to suggest a higher spiritual reality which penetrates all physical being. More recently, in, say, the poetry of Sylvia Plath, the same pattern of imagery has grown into a vision of all physical substance as grotesquely alien to the perceiving consciousness, the body a dead husk imprisoning a sickened spirit, things endowed with terrifying life. While obviously closer to Thoreau, Bly is essentially similar to neither. His animism stems from a perception of vitality in things which connects with the vitality in the body, but which is neither separable from states of physical being nor basically alien to consciousness. Dying into the darkness at the heart of Bly's poetry is not a transcendence of the body but an immersion in the body in turn immersed in the corporeal flow of things. If this elusive immersion is achieved, the body in its fullness contains and is contained by "the inner world," which is this world, not illuminated but condensed to its deepest indivisible essence.

So behind the traditional mystical paradox—the praise of ordinarily negative states, grief and "the death we love," as avenues to holy joy—there exists in Bly the further paradox that spiritual union with the universe must be sought in physical terms. Perhaps for this reason trees play a constant symbolic role in *Silence,* reaching toward emptiness, but always rooted in the earth. In "Poem in Three Parts":

> The strong leaves of the box-elder tree,
> Plunging in the wind, call us to disappear
> Into the wilds of the universe,
> Where we shall sit at the foot of a plant,
> And live forever, like the dust.

The dust, which appears frequently in Bly's poetry, suggests the most corporeal vision of union with the cosmos, a union spiritually more meaningful than the traditional theological dreams of death if only because of its physical inevitability. Bly compares the two visions in "At the Funeral of Great-Aunt Mary."

> The minister tells us that, being
> The sons and daughters of God,

We rejoice at death, for we go
To the mansions prepared
From the foundations of the world.
Impossible. No one believes it.

III
Out on the bare, pioneer field,
The frail body must wait till dark
To be lowered
In the hot and sandy earth.

The sense of death as physical union with everything becomes
a spiritual or moral force in life because it celebrates a loss of self
into the other which is more absolute than the ego-loss presumably implied by the death of transcendence; the traditional mystic soul united with god as often seems swollen as lost in
oneness. Also the sense of corporeal dissolution of self is, Bly
suggests, always with us. Every sleep is a bodily premonition of
death. Much of *Silence* concerns periods of transition between
waking and sleep, between light and darkness. During such periods the deep image comes close to the surface because the mind
sinks to the depths of the body, the body opens to the world.

The day shall never end, we think:
We have hair that seems born for the daylight;
But, at last, the quiet waters of the night will rise,
And our skin shall see far off, as it does under water.
("Surprised by Evening")

Perhaps it no longer seems paradoxical that the state of "approaching sleep" is most fully described in "Awakening."

We are approaching sleep: the chestnut blossoms in the mind
Mingle with the thoughts of pain ·
. . . .
Bodies give off darkness, and chrysanthemums
Are dark, and horses, . . .
. . . .

> As the great wheel turns around, grinding
> The living in water.
> . . . .
> . . . the living awakened at last like the dead.

In his second collection of poems, *The Light Around the Body,* Bly's paradoxes are deepened because much of his poetry spreads into another world. Like various other American mystics, most conspicuously Thoreau, Bly becomes interested in the politics of American imperialism, a subject at least superficially uncongenial to mysticism. All but one of the sections of *Light* begin with quotations from Jacob Boehme, the Protestant mystic who influenced the American Transcendentalists (through Emerson, who knew him as "Behemen"). "For according to the outward man, we are in this world, and according to the inward man, we are in the inward world. . . . Since then we are generated out of both worlds, we speak in two languages, and we must be understood also by two languages." The poems of *Light* concern the conflict between the two worlds, in the poet, and in America. So inevitably these poems bring together the two languages of which Boehme speaks, doubling Bly's paradoxes, sometimes confusingly. *Light* still praises grief and maps the progress of the body toward that death which is fulfillment, but while *Silence* emphasized intimations of ultimate union *Light* focuses on obstacles to the good death, one of which is, paradoxically, another sort of death. "Smothered by the World" describes a purgatory between life and death.

> Once more the heavy body mourns!
> It howls outside the hedges of life,
> Pushed out of the enclosure.
> Now it must meet the death outside the death.
> Living outside the gate is one death,
> Cold faces gather along the wall,
> A bag of bones warms itself in a tree.

This death results from basic spiritual distortion in the world. Bly describes it in the same physical terms he used to connect the body and the world, but here the connection has become grotesque. Human consciousness inhabits objects only to suggest a general despair, as in "Those Being Eaten by America."

> The wild houses go on
> With long hair growing from between their toes
> The feet at night get up
> And run down the long white roads by themselves

> The dams reverse themselves and want to go stand alone in the
> desert

The sterile death that follows this despair is occasionally described in terms of whiteness, often snow, but even the darkness which in *Silence* was always the medium of visions has in *Light* changed, become corrupted. "There is another darkness," Bly writes in "Listening to President Kennedy Lie about the Cuban Invasion." "There is a bitter fatigue, adult and sad."

The other darkness, in poems like "Hatred of Men with Black Hair," is described as inhabiting the same deep realms as the darkness of vision.

> The State Department floats in the heavy jellies near the bottom
> Like exhausted crustaceans, like squids who are confused,
> Sending out beams of black light to the open sea

Both darknesses exist at the root of the mind, which is the source of politics as well as poetry. As the title of "Hatred" suggests, the destructive darkness results from a refusal to acknowledge that more primitive darkness which is the way to union. The American dream of self-proclaimed innocence, so shot through with unacknowledged blackness, leads to a death which cannot reinforce life, if only because it strikes so unnaturally. This vision is dramatized most fully in Bly's later poem "The Teeth-Mother Naked at Last," but it is suggested in "At a March against the Vietnam War," which appears in *Light*. Bly says of "a boat/ Covered with machine guns:"

> It is black,
> The hand reaches out

And cannot touch it—
It is that darkness among pine boughs
That the Puritans brushed
As they went out to kill turkeys

At the edge of the jungle clearing
It explodes
On the ground

We long to abase ourselves

We have carried around this cup of darkness
We have longed to pour it over our heads

Always, however individually, the poet reflects his time. Primarily *Silence* contains poetry written in the 1950s, a time of comparative political innocence (or naiveté) for American literature, when literary rebellion against America was usually considered a rather solitary and apolitical experience. *Silence* is a book of solitude, of Bly alone with the world; even its few love poems do not involve a recognizable other. *Light* is a book of the sixties, a predominantly political book, like many other books of poetry published since 1966 (the year Bly organized American Writers Against the Vietnam War). But while Bly's development must obviously be understood in terms of our recent history, he might probably have undergone similar changes in any historical context, for in *Light* he is only dramatizing a tension implicit in the paradoxes of *Silence*.

Traditionally, mysticism has existed in potential or actual conflict with more earthly approaches to morality; the conflict surfaces when the mystic theorizes about evil. Having accepted grief and the dissolution of his body as aspects of a vital flow into "the wilds of the universe," Bly must logically confront experiences of grief and death, perhaps unnecessary grief and premature death, much less palatable to those who suffer them. The mystic always returns to the world of men. The perception of dominant and perhaps inherent evil there can blunt his mystic acceptance, or it can become the basis for more strenuous efforts toward transcendence, a denial of the essential reality of certain aspects of the world in favor of higher realities. Allen Ginsberg, for instance, plays more or less seriously with the latter response when he chants, in "Wichita Vortex Sutra": "I here declare the end of the War / Ancient days' Illusion." But because Bly's mysticism remains untranscendental ("The two worlds are both in this world") neither traditional response is really possible. The social fact of pointless death forces a deeper examination of the idea of death as a spiritual good, but Bly is unwilling to deny either vision.

What he attempts to do instead, besides suggesting how the primitive sense of union has been lost, how death has been corrupted, is to create a vision of process toward a new world in which paradoxes resolve themselves. But the approach of this world is itself paradoxical, a terrible movement toward communal death which, like the individual death of *Silence,* is also the approach of birth. As the tension between inner and outer worlds grows more extreme Bly suggests that the center will not hold; however the approaching apocalypse is also described as evolution. The final section of *Light* is called "A Body Not Yet Born." Like the rest of the book it contains images of despairing death, as in "Hurrying Away from the Earth."

> Some men have pierced the chest with a long needle
> To stop the heart from beating any more;
> . . . .
> The time for exhortation is past, I have heard
> The iron chairs scraping in asylums,
> . . . .
> Men cry when they hear stories of someone rising from the dead.

If the dark night of the soul has become a universal darkness, it carries implications of universal illumination. In "When the Dumb Speak," Bly describes

> . . . a joyful night in which we lose
> Everything, and drift
> Like a radish
> Rising and falling, and the ocean
> At last throws us into the ocean

One ocean flows from the waters of inner experience described throughout much of *Silence,* but the other spreads through time as well as space. "When the Dumb Speak" ends with "images" which evoke traditional Christian visions of the world ending in apocalypse:

> Images of the body shaken in the grave,
> And the grave filled with seawater;
> Fires in the sea
> . . . .
> The house fallen,
> The gold sticks broken

But "Evolution from the Fish," as its title indicates, describes what is to come not as a Christian end but as an evolutionary change which parallels earlier changes. Here the loss of "everything," which is a loss of self, becomes a participation in the physical development of life from the beginning. "The grandson of fishes" is described

> . . . moving toward his own life
> Like fur, walking. And when the frost comes, he is
> Fur, mammoth fur, growing longer
> . . . .
> He moves toward the animal, the animal with furry head!

As the poem moves into our time the furry-headed one becomes specific, individual, "this long man with the student girl," but in the end he is embarking on another voyage, in darkness, through sleep.

> Serpents rise from the ocean floor with spiral motions,
> A man goes inside a jewel, and sleeps. Do
> Not hold my hands down! Let me raise them!
> A fire is passing up through the soles of my feet!

An earlier version of "Evolution" appeared in 1962 in a brief anthology of poems by Bly, Duffy, and Wright, *The Lion's Tail and Eyes.* Indicatively, it included one additional last line: "I am curving back into the mammoth pool!" By omitting the backward curve Bly alters the final direction of the poem from the past to the future; now the subject is not repeating cycles of existence but a continuing upward spiral into new states of being.

Bly is at his most difficult, to follow and to accept, when he begins to describe the particular nature of the apocalypse to come, and the evolution it heralds. A premonitory poem in *Light,* "Romans Angry about the Inner World," describes that world as "A jagged stone / Flying toward them out of the darkness" and suggests the final articulation of Bly's evolutionary vision. In the poem "executives" watch Roman executioners torture "a woman / Who has seen our mother / In the other world." Specifically the lines refer to the mystical cult of Magna Mater, eventually suppressed by the Romans. But the anachronistic presence of the executives implies a comparison between imperial Rome and neo-imperialist America, a comparison that goes beyond ordinary politics. Later Bly will elaborate the theory that the mother-goddesses smothered by one empire are returning to haunt the psyche of the other. In his long introduction to "The Teeth-Mother Naked at Last" at the Antioch reading, Bly explained a vision of mythic development largely based on the psychological and historical investigations of Jung's disciple Erich Neumann. Originally, as Bly explains Neumann, the world's great religions were based on worship of the female principle, the Great Mother; the Romans and the Jews fought to substitute male gods for the female goddesses, beginning the long western tradition of primacy of the masculine consciousness. Bly defines sexual consciousness in Jungian terms: masculine consciousness involves logic, efficiency, the advancement of material civilization, repression, and control of the natural world; and feminine consciousness involves intuition, creativity, mystic acceptance of the world. Because only women are biologically creative, it is usually the man who feels the aesthetic urge to create with materials outside his own body. However he is truly inspired only if he makes "the great turn" toward the mother, accepting the guidance of the (always female) Muse, and exploring his own feminine consciousness

(Jung's anima). Now, though, not only artists but the whole culture is beginning, psychologically, to turn to the Great Mother. "America looks down in the psyche now," Bly said at Antioch, "and it sees the mothers coming up." "That's what's been happening in America in the last fifteen years, that the father consciousness civilization is dying and the mothers are returning."

As the mythic forms of the mothers suggest, this can be a destructive as well as liberating process. Drawing on various mythologies for examples Bly describes the four great mothers in opposed pairs, constructive and destructive: the mother of fertility (Demeter) balanced by the mother of destruction (Kali), the ecstatic mother (Artemis) balanced by the stone mother (Medusa). In this relation to each other they form a cross, or the four main compass points of a circle, and the teeth mother hovers on the circumference between death and stone mothers. To prove his theory, Bly cites widely various bits of evidence of the return of the different mothers. One manifestation of the destructive mothers in the aesthetic consciousness appears, for instance, in de Kooning's paintings; Bly is perhaps thinking of works like "Woman I." In a very different sphere, Bly attributes the American violence of Vietnam, often directed against women and children, to our pathologically masculine soldiers' fear of the female, of the mothers, whom they see only in the form of the death mother or the teeth mother. On the other side, Bly sees in hip and liberated life styles the influence of the ecstatic mother, though he explains that the search for the ecstatic mother can fail in a long fall toward the stone mother—the use of drugs, too, dramatizes this paradox, and Bly the comedian does not hesitate to play on the colloquial sense of "stoned."

To those moved by the visionary qualities of Bly's poetry, this theory may present serious problems. How much of it is really believable, how literally does Bly intend it, how necessary is it as a basis for his poetry? Indicatively, little of the theory actually appears in "The Teeth-Mother Naked at Last," though it provides a striking title. Bly's vision of the great evolutionary change is felt more convincingly in his poetry—explorations into "the inward world . . . thoughts we have not yet thought" which involve little detailed reference to the mothers—than in his spoken and very explicit explanations of what he thinks now. Bly the performer is enormously compelling, a constantly disarming mixture of vaudeville comedian and oracle, but in retrospect, beyond the range of his personal vibrations, his archetypal sociology does not fully convince. Perhaps in our time any extreme definition of the opposition between male and female consciousness must seem suspect. More important, though, is the tension between Bly's use of the old Jungian archetypes to describe our future, and the constant suggestions in his poetry that the present movement of human consciousness is something new, now hardly dreamed of. Somehow it seems inadequate to describe "the body not yet born" in terms of ancient myths, however they are blended or transmuted to define the world to come. Better to accept Bly's explanations as metaphor, his poems as reality.

For it is the sense of deeply perceived reality in the poetry that leads us in the first place to consider the prose articulation of the theory, and in fact Bly the poet, as he points out, was using the conflict between "masculine" and "feminine" as a metaphor long before he read Neumann and developed his theory. In *Light,* for instance, "The Busy Man Speaks" defines "the mother" in terms of "art," "sorrow," "the ocean"; and "the father" in terms of "the stones of cheerfulness, the steel of money." Still earlier, in *Silence,* women are often associated with liberating death, as in "With Pale Women in Maryland": "Like those before, we move to the death we love / With pale women in Maryland."

To see Bly's poetry as dependent on anyone's theory, on Jung's, Neumann's, or even Bly's own, is not only to deny his belief in the irrational psychic sources of poetry but also to dilute the unique force of his poems. If we turn to Jung for explanations, we can say simply that the origin of Bly's deep images is the collective unconscious, that the conflict between the inner and outer worlds is a conflict between anima and persona, that Bly's water imagery is, given his concerns, predictable. Water, Jung says in "Archetypes of the Collective Unconscious," is "no figure of speech, but a living symbol of the dark psyche," the realm "where I experience the other in myself." Even Bly's paradoxical discovery of vitality in death can be explained in terms of Jung's contention, in "Psychological Aspects of the Mother Archetype," that "nothing can exist without its opposite; the two were one in the beginning and will be one again in the end. Consciousness can only exist through continual recognition of the unconscious, just as everything that lives must pass through many deaths." But to interpret Bly basically in these terms is to oversimplify his paradoxes without really explaining them, as Jung's archetypes inevitably tend to reduce and oversimplify complex individual states of being. Descending into realms initially explored by Jung and later by Neumann, Bly goes beyond both. His greatest strength is his ability to discover in the darkness images that are not archetypal, at least not in the Jungian sense, because they are only beginning to loom into view.

But even if we remain unconvinced by the details of Bly's theory we cannot deny that it remains a fascinating metaphor for states as yet not analytically describable. More important, the mothers metaphor enables Bly to develop and enrich the paradoxes that float up from his inner darkness. He has constructed a vision of mystic evolution that not only refuses to deny but explains the moral dissolution that forms the primary vision of *Light*. The tension between the ecstatic mother and the stone mother provides a theoretical basis for Bly's double conception of darkness, the inspiring darkness of the inner world held in suspension with the terrifying blackness of the outer. "The Teeth-Mother Naked at Last," a map of the psychological politics behind an imperial war, is also a record of the collision between inner and outer worlds.

"Teeth-Mother," though marked throughout by Bly's characteristic surrealist imagery, differs basically from his earlier poetry. So far it is his only really extensive poem, and its coherence is more theoretical than imagistic. Frequently its deep images give way to flat, almost prosy statement, often far less striking than the visions of *Light*, but in some ways more moving. Bly adopts different tactics in this poem partly because he is writing a sort of propaganda based on juxtaposition of certain facts, but also because it seems impossible, and probably not desirable, to assimilate the actuality of Vietnam into poetry as Bly has previously written it. The Vietnam poems in *Light* primarily concerned the reverberations of war; "Teeth-Mother" is often a simple contemplation of unbearable facts. But it also implies an explanation.

> Helicopters flutter overhead. The death-
> bee is coming. Supersabres
> like knots of neurotic energy sweep
> around and return.
> This is Hamilton's triumph.
> This is the advantage of a centralized bank.

Destructive—"neurotic"—machines dominate the poem; despite his moral revulsion, Bly's ability to immerse himself in things enables him to evoke the alien world of machines and mechanical men as fully as he evokes the inner world. Vietnam represents the desperate end of the "masculine" rage for order, the force that created American prosperity but a force basically corrupted by its denial of the inner world. The warrior mentality, recreating itself in machines, opposes not only nature ("800 steel pellets fly through the vegetable walls") but the dark flow of its own humanity, its movement toward the death which completes life. The desire for death as fulfillment, corrupted, becomes a desire for death as grotesque destruction.

> The ministers lie, the professors lie, the television lies,
>   the priests lie. . . .
> These lies mean that the country wants to die.
> . . . .
> It's a desire to take death inside,
> to feel it burning inside, pushing out velvety hairs,
> like a clothes brush in the intestines

In a series of awkward but often striking juxtapositions, Bly suggests that the American rejection of grief and darkness, made possible by wealth, creates the grief of Vietnam. It is:

> because we have so few tears falling on our own hands
> that the Super Sabre turns and screams down toward the earth

51

In the face of this there appears no adequate response, no praise of the grief that follows the denial of grief, no mystical acceptance. Bly the political moralist presents, ironically undercut, the plea of the contemplative dreamer, who sees the corporeal flow of existence very much in terms that suggest *Silence*.

> Tell me about the particles of Babylonian thought that
>   still pass through the earthworm every day.
> Don't tell me about "the frightening laborers who do
>   not read books."

But the dehumanizing outer darkness prevails:

> . . . if one of those children came near that we have set on fire,
> came toward you like a gray barn, walking,
> you would howl like a wind tunnel in a hurricane,
> you would tear at your shirt with blue hands

No response to this, and yet, paradoxically, Bly suggests a response, or at least a way of understanding it. The horribly catalogued violence against human and vegetable nature can be seen in a more distant sense as a natural aspect of the apocalyptic evolutionary change described in more positive terms in the final pages of *Light*. One voice in "Teeth-Mother," looking for solace, suggests of the violence of "the Marine battalion," "This happens when the seasons change / this happens when the leaves begin to drop from the trees too early." Bly undercuts the suggestion of solace, but the comparison remains. Vietnam, in some sense the death of American dreams, is not an end but a transition, in which the teeth mother necessarily appears as an aspect of the ecstatic mother.

> Now the whole nation starts to whirl
> . . . .
> pigs rush toward the cliff,
> the waters underneath part: in one ocean luminous globes
>   float up (in them hairy and ecstatic rock musicians)—
> in the other, the teeth-mother, naked at last.

The balance, and the sense of cycles evolving, provide no cure to present agony. Bly knows it is the false transcendence of agony, with its attendant repression, which distorts human consciousness in the first place. But the vision of evolution enables Bly to sustain his paradoxical suspension of despair and mystic hope, his sense of death as life. Perhaps that paradox will always defy resolution, but in his latest poetry Bly continues to offer hope for evolution into a state of consciousness in which despair can be replaced by that grief which attends the natural movement of life, which is not inconsistent with joy. At the end of a recent poem read at Antioch, Bly suggests, through paradox now expressed with a clear simplicity, that the conflict between the father and the mother may be resolved by that consciousness now being born.

> More of the fathers are dying each day.
> It is time for the sons.
> Bits of darkness are gathering around them
> The darkness appears as flakes of light.
>
> ("Six Winter Privacy Poems," no. 3)

JAMES F. MERSMANN

Robert Bly
Watering the Rocks

> I am the poet of the woman the same as the man,
> And I say it is as great to be a woman as to be a man,
> And I say there is nothing greater than the mother of men.
> . . . .
> I am he that walks with the tender and growing night,
> I call to the earth and sea, half-held by the night.
>
> —Whitman, "Song of Myself"

The energy with which the Minnesota poet Robert Bly unreservedly gives himself to his ideas, or in some cases, his prejudices, makes him both one of the most annoying and most exciting poets of his time. Objectivity and judiciousness are not nice words in Bly's vocabulary: "Men like Whittemore or Nemerov can never write anything new because they are on-the-other-hand-men. If you say, the Christian Church is corrupt, they would say, 'On the other hand. . . .' If you say, 'John Foster Dulles was as close to being crazy as most statesmen get,' they would say, 'On the other hand. . . .'"[1] There is little danger that Robert Bly will ever be ridiculed as an "on-the-other-hand-man." Compared with the intense flex and balance of Denise Levertov, Bly sometimes seems like a frenetic farm boy shying rocks impulsively at anything that moves; but he can often be stingingly on target, and has probably brought home more game politically than any other poet besides Allen Ginsberg.

Bly is a natural *antagoniste*. From the first issue of *The Fifties* in

From *Out of the Vietnam Vortex: A Study of Poets and Poetry Against the War* (Lawrence, Kansas: The Regents Press of Kansas). Copyright © 1974 by the Regents Press of Kansas. Reprinted with permission.

1958, it was evident that Bly was a noisome gadfly to be reckoned with. Readers could sense that no one and nothing was to be immune from criticism, which instead of observing the polite rules of "on the other hand" attacked with what sometimes seemed a sophomoric energy. Though "Crunk," who is usually the pseudonymous shadow of Bly as Thersites, is here particularly mild, this first *Fifties* nevertheless draws blood from Yvor Winters, Allen Ginsberg, Henry Wadsworth Longfellow, the *Western Review,* John Ciardi, Chicago newspapers, and the *New York Times Book Review,* and gets in shots at rhyming, imageless poetry, universities, advertising, Christianity, the Atomic Energy Commission, and indeed, everyone, because "everybody" thinks "America is in strong moral condition." Bly and Crunk warm to their task in subsequent issues, taking on poets, institutions, and ideas of every kind with a wit that, though sometimes shallow, is always vigorous and exciting. Bly is, like the Supersabres he campaigns against, a "knot of neurotic energy"; and his voice, like "the whine of jets, pierces like a long needle" whether in prose, in person, or as "voice" in his poems. Bly is skilled both with needle and with ax, for to describe what happens in the shambles of "Madame Tussaud's Wax Museum," "Wisdom of the Old," and "The Order of the Blue Toad" (regular features of *The Sixties*) one has to reach for the metaphor of the ax. Whether or not it is true that Bly "started out completely surrounded by enemies," he has over the years offered nearly everyone an excuse to claim that status. "It's a wonder he's alive," exclaims Kenneth Rexroth.[2] But Bly has not only survived, he has thrived.

I

Most artists are, of necessity, "outsiders" to the larger society and its values, but Bly has been something of an outsider to his fellow poets as well. He has come by this chiefly for two reasons. The first can be called by different names: integrity. independence, stubbornness, egoism. One suspects that many of the critical remarks offered against Bly by his colleagues during the sixties (his theatricality, carelessness of form, lack of music, dilettantism) are only "acceptable" expressions of "unacceptable" irritations and antagonisms they felt toward him. Bly is "no respecter of person," and often does not play according to the polite rules, whether the game in question belongs to the establishment or the anti-establishment. He is like the pesky student who keeps asking the professor troublesome questions and will not be intimidated. Such traits alone are sufficient to alienate many, but even beyond this, there is something about Bly in person or print that often makes people uneasy. He is a man with disturbing energy and self-confidence, and an unreserved commitment to the things he does. Earmarks of integrity? or egoism?

Secondly, Bly stands as an "outsider" in that he has been without the support of anything like a Black Mountain, San Francisco, or New York coterie of fellows and followers. (Though a few poets have had affinities with Bly's poetic manner and ideas—Robert Kelly, James Wright, Louis Simpson, Jerome Rothenberg—he stood mostly alone before the *Kayak* poets began to make themselves heard.) Bly's allegiance has been to poets of other languages and of another imagination— the German poets Georg Trakl and Gottfried Benn, the French René Char and André Michaux, the Swedish Gunnar Ekelöf, and especially the Spanish Cesar Vallejo and Federico García Lorca, and the Chilean Pablo Neruda. This inspiration, and the "new imagination" of the poetry that Bly promotes and practices, demands more than casual reading. Bly's poetry is perhaps not so much misread or unread as shallowly read and put easily aside as poetry of the *deep* or *subjective image*. It has been an uncrowded and easy category, a convenient pigeonhole for disposing of poetry that challenges poetry-reading habits. Because the form is strange, it can be focused upon for comment and used as an excuse to avoid a difficult and profoundly unsettling content. Bly has been, then, generally regarded as that poet whom one wishes would take more care "with how things go together,"[3] whom one hopes will take more notice of *melopoeia* and *logopoeia* and give up his obsession with *phanopoeia*,[4] whom one wishes would put a little more trust in the power of "art," and give less energy to polemics.[5]

Bly's interest has always been with content rather than form, and life rather than "art." (Though these pairs are properly not polarities but are related as *ends* and *means,* poets and schools of poetry persist in arranging themselves on one side or another of the dichotomy.) His quarrel with traditional forms and their recent American substitutes is that they cannot carry the content of modern life. That content, he feels, is "the sudden new change in the life of humanity, of which the Nazi Camps, the terror of modern wars, the sanctification of the viciousness of advertising, the turning of everyone into workers, the profundity of associations, is all a part."[6] The "men of 1914" and Eliot in *The Waste Land* made one large raid into this life, but did not persist or widen their foraging; and, in fact, they finally retreated. Bly's view of the modern world is one, then, that focuses on an ugliness that is wider and deeper than that exposed by *The Waste Land,* and which in 1958 had "still not been described."[7] That reality, he suspected, could never be described in the restraints or prettinesses of rhyme, the decorous regularity of iambic meter, the four-letter words of Beat poetry, the vague suggestiveness of the *symboliste* mode, the impeccable order of poems for *Kenyon Review,* the narrowness of personal or confessional poetry, or the abstract tendencies of contemporary British poetry. What was needed was something at once more vigorous, more powerfully physical, more capable of reaching down into the darknesses and nightmares of the modern sickness. All these are implied in the metaphors with which he describes Spanish poetry, where he finds a power that "grasps modern life as a lion grabs a dog, and wraps it in heavy countless images, and holds it firm in a terrifically dense texture."[8] American poetry was incapable of this because it had sidestepped and never really gone through the experience of Surrealism:

Beginning with Baudelaire, French poetry went through a dark valley, a valley filled with black pools, lions, jungles, turbid rivers, dead men hanging from trees, wolves eating the feathers of birds, thunder hanging over doors, images of seas, sailors, drunken boats, maggots eating a corpse with the sound of a sower sowing grain, endless voyages, vast black skies, huge birds, continual rain. This immersion has given French poetry its strength, its rich soil, whereas our soil is thin and rocky, and the poetry of the 30's and 40's increasingly resembles a flower cut off above the ground and slowly withering.[9]

The last line hints at Bly's bias against the conscious mind, against the cerebral and the abstract. A poetry that grows from the intellect is like the plant deprived of its soil: true poetry springs from a deeper self, unknowable by the machinery that sorts and labels the produce at the top of the head and makes rational cases for whatever it wishes. The deep imagination swells up from the edges of hallucination and fantasy to produce Picasso's *Guernica,* while the superficial imagination finds satisfaction with the usable representational art of Marines planting the flag on Iwo Jima. The images that Bly calls for are not, then, the pictures of Ezra Pound and the Imagists, "petals on a wet black bough," but the images that writhe in the fogs halfway between deep and inarticulate passions and conscious thought. For Bly, the Chilean poet Pablo Neruda is the greatest poet of the deep consciousness and imagination, the possessor of a gift "for living in the unconscious present. Aragon and Breton are poets of reason, who occasionally throw themselves backward into the unconscious, but Neruda, like a deep sea crab, all claws and shell, is able to breathe in the heavy substances that lie beneath the daylight consciousness. He stays on the bottom for hours, and moves around calmly without hysteria."[10] Bly, one feels, is not by nature such a deep-sea crab, nor entirely or always securely beyond the tentacles of hysteria; but if he remains a poet of reason—as his heritage and Harvard experience perhaps force him to be—he does nevertheless sometimes swim deeply into the dark waters of the individual and the national psyche.

Bly chooses the poetry of the subjective image because it can carry the content he wants. But is there, perhaps, a closer relationship between the form and the nature of the content it carries? Does the deep image by its very nature, as revealed in the metaphors with which we describe it, lend itself necessarily to a dark, pessimistic, "anti-" or protest poetry? One does not swim downward into light, but into darkness; and one expects the ocean floor to be inhabited not by delicate and docile creatures, but by horrifying and grotesque forms. Thus a mode chosen to reach into these depths may end by compelling one to stay there, and a way of expressing what one sees may end in becoming a way of seeing whatever one would express. In other words, if we draw images and metaphors from an irrational and chaotic field, will the world they attempt to express be found to be more grotesque and horrible than it perhaps really is? (One thing is at least beyond question—the deep image is by its nature not well suited to saccharine, romantic, or patriotic poetry.) The importance of the question is that, ultimately, one wonders whether Bly's form is a result of his vision, or his vision the result of his form; whether he achieves a more powerful protest because his agonies are deeper, or whether they only seem so because expressed in a more profound form. One is at least confident in claiming that the two influences have reinforced and deepened one another, and that content and form join with a potency that justifies Bly's emergence as one of the most important poets of the sixties.

II

Bly's first book of poems, *Silence in the Snowy Fields,* is full of rural quietnesses, farmyards, fields, solitudes, and silences.[11] Peaceful and strangely satisfying, the poems attest to a wholeness in the poet who speaks them. The few troubled poems are easily carried by the calm of the rest. But there are touches of discontent here already, and, though far from the spirit of protest animating later work, they do raise themes that become important in *The Light Around the Body.*[12]

In "Unrest" (*Snowy Fields,* p. 25), Bly offers us a "state of the nation": youth blighted in a landscape of cold darkness, barren trees, baboons, and insects. Stereotyped bankers and businessmen appear first as culprits, and ultimately as fellow sufferers. The poem speaks of a "lassitude" that "enters into the diamonds of the body," and thus looks forward to "the light in children's faces fading at six or seven" ("Those Being Eaten by America," *Light,* p. 14), and to Bly's magnificent images of defeat in "Come with Me" (*Light,* p. 13).

In "Awakening" (p. 26), the poet communicates a fear and foreboding that evokes Yeats's "Second Coming" and the beast moving its slow thighs. A storm is coming, a darkness, apocalyptic, threatening. creeping through the grass, making the water in wells tremble, piling up in the shadows of church doors, seeping into the corners of barns, coming, coming. Indeed it is a darkness that makes us "want to go back, to return to the sea" ("Return to Solitude," p. 12), or to dive into that other darkness and "sea of death, like the stars of the wheeling Bear."

Unlike Levertov, in whose poetry death becomes alluring only after the war has undercut a previous vitality, Bly seems always to have sung soft songs to death. "Return to Solitude," "Depression," and "Night" are a few of the poems in *Snowy Fields* where death enters more as friend than intruder. It is as if death were at last the full granting of the solitude and silence that man grabs fleetingly from the night and the fields when he is able momentarily to forget his daylight awareness of man's inhumanities to man. To die is also to be absolved from returning to the agony of moral confrontation and impotence. Death is, moreover, an escape from the self ("My body hung about me like an old grain elevator, / Useless, clogged, full of blackened wheat" p. 37), and from the future into which

> . . . we are falling,
> Falling into the open mouths of darkness,
> Into the Congo as if into a river,
> Or as wheat into open mills.

(P. 31)

But despite these signs of a Marlovian consciousness, the dominant vision of *Silence in the Snowy Fields* is convincingly positive. Much more prevalent than shadow is luminescence; much more prominent than negation is affirmation:

> It is good also to be poor, and listen to the wind.

(P. 28)

> I am full of love, and love this torpid land.

(P. 33)

> There is a privacy I love in this snowy night.

(P. 38)

It is a joy to walk in the bare woods.

(P. 45)

I have awakened at Missoula, Montana, utterly happy.

(P. 47)

How beautiful to walk out at midnight in the moonlight
Dreaming of animals.

(P. 54)

Nor is it nature alone that Bly finds satisfying. There are also friends, "men and women I love," the human face that "shines as it speaks of things" (p. 58). The poet's peace is extremely attractive and yet perhaps a peace "in spite of," a "separate peace" concluded between the poet and a world that is necessarily restricted. This personal and local poetry is at times very much like Levertov's "poetry of the immediate." Just as one eventually learns from Levertov's poetry what can be seen from her kitchen window, one learns in reading *Snowy Fields* that nearly all the trees in Bly's farmyard must be box elders.

The apparent contradiction between the personal poetry of *Silence in the Snowy Fields* and Bly's *Fifties* campaign for a poetry that grasps the whole of modern life like a lion can perhaps be explained as his attempt to set his own house in order before setting out to correct the world's. Or it may be that, prior to the political assassinations of the sixties and the onset of the Vietnam war, Bly still secretly hoped that a private poetry and an escape from ugly political realities were possible. He doubted from the first, however, that "the small farmhouse in Minnesota" would be "strong enough for the storm" (*Snowy Fields*, p. 26). The tornadic emotionals of Vietnam destroyed the "farmhouse," and convinced Bly that the inward man could not survive unless the outward man spoke out. Poets could not, like trees, be nonpolitical and flourish as well under one administration as another.[13]

Whatever explanation accounts for the private and personal nature of the early poetry, that poetry no doubt increased Bly's understanding and furnished the reservoir of spiritual strength to sustain his political and public energies in *Light Around the Body*. The epigraph to *Snowy Fields*—"We are all asleep in the outward

61

man" (Jacob Boehme)—suggests Bly was digging inward, exploring the solitary "insular Tahiti" of the soul, in order to *awaken* the self. He later argues that "paradoxically what is needed to write true poems about the outward world is inwardness."[14]

III

In *Light Around the Body* the specific detail of *Snowy Fields* becomes the generalized subjective image, the inwardness becomes a window on the world, and the "I" becomes "we," or appears only as a point of vision ("I hear," "I see") or a means of introducing the image. The "I" of the private vision and of the self apart from the mass of men becomes the "we" of public vision and of the self as part of the community of mankind. Just as there is an inner and an outer man, there is a private and a public man, and similar laws of union and alienation apply to both: "For according to the outward man, we are in this world, and according to the inward man, we are in the inward world. . . . Since then we are generated out of both worlds, we speak in two languages, and we must be understood also by two languages" (Jacob Boehme, epigraph to part 1, *Light,* p. 7). In *Light Around the Body* Bly is speaking in the other of his two necessary languages, about the other of his two necessary selves. The private vision of *Silence in the Snowy Fields,* if persisted in, would have atrophied into a wrinkled Wordsworthian natural mysticism evasive of modern realities; the focus of *Light Around the Body,* pursued exclusively, threatens to deteriorate into noisy rhetoric.

Maintaining a healthy balance and interchange between inner and outer worlds is not easy: most men eventually fall toward an "other-worldly" pseudomysticism or a "this-worldly" utilitarian cynicism. True mystics—St. Paul, Meister Eckhart, St. John of the Cross, Jacob Boehme—are distinguished by their ability to use the resources of the inner world for the practical concerns of everyday existence. The inner world is not a rejection or escape but a source of strength and illumination that transforms the outer world. The genuinely spiritual man accepts both worlds; "he knows that his mortal life swings by nature between Thou and It [the divine and the mundane], and he is aware of the significance of this. It suffices him to be able to cross again and again the threshold of the holy place wherein he was not able to remain."[15]

Bly may not be a mystic, but he seems to be a genuinely spiritual man who has learned to use the resources of the inner life to energize his work in the outward world. Furthermore, there are convincing signs that Bly at least *understands* mysticism. That is itself a rare gift. He also seems to have learned, in Eliot's words, "to care and not to care," that difficult passivity that leads to revelation. His poem "Watering the Horse" records one such instant of clarity:

> How strange to think of giving up all ambition!
> Suddenly I see with such clear eyes
> The white flake of snow
> That has just fallen in the horse's mane!
>
> (*Snowy Fields,* p. 46)

That kind of "letting go," generally foreign to rational Western man, is usually learned through pain and defeat. Bly, who nowhere shares with his reader the details of his particular personal suffering, has somehow come to the mystical wisdom of passivity:

> There is a joyful night in which we lose
> Everything, and drift
> Like a radish
> Rising and falling, and the ocean
> At last throws us into the ocean
>
> ("When the Dumb Speak," *Light,* p. 62)

This understanding, necessarily experiental and not the mere acceptance of the idea by the conscious mind, is for Westerners, if not "mystical," at least a great epiphany. (Denise Levertov's denial of the vain will is a parallel illumination. Allen Ginsberg may not yet have learned to float like a radish, and continues to fling himself against the door that, as Levertov has learned, opens outward.) If the reader bothers to become aware of this spiritual depth in Bly, he is less apt to assume he has read Bly when he has read him only superficially.

IV

Bly's great energy has often earned for him the image of reckless dilettante. In the few public poems of *Snowy Fields* and in nearly all poetry during the war, Bly set for himself the task of jumping up out of the self "like a grasshopper" into the larger soul of the nation to "entangle" in words and bring back some of the strange plants and animals that inhabit it.[16] By seeking to explore the origins and effects of the impulses that make America and Americans physically and psychically what they are, Bly has found himself in the role of "psychologist." Armed necessarily with only a layman's knowledge of Freud and Jung, an imperfect secondhand knowledge of his patient's history, and an inability to hide the simplicity of his thought in arcane official jargon, his analyses have inevitably struck many as foolish and simplistic:

> I think the Vietnam war has something to do with the fact that we murdered the Indians. We're the only modern nation that ever stole its lands from another people. And killing the Indians seemed like a wonderful idea at the time: everybody used to shoot them out of trains and have a grand time. But it doesn't seem so funny anymore.
>
> But as Freud says, when you commit a crime. . . . Supposing you're a five-year-old boy; you beat up some kid next door—he's two years old—and you put out his eye and what happens? Your parents smooth it over and everything, and it's all o.k. and you forget about it, and everything goes fine—until you get about thirty-five years old and you get married and it turns out that everytime you get in a quarrel with your wife, you beat her up. So finally you both go to the psychiatrist and the psychiatrist talks for about six years and finally the story about the little boy comes out, and then he says, "Could I see photograph of the little boy?" and you go back to your mother and get photograph of the little boy, and

then the doctor says, "Did you ever notice the resemblance between that little boy and your wife." As Freud said, when we commit a crime we don't atone for it as the Catholic Church thought we would. What you do first when you commit a crime is you forget it and then you repeat it. So therefore in my opinion what we're doing is repeating the crime with the Indians. The Vietnamese are our Indians. We don't want to end this war! We didn't want to quit killing the Indians but we ran out of Indians, and they were all on reservations.[17]

Similar readings of American history are behind many of Bly's poems, and have frequently been offered between poems at his readings. Moreover, in exploring the American psyche Bly sometimes comes to conclusions that, contrary to all accepted rules of poetry, he baldly offers in the poems themselves free of charge. These must be acknowledged as disturbing weaknesses: in *Light,* "Men like Rusk are not men" (p. 30), "We distrust every person on earth with black hair" (p. 36), "No one in business can be a Christian" (p. 43); and in *Teeth-Mother,* "The ministers lie, the professors lie, the television lies, the priests lie" (p. 10). Even though perhaps true, these are prose opinions and not poetic insights. Political poetry is always in danger of being taken literally as prose, and the presence of prose passages such as these has helped insure misreadings of Bly's poems. Read as prose, the poems seem more strident and fantastic than they really are.

It is not difficult to understand why many have been offended by Bly and why his efforts have sometimes been dismissed as "theater." But are the faults just mentioned really the source of the dissatisfaction? Or is it that we suspect it is "highly improper" for "a poet" to talk and act as Bly does, "forgetting his art" and speaking out in areas where he is "not qualified"? Would we readily embrace the same analyses, garbed in an esoteric lingo we only half understand, coming from an "experienced psychologist" with "credentials"? Is it perhaps that our culture has always assumed and tacitly demanded that its poets should "stick to 'poetry'" and remain political eunuchs? Is it perhaps that Bly's openly subjective readings offend against New Criticism, value-neutrality, and "the myth of the objective consciousness"?

But Bly and his work are deeper than they at first seem. Bly may simply be wrong in asserting that we kill the Vietnamese because we have run out of Indians and because "underneath all the cement of the Pentagon / There is a drop of Indian blood preserved in snow" ("Hatred of Men with Black Hair," *Light*, p. 36); but there can be less doubt that the two are connected, and that killing of Indians and Vietnamese are both related to the same complex disposition and world view. In fact, even the objections to Bly's political energies grow out of the very same set of values, and it is at these values as much as at the war that Bly directs his protest.

Like Allen Ginsberg, Bly began his protest against the war long before this country's fighting in Vietnam began. He sensed early that although oppression in all countries was increasingly invisible, it was nevertheless increasingly experienced—"even in America, [oppression] is as common as beauty, for those who have senses which can grasp it."[18] The protest against the war has been for Bly as for Ginsberg (as it was not for a long while for Levertov) part of a larger revolt against the disposition that occasions war and oppresses the human spirit. Bly senses that somewhere hidden in present values and in the American psyche is a dark and terrible cancer, a core of rottenness and disorder. Louis Simpson feels the same truth and suggests that just when America seems to have realized its dream—

> Priests, examining the entrails of birds,
> Found the heart misplaced, and seeds
> As black as death, emitting a strange odor.[19]

It is this darkness and disorder that Bly seeks to explore, understand, and expose—toward the end that it may heal.

Does this darkness grow out of the black seeds of a national and international malaise, or is it something so pervasive as to hint of a darkness in human or cosmic nature? Is this darkness and this terror, which eventually drives man to "tear off his own arms and throw them into the air," innate in man and the cosmos or in man's political and social structures? The question of Bly's philosophy of man and nature is not immediately easy to answer. He is neither a Hobbesian who believes that man is, except for law, a wolf to man, nor a Rousseauist who sees man as a noble savage diseased with civilization. Nor can he be easily categorized as a Jeffers or a Conrad or a Hardy—he is neither a skeptic nor a pessimist, but senses a darkness in both man and the cosmos that he does not understand. The third stanza of "Johnson's Cabinet Watched by Ants" gives the reader a feeling that evil may be timeless and very much at home in the universe, that it is an old story, ineluctable, cotemporal with the primeval ooze:

> Ants are gathered around an old tree.
> In a choir they sing, in harsh and gravelly voices,
> Old Etruscan songs on tyranny.
> Toads nearby clap their small hands, and join
> The fiery songs, their five long toes trembling in the soaked earth.
>
> (*Light,* p. 5)

Perhaps man has always alternated between demonic nights in the forest and days of faith; perhaps he always will. Bly knows that evil is real, and should not be underestimated. Thus in Bly's protest, visions of a New Day (Ginsberg's *TV Baby Poems,* and Lawrence Ferlinghetti's "After the Cry of the Birds") give way to more modest visions:

> The world will soon break up into small colonies of the saved
> ("Those Being Eaten by America," *Light,* p. 14)

> they will abandon their homes
> to live on rafts tied together on the ocean;
> those on shore will go inside tree trunks
> ("Written in Dejection near Rome," *Light,* p. 15)

Generally, of course, Bly's poetry does not seek to uncover the ultimate nature of the universe, but to find the more immediate sources of darkness in man's present society. Some evil may be inevitable, but the poet of *Silence in the Snowy Fields* knows also that man is capable of peace, wholeness, and joy, and that most of the darkness and joylessness of modern man is unnatural. The American psyche Bly finds especially afflicted.

V

Before we approach Bly's poetic diagnosis of the cause of America's illness, we will do well to examine the symptoms he notices. The most egregious symptom is, of course, the Vietnam involvement itself, but closely related are manic fatigue, hysteria, and desire for self-mutilation and death.

The war and the unavailing protest against it has deepened the "lassitude," and that dulls "the diamonds of the body" (one recalls Ginsberg's "Moloch that enters the mind early"). This oppression-spawned acedia has been especially pervasive in the antiwar movement and in poetry itself. It coexists in a schizophrenic tension with outrage: the uncontrollable necessity of "raging out" (as Robert Duncan puts it) and the sense that it will do no good, that the evil is too large and inexorable. Or perhaps the soul corrodes into the catatonic depression of Levertov's "Cold Spring" because it is overcome with the surfeit of ugliness and horror. In the protest poets themselves, and in their vision of America, there is a prevalent taint of "the Bartleby syndrome," the despair that comes from impotently facing up to the massive wall.

Apathy and paralysis can result from conflicting impulses, from frustration of intense desire, and also from alienation of one part of the self from another. In our culture we are paralyzed and defeated because the outer man has lost touch with the inner man. The only images that now express us are "those things that have felt this despair for so long," things that man has used, worn out, given to the refuse heap, or simply ignored like "curly steel shavings, scattered about on garage benches" ("Come with Me," *Light,* p. 13).

Despite his own personal energy and strength, Bly is the supreme poet of defeat—defeat expressed in deep images of maniacal fury and total inertia. Poems such as "Come with Me" make their impact immediately without need of explication. Something in us readily identifies with

Those removed Chevrolet wheels that howl with a terrible
    loneliness,
Lying on their backs in the cindery dirt, like men drunk, and naked,
Staggering off down a hill at night to drown at last in the pond.
Those shredded inner tubes abandoned on the shoulders of thruways

These images are so right and familiar that we are apt to pay too little attention to their richness. Not only in his choice of image, but in his choice of particular words, Bly exactly captures the loneliness, degradation, defenselessness, disorientation, suffocation, defeat, and isolation of modern man. Moreover, we see in these images that man is impelled headlong by forces he does not understand or control, that instead of being in the driver's seat he is driven by a larger impersonal machine and is a commodity that has no value except that it can be used up. The appropriateness of Bly's images are perhaps proven by the fact that we can hardly speak about them without falling into puns. Men are the wheels of a society that oppresses, and they carry its burdensome machinery on their backs. Like the inner tubes, they are worn down or defeated in time because the pressure is too great. Like any expendable material, valuable only as it serves the great work of commerce, progress, or the Gross National Product, the defeated and destroyed individual is left by the roadside to rot while the great business of the world roars on. If even this much explication seems too much, it may at least suggest that the "rightness" we feel in Bly's images is not accidental. One can no more rationally explain how it feels to be a tire than one can explain the oppression the Vietnam War has brought to the human spirit, yet both are immediately known when the poet writes, "We all feel like tires being run down roads under heavy cars" (*Teeth-Mother*, p. 16). And even the use of the passive voice here could not be otherwise. Man no longer acts but is acted upon by external forces.

Bly's deep images, so well suited to carrying the sense of the grotesque, light up other dark corners of American life, and make the reader feel he is watching strange old movies out of the American past:

> We have a history of horse-beaters with red mustaches
> knocked down by a horse and bitten.[20]

> . . . these are the men who skinned Little Crow!
> We are all their sons, skulking
> In back rooms, selling nails with trembling hands!
> > ("Hatred of Men with Black Hair," *Light,* p. 36)

> The janitor sits troubled by the boiler,
> And the hotel keeper shuffles the cards of insanity.
> > ("The Great Society," *Light,* p. 17)

Though these images are still close to the surface imagination, one can already feel in them an ominous and terrifying note that elsewhere explodes from the deep unconscious with hysterical force:

> > One leg walks down the road and leaves
> > The other behind, the eyes part
> > And fly off in opposite directions

> > Filaments of death grow out.
> > The sheriff cuts off his black legs
> > And nails them to a tree
> > > ("War and Silence," *Light,* p. 31)

> Wild dogs tear off noses and eyes
> And run off with them down the street—
> The body tears off its own arms and throws them into the air.
> > ("Watching Television," *Light,* p. 6)

Such images haunt *The Light Around the Body* and carry a fantastic horror and degradation. The impossible spectacle of the body tearing off its own arms and throwing them into the air (it has all the mind-crushing-paradox qualities of a Zen *koan*) is the ultimate expression of extreme self-revulsion and longing for mutilation and annihilation.

Because we have been captured by "death," the death-in-life of the outward man cut off from his vital center, Bly believes we long for real death, an annihilation of the alienated self. Undoubtedly influenced by Freud,[21] Bly finds in our hatred and desire to kill others a double proof of our own self-hatred and death wish. According to Freud's theory of projection, we attribute to our enemy the hatred for us that we feel toward ourselves. We thus need to destroy the enemy because we are paranoiacally sure he is trying to kill us. And by a second law of sublimation and transference, we satisfy our desire for self-destruction by violence against our enemy. Out of such understandings come those sections of *The Teeth-Mother Naked at Last* in which Robert Duncan thinks Bly has captured the truth behind the Vietnam War.[22]

> It is a desire to eat death,
> to gobble it down,
> to rush on it like a cobra with mouth open,
>
> It's a desire to take death inside,
> to feel it burning inside, pushing out velvety hairs,
> like a clothes brush in the intestines
>
> (*Teeth-Mother*, p. 10)

An even more powerfully haunting version about death occurs in a portion of the poem published in the *Nation* but strangely does not appear in the City Lights edition of the larger poem:

> As soon as Rusk finishes his press conference,
>   Black wings carry off the words,
> bits of flesh still clinging to them; somewhere
> in Montana near Hemingway's grave,
> they are chewed by timid hyenas[23]

Bly's poems suggest multiple reasons for his and America's obsession with death. Death is variously looked on as the complete solitude and silence, as escape from self and weary realities, as schizophrenic catatonia, as avoidance of the imminent apocalyptic darkness and cataclysm, as annihilation of the alienated outward self, as projected and sublimated self-hatred. Bly further suggests that we desire death as punishment for the guilt of past evils, and as the culmination of our strong antilife impulses.

We seek death as expiation of the burden of guilt accumulated from the rape of the frontier and the ecology, from puritanical morality and discipline, from killing Indians, from a history of violence and socioeconomic inequities—Bly's hysterical images of mutilation seem to spiral out of guilt-frenzy. There are antilife forces at work throughout the modern world, but Bly senses that they have developed most strongly in America because our "progress" has been more rapid.

VI

The temptation is to throw sticks at someone, to blame someone for all this guilt and evil, and Bly does not resist. The nearest targets are "merchants," "executives," "bankers," "dentists," and "sportsmen." Michael Goldman and Louis Simpson are right when they complain that Bly's executives and bankers are all stereotypes, and that his depiction of them is full of clichés.[24] But Bly, of course, is not interested in the psyche and personality of the individual banker; he is interested in the national psyche, of which "banker" is one aspect. It is nonsense to imply that Bly's poetry fails because all bankers are not really the bad men Bly paints them to be. Bankers as stereotypes ("stereotypes" are after all formed by induction) do have common values that *are* indeed clichés that keep the machine of state running. Moreover, Bly's poetry everywhere *intends* to imply that life in America *is* a cliché: "Dentists continue to water their lawns even in the rain" ("The Great Society," *Light,* p. 17).

It is true that poetry, even since Pound and Eliot, has been overrun with images of philistine bankers and joyless typists; but because the evils of commercial society are still upon us, poets are probably impelled to rage on against them even if there are no longer fresh ways to do so. Still, we are rightly tired of hearing "No one in business can be a Christian," even if, in the way Bly means it, it is undeniably true.

There is also in Bly a Poundian tendency toward easy economic readings of political and social evils. In *The Teeth-Mother Naked at Last,* after a description of the massive armaments that crush Vietnam, we are told: "This is Hamilton's triumph. / This is the advantage of a centralized bank" (p. 5). We have a right to feel less pleased with this element of Bly's poetry because it may seem to us, as Pound's economic theories seem to Louis Untermeyer, "not only ineffectual but absurd."[25] But, although it is easy to overlook, Bly's analysis goes further than Pound's and in an exactly opposite direction. Pound was, after all, a reactionary and eventually a fascist of sorts; Bly has none of his tastes for "kulchur," power, order, or violence (see "Sestina Altaforte"). Moreover, unlike Pound, Bly sees the centralized bank and commercialism as a symptom rather than a cause of the modern disease:

> It's because a hospital room in the average American
>   city now costs $60 a day that we bombed hospitals
>   in the North
>
> It's because the aluminum window-shade business is
>   doing so well in the United States that we roll fire
>   over entire villages
> . . . .
>
> It's because we have new packaging for smoked oysters
>   that bomb holes appear in the rice paddies
> (Teeth-Mother, p. 14)*

Though these and other such lines seem to be a condemnation of material wealth, they are something more than that. Added together they show an artificiality, a passion for order and precision, a remoteness from experience, a coldness, a hardness, and an antiseptic quality in our lives. What seems at first an inane economic prose argument—"It's because tax-payers move to the suburbs that we transfer populations"—becomes, with the

---

*City Lights Books edition, 1970.—ED.

added thought we grant to poetry, a statement about attitudes that grow out of our own rootlessness and externality, our loss of sense of place, our distaste for the darker, more sensual (less external) "uncivilized" populations of the inner cities, and the loss of uniqueness and identity that makes us forget "populations" are composed after all of individuals.

It is the externality, the living in the outward man, that Bly quarrels against: "O dear children, look in what a dungeon we are lying, in what lodging we are, for we have been captured by the spirit of the outward world; it is our life, for it nourishes and brings us up, it rules in our marrow and bones, in our flesh and blood, it has made our flesh earthly, and now death has us" (Jacob Boehme, epigraph to part 4, *Light,* p. 39).

VII

The inward-outward, spiritual/material dichotomy in Jacob Boehme's writings eventually merges for Bly with the parallel *anima/animus* dichotomy important in the psychology of Carl Jung. Marx made us aware of the laborer's alienation from his labor; Ivan Illich now shows us, in his "deschooling" campaign, the learner's alienation from what he learns; Robert Bly, taking his inspiration from Boehme, and ultimately from Jung, helps us understand the present alienation of the inward and the outward man.

In perhaps the most finely realized poem of *Silence in the Snowy Fields,* "A Man Writes to a Part of Himself," Bly serendipitously "figures" the inner and outer selves as wife and husband—the wife starved, hiding in a cave, "Water dripping from . . . [her] head, bent / Over ground corn . . ."; and her husband

> On the streets of a distant city, laughing,
> With many appointments,
> Though at night going also
> To a bare room, a room of poverty.
> To sleep among a bare pitcher and basin
> In a room with no heat
>
> (*Snowy Fields,* p. 36)

The contrasting images are of primitive and modern man, of primitive and native spirituality neglected and atrophied in favor of commerce and a joyless sensuality that, in the end, is barren and unsatisfying even to the outward man.

We cannot know how much Bly consciously intended in this poem, but like any good poem it continues to throw off multiple radiations. Bly claims not to have read Jung until later, but the poem is nevertheless rich with the symbology of Jungian psychology and offers something of a key to the rest of Bly's work.* Rather than being consciously influenced by Jung, the poem is probably another piece of spontaneous evidence for the validity of certain Jungian archetypes. It is, first of all, significant that Bly should choose to represent the inner self as a woman and the outer self as a man. If we look closer, we notice that the wife is hiding in a "cave," and though she may be starving, is nevertheless bent over a bowl of grain (the bowl, though not named, is necessarily imaged in the adjective of "ground corn"). Water drips from her head and she looks out over another concavity or bowl, "into rain that drives over the valley." Despite her loneliness and poverty in her husband's absence, these are images of fertility and life, of soil to be planted, of seeds waiting in the dark earth, of sensuousness and female sexuality. Though it is evoked with amazing economy, one even senses deep emotion in the wife: "you raise your face into the rain."

In contrast to the fertile valley are the "streets" of the city; in contrast to the visceral emotions of the wife are the superficial emotions of the husband "laughing, with many appointments." The husband's room, futhermore, is one "with no heat" and no running water. The pitcher and basin, important parallel symbols for male and female, are barren—"bare" being twice repeated in the stanza. Instead of returning at night to the wife's

---

*This peom and also "The Busy Man Speaks" were written, Bly claims, before he started reading Jung. But the Jungian influence on the rest of *Light Around the Body* is at least partly conscious, and Bly seemed pleased (personal interview, Oct. 28, 1971) to confirm the patterns that I had discovered in his imagery (as developed here in the last half of this essay). In his new book, *Sleepers Joining Hands,* Bly himself briefly explores in prose this fascination with Jung and the earth and stone mothers.

warm, dark, wet, fecund cave, he goes to the "bare room," light, dry, antiseptic, without heat or water.

Though the outward man may necessarily seem to bear the brunt of the blame for the loneliness and estrangement, Bly's poetry seeks a balance that refrains from disparaging the outward man. In this indirect "dialogue of body and soul" there are no recriminations: the spiritual/emotional/sexual is not put on a pedestal, the material/active/external is not damned—both are deprived of the natural ecstasy that can come only when they are united as one. Even the central metaphor of marriage indicates Bly's understanding of the necessary balance of masculine and feminine forces in all considerations of life. This awareness saves his protest from the antinomian heresies of fun, flesh, and frolic marking Ginsberg's work. Bly, too, knows that the flesh is holy, yet he shows no signs of Ginsberg's excessive, almost tantric faith in sanctity through sexuality, nor any utopian visions of mankind made ecstatic by schooling in the "college of the body." The Beat Generation's treatment of the order-orgy dichotomy sometimes forgets that the two are simply out of balance and that order is not all bad or orgy all good. Bly shares a similar revolt against the "intellect" and a campaign for restoration of emotional and sensuous life, but with the implicit understanding that order, objectivity, law, restraint, authority, material goods, and social conventions are not to be destroyed and abandoned, but brought back into proper proportions with freedom, subjectivity, impulse, spontaneity, and spirituality.* Perhaps this makes Bly a traditionalist, yet the "balance" he seeks is not a lukewarm halfway point; he seems to understand that such polarities are not really antagonistic but can paradoxically come together in a union that increases and enhances both.

When Bly in later poems condemns the outward world, it is

---

*Bly complains in an early issue of *The Sixties* about the abstract language of modern poetry, and includes a portion of *Howl* as an example. He has consistently claimed that Beat poetry, in spite of its predilection for four-letter words, uses an abstract diction. Perhaps proof that Bly has found a more concerete language—we are very much aware that Ginsberg's poetry is about the two long strings of abstractions listed in the above paragraphs, but we have first to carefully analyze the images and motifs of Bly's poetry before we see that it is equally concerned about these same abstractions.

never the physical and social "man" that he condemns, but rather the implicit assertions of modern life that this is the only man there is. Though the modern world gives itself to the "husband," the outward man, he too is nevertheless starved, and like so many things "howls outside the hedges of life" ("Smothered by the World," *Light,* p. 7), because he cannot really *live* except in union with his "wife."

Importantly related are the series of contrasts in "The Busy Man Speaks," the second poem of *Light Around the Body*. Here the modern busyness-man, like the accountant of stars in Antoine de Saint Exupéry's *Little Prince,* is devoted to *matters of consequence* and refuses to give himself to the "mother" (significantly) of solitude, tears, ocean, sorrow, humility, suffering, open fields, night, crickets, Christ. He will give himself instead to the upright "father" (significantly) of all things hard, angular, and artificial:

> But I will give myself to the father of righteousness, the father
> Of cheerfulness, who is also the father of rocks,
> Who is also the father of perfect gestures;
> From the Chase National Bank
> An arm of flame has come, and I am drawn
> To the desert, to the parched places, to the landscape of zeros;
> And I shall give myself away to the father of righteousness,
> The stones of cheerfulness, the steel of money, the father of rocks.
>
> ("The Busy Man Speaks," *Light,* p. 4)

Bly parodies the modern religion of commerce and money by suggesting a mystical relation between the busy man and his modern God: the flash of holy fire comes not from the heavens but the Chase National Bank. Though devotion to this God surrounds modern man with a "desert," his days in the desert, unlike Christ's, bring him not spiritual food, but spiritual starvation.

Such divisions of the masculine and feminine occur under subtle and sometimes covert forms throughout Bly's protest poetry, and become the most important unifying theme. What for Ginsberg becomes an Apollonian-Dionysiac or order-orgy conflict, becomes for Bly a conflict between masculine and feminine, hard and soft, rigid and flexible, rock and water. The related polarities or subforms are many, and include reason-emotion, active-passive, barren-fertile, cold-warm, angular-curved, stars-moon, frozen-fluid, domination-submission, discipline-love, power-weakness, and light-dark.

Never an "on-the-other-hand" poet in his commitment, Bly characteristically uses an "on-the-other-hand" conjunction and contrast of images that involves some aspect of the masculine/feminine tension. Sometimes they are subtle and concealed, and yet they are usually strange enough to make us think they can hardly be accidental: "The Marines think that unless they die the rivers will not move" (*Teeth-Mother,* p. 18).

While a good deal of the symbolism one finds as a result of the *anima/animus* key may be fortuitous rather than consciously managed by Bly, it is nevertheless part of a particular disposition and consistent manner of seeing. The opening image of *Light Around the Body,* for example, may have been chosen for no other reason than its signification of great numbers: "Merchants have multiplied more than the stars of heaven" ("The Executive's Death," p. 3). Perhaps Bly was not at all thinking of the connotations stars have in Blake's "Tyger," Yeats's "Who Goes with Fergus" (and Yeats's system), or Stephen Crane's "Open Boat," yet these meanings work perfectly with the poem's juxtaposition of high and low, cold and hot, sterile and prolific; with the contrast of merchants and executives against crane handlers, taxi drivers, and commuters. The executives walk "high in the air" on "cool floors" and dream of a death that calls up thoughts of Hemingway's leopard in "The Snows of Kilimanjaro"; the commuters are compared to "moles" and "hares" living close to the earth, with the "sound of thousands of small wings."

VIII

What does Bly see as the historical roots and parallels of the lopsided masculine emphasis of modern life? Among others, the poetry seems to implicate such figures and forces as Plato, the Old Testament, the Roman Empire, Hegel, the Catholic Church, Puritanism, Locke, Andrew Jackson, and Teddy Roosevelt. It seems most convenient here to start with the more recent and move backward in time.

Theodore Roosevelt is one of the "Three Presidents" (*Light,* p. 19) along with John Kennedy and Andrew Jackson. The advocate of carrying a big stick is here imagined as wanting to be a stone laid down thousands of years ago, one so dry that it is filled with invisible cracks. It is apparently an anti-orgiastic stone, too, for it "gets up and runs around at night, / And lets the marriage bed fall"; and though it leaps into water, it does so only for the purpose of "carrying the robber down." To the Rough Rider who "crushed snails with . . . [his] bare teeth," Bly contrasts Kennedy. (Bly wanted to idolize Jack Kennedy— see the sorrow of "Listening to President Kennedy Lie about the Cuban Invasion," *Light,* p. 16.) When he reads the "Three Presidents," Bly's voice shifts from a harsh, aggressive, mocking energy in the Roosevelt section to a liquid, smoothly flowing serenity in the Kennedy portrait. Unlike Roosevelt, Kennedy does not want to be a stone, but a "stream of water falling," "able to flow past rocks," to "carry boulders with me to the valley."

Andrew Jackson appears in "Three Presidents" only briefly, and although his desire to be a white horse is perhaps muscular and masculine enough, it is not really a negative image. But there can be little doubt of Bly's intentions in "Andrew Jackson's Speech" (*Light,* p. 24). Jackson has been reading Virgil, who, we recall, wrote the *Aeneid* in behalf of "duty," "law and order," the divine right of Augustus Caesar, and the glory of the Roman Empire; and who was chosen by Dante to serve as "Reason" in the Divine Comedy. The passage of Virgil at hand—"I have broke faith with the ashes of Sichaeus!" argues a loyalty to the dead past at the cost of sensuous love and domestic happiness. Andy Jackson, known for his quarrels and duels in defense of the "sacred name" of his wife, Rachel, here claims he would kill to save the honor of his people as readily as he did for his wife. The poor of Detroit are pictured, interestingly enough, as people who had been warned by Washington "never to take another husband." The Detroit riots, it is implied, must be put down at whatever cost to save the honor of the dead and moldering American dream, the attitudes toward enterprise and order that no longer serve the people's present needs any more than the dead Sichaeus serves Dido's daily needs of spiritual and sensual love.

Bly's obsession with Jackson erupts again in his National Book Award acceptance speech. Bly remarked that, of late, books concerning the killing of Indians seemed to jump into his hands when he entered bookstores, and from them he discovered that Andrew Jackson was the "Westmoreland of yesterday," one who was guilty of a scorched-earth policy and "recommending murder of a race as a prudent policy, requiring stamina."[26] Both "prudence" and "stamina" are, in such a context, obviously distasteful "masculine" qualities that remain as forces behind the mentality of the Vietnam War.

In "The Current Administration" (*Light*, p. 22), Bly employs his favorite technique of contrast, posing the hard and abrasive against the soft and the yielding, the spiritual and the human against the material and the mechanical. Among other signs revealing blindness and lack of understanding during the Current Administration, "A rose receives the name of 'The General Jackson.'" Here in nine words Bly catches the insane unreality of official thinking, the corruption of language, the refusal to see any meanings beyond one's own purposes and prejudices. The rose, the symbol for poets of Eternal Beauty, of Love, of Absolute Good, of Dante's mystical vision; the rose, in nature the most fragile, soft, delicate of flowers—here, with the complacent mindlessness of pseudo-Southern charm, becomes "The General Jackson," both "Old Hickory" and "Stonewall" himself. ("O rose, thou art sick, / the invisible worm / That flies in the night . . .")

No doubt Jackson was "not all bad," but the point is that Jackson is, for Bly, an effective shorthand symbol of certain qualities that decimate American life. That, too, is the case with most of the other figures and institutions Bly implicates. The Roman Catholic Church in Bly's poetry is not the church of Thomas Merton, Teilhard de Chardin, or Good Pope John, but the hierarchical, authoritarian, excommunicating, fear- and guilt-instilling church of the Inquisition. Bly knows that this Church is not the whole reality, but that it still is a *part* of the reality and feeds the attitudes that create Vietnams. It is also a ready symbol of the establishment and of the past, against which may be posed the revolutionary antiwar "Protestant tied in the fire" (*Teeth-Mother,* p. 22). The Inquisition affords a convenient parallel to the questioning of Viet Cong prisoners (*Teeth-Mother,* p. 9, and *Light,* p. 37), and the Church's guilt, historically, of simony can be used as excellent indirect criticism of modern governments that are likewise guilty. Thus, President Johnson might expectedly be a defender of the Church, and include in his "lies," "that only the Protestants sold indulgences" (*Teeth-Mother,* p. 11).

With this general attitude in mind, one sees the significances Bly intends in the following lines: "and with a lily the Pope meets / a delegation of waves, and blesses the associations / of the ocean." More strange occurrences of "The Current Administration"! The first contradiction is between the symbolic Pope and the lily-waves-ocean. Hers is the "rock" that so often finds juxtaposition with water in Bly's protest poetry. The Rock of Peter, the foundation of the Church, itself a rock against which floods shall not prevail, here officiously blesses the waters and inevitably thinks of them as "delegations" and "associations." Not only is there a provocative contrast between the static and the fluid, the motionless and the motionfull, but also, seemingly, an insidious encroachment of the institutional order and hierarchy into the realm of the wet and the free.*

Sharing the guilt with Roman Catholicism is Puritanism: whereas the first is the primary symbol of institutional evil, the second is the primary symbol of a harsh and repressive morality. Puritanism imposed both a terrible guilt and a terrible need to punish; promoted a judgmental disposition; caused men to look on one another with jaundiced eyes; encouraged a hiding of the inward self by external masks; outlawed ecstasy and denied the flesh; reduced the world to blacks and whites; and sent men on hunts for witches and Communists. It is partly responsible for the darkness haunting Bly's poems:

---

*William Everson, in David Kherdian's *Six Poets of the San Francisco Renaissance* (Fresno: Giligia Press, 1965), pp. 131–51, has some brief but interesting remarks on the Church's masculine spirit, and her neglect of the feminine Sophia, the Divine Wisdom.

It is that darkness among pine boughs
That the Puritans brushed
As they went out to kill turkeys
("At a March against the Vietnam War," *Light*, p. 34)

That same darkness, fear, and guilt make Bly, during the march on Washington (November 27, 1965), imagine

. . . something moving in the dark somewhere
Just beyond
The edge of our eyes: a boat
Covered with machine guns
Moving along under trees

(*Light*, p. 34)

Because the Puritan's devil is after us always, we must always seek to kill the "devils." Bly, were he to comment on this poem, might as easily say (as he did about "running out of Indians") that we kill the Viet Cong because we have run out of witches and devils.

Behind both Catholicism and Puritanism, as Bly conceives them, is an essentially Old Testament mentality. Old Testament Yahweh was a jealous God, a God of the Hebrews who demanded complete obeisance, and in return helped the righteous Jews slay their enemies. He was the God who asked Abraham to slay Isaac (see Marge Piercy's "Fathers and Sons" in her *Hard Loving*), who sent plagues upon evil-doers, and who might, to embarrass the devil, send plagues upon just men. These are the images, tending toward caricature, that Bly intends in "the last haven of Jehovah, down from the old heavens, / Hugged a sooty corner of the murdered pine" ("The Current Administration," *Light*, p. 22); and "they are dying because the President has opened a Bible again" (*Teeth-Mother*, p. 18).

The Old Testament Yahweh was a God of patriarchy and hierarchy, was a God above and remote, having the relation to his people that a Victorian father had to his children. This hierarchical pattern or pyramidal structure mirrors that of a strong president to his constituency (and, in fact: of a professor to his pupils all in rows; of the pope to his laymen; of reason to the other faculties in the Renaissance–neo-classical scheme of "order and degree"; of God to the Great Chain of Being; and of the powerful United States to the lesser nations). Though he never poses *hierarchy* against *community* as Robert Duncan does, Bly similarly revolts against such "fathers" and such hierarchy. Bly apparently intends to pose the president and Yahweh as interchangeable entities in his Jack-and-the-Beanstalk description of "the giant's house":

> . . . Chairs
> In the great room, hacked from redwood.
> Tiny loaves of bread with ears lie on the President's table.
> Steps coming! The Father will soon return!
>
> ("The Current Administration," *Light*, p. 23)

The Bible that the President "has opened" again and which causes the dying is obviously an Old Testament. But there is more to the Bible than the Old Testament—Christ brought a new covenant of *grace* that was to replace the covenant of *law*:

> I know that books are tired of us.
> I *know* they are chaining the Bible to chairs.
> Books don't want to remain in the same room with us anymore.
> New Testaments are escaping! . . . Dressed as women . . .
> they go off after dark.
>
> (*Teeth-Mother*, p. 17)

Presumably the Old Testament would not have to be chained but would be comfortable in the same room with modern man. Is it accidental that Bly has this book—of forgiveness, freedom, and the love that counsels "resist not evil," "if a man takes your coat, give him also your shirt," and "move as the Wind of the Spirit moves you," that teaches strength in weakness, victory in defeat, and life in death—can it be accidental that Bly has this book go off "after dark" dressed as a "woman"?

There are forces in the secular realm as well that oppose the spirits of the wind and the water:

> . . . I walk with a coarse body through winds
> That carry the birds on their long roads to the poles,
> And see the ghost of Locke above the railroad tracks.
>
> $\qquad\qquad\qquad$ (*Light*, p. 22)

The poet obviously regrets his coarse body and his inability to share the fluid wind-paths of the birds, and almost implies that this ability is not foreign but has been lost. The road of the birds, the river of wind, contrasts with the iron rails, heavy cross-ties, and inflexible direction of the modern railroad. The ghost of Locke that hovers over this hard fact is not the Locke who sometimes defended religious and political liberty or battled against Cartesian abstraction, but the Locke associated with the "association of ideas," the "tabula rasa," materialism, and positivism. The Holy Spirit quietly implicit in the images of birds and wind has been replaced for modern man by the spirit of Locke—antimystical, antimiraculous, anti-Enthusiasm (*en=*, in + *theos,* God; in God or possessed by God; poetic ecstasy). The "coarse body" here deserves comparison with the "heavy body" in "Smothered by the World" (*Light,* p. 7) and the "body burdened down with leaves, / The opaque flesh, heavy as November grass, / Growing stubbornly, triumphant even at midnight" in the poem "In Danger from the Outer World" (*Light,* p. 47). Locke and his ideas have helped as much as puritan morality to reduce the body to a joyless mass and rob it of the light that both *lights* and *lightens* it (Bly obviously understands the idea of grace in Dante, and in Simone Weil's *Gravity and Grace*):

> I have risen to a body
> Not yet born,
> Existing like a light around the body,
> Through which the body moves like a sliding moon.
>
> $\qquad\qquad$ ("Looking into a Face," *Light,* p. 53)

Significantly, the body moves through and with a light not like the sun, but "like a sliding moon" (Diana, not Apollo). It is the light of the imagination and the interior mysterious soul that gives all things an awesome significance, and not the hierarchical sun of reason that denudes all things with cold analytical light.

Rather than unifying or synthesizing, science analyzes, dissects, reduces things to components and numerical quantities, and is concerned with bodies as mass. The "heavy body" figuring so prominently in Bly's poetry, and the persons reduced to numerical quantity ("Arabic numerals / walked the earth, dressed as bankers and sportsmen" ["The Current Administration," *Light,* p. 22]) are perhaps related to Locke's teachings that matter can be expressed in terms of mathematical quantity, and that even the secondary qualities of bodies ultimately depend upon "the bulk, figures, number, situation, and motions of the solid parts of which the bodies consist."[27]

What Locke effected in the world of physics, Hegel effected in metaphysics. Hegel's teachings, when overly simplified, reduced man to a small cog in a vast scheme and pattern. The universe had purpose and direction, and man was part of the process, but not the end and raison d'être of creation. Hegel, now generally out of favor, has been replaced by Sören Kierkegaard, the father of modern existentialism, who argued against the Hegelian Grand Design and for the freedom and responsibility of the individual. But Bly evidently still finds Hegel culpable for the modern inclination to make external abstract considerations—honor, progress, power, "national purpose"—more important than persons:

> Accountants hover over the earth like helicopters,
> Dropping bits of paper engraved with Hegel's name.
> Badgers carry the papers on their fur
> To their den, where the entire family dies in the night.
> ("A Dream of Suffocation," *Light,* p. 8)

Here again in characteristic association are the numerical, commercial, mechanical, military, external, and abstract hovering over and bringing death to the underlings, here "badgers" (elsewhere moles and hares) living undergound but nevertheless fatally tainted and infected. Hegel's killing power is indeed frightening, for even his name on a scrap of paper can kill the whole family of badgers.

In the Roman Empire, known for its persecution of early Christians, its lust for power, order, duty, propriety, and in its later stages, its corruption and disintegration, Bly finds an apt commentary on the present United States. The Romans were the first people to get along without gods; having lost any real interest in their pagan deities, they were nevertheless determined to suppress the God of the Hebrews and Christians. They are ready images for modern pragmatism and coercion and for contemporary persecutions of any lingering or fresh spirituality. The time setting within poems in which Bly uses the Romans cannot be determined, and, one may infer, is unimportant: the American enterprise and the Roman enterprise are the same. Thus in lines obviously dealing with the torture of Viet Cong prisoners, "excellent Roman knives slip along the ribs" (*Teeth-Mother,* p. 9), and in "Romans Angry about the Inner World" (*Light,* p. 9), executives, executioners, and Romans blend into one. The young girl the "Angry Romans" torture could as well be an early martyr, a modern occultist, or a transtemporal symbol. In the last-mentioned poem it is once again noteworthy that the poet, who might have chosen a St. Stephen, picks a female as his advocate of the inner life, as the victim of the stern hardness of the Romans for whom

> The other world is like a thorn
> In the ear of a tiny beast!
> The fingers of the executives are too thick
> To pull it out!
>
> (*Light,* pp. 9, 10)

These executioners, who know nothing of children, of ecstasy, of "a leaping of the body, / the body rolling,"

> Move toward Drusia. They tie her legs
> On the iron horse. "Here is a woman
> Who has seen our mother
> In the other world!"

The horse has often been used as a symbol of masculine sexuality, certainly in D. H. Lawrence and Robinson Jeffers. The horse here, however, is not an image of living and sensual potency, but an iron horse, an instrument of torture, an appropriate symbol of a cold and barren force, a masculinity gone awry. On this iron horse the devotee of the inner world is broken because she continues to testify that these men have a "mother" in the inner world.

Because modern Western society has wrongly associated masculinity with toughness and power, Bly connects it with images of irons, teeth, rocks, mountains, ice, and passionlessness. The defective modern attitude thinks of Christ as "effeminate," in sharp contrast to the insights of Hopkins or Donne. For Hopkins, Christ is both the falcon riding the river of wind and "a stalwart stallion, very-violet sweet." Biblically, Christ is the sensual lover prefigured in the Song of Solomon and the bridegroom for whom the maidens light their lamps. In Donne's Holy Sonnet number 14, God is a phallic force or battering ram seeking to enter the walled city that "labors to admit" him. This masculine vitality, however, by ravishing and enthralling the city (the self), makes "her" chaste and free. In place of this potent and fertile masculinity, compatible and in fact paradoxically identical with feminity, the modern world poses a harsh and sterile travesty. Ironically, the very railroad over which the spirit of Locke hovers carries, too, its "iron horse," as much an incarnation of the God of Science and Industry as the "stalwart stallion" of the God it replaces.

If proper masculinity is somehow an incarnation of spiritual power mysteriously *creating* through warlike "destruction" and *making whole* by "annihilation," then we might readily expect a pseudo-masculinity to destroy what it would pretend to create, and annihilate what it would make whole. Such reflections throw an interesting light on war, including the first war in literature, Homer's Greeks on the beaches of Troy. Though Achilles may have been the offspring of the sea goddess Thetis, he is inflexible, intractable, armored man. As barren, barbaric, alienated power, who treats women as concubines, Achilles chases Hector, the devoted husband and Troy's physical and spiritual bulwark, around the walled city and, embarrassingly, through the "laundry" (the hot and cold springs where the women do their washing when the city is not under attack). One kind of masculine power defeats another, and associates it disgracefully with the feminine. Furthermore, Odysseus, the man of reason, in the artificial wooden horse—pretenced as a spiritual offering to the gods—gains entrance to the walled city, not surely to make it chaste and free, but to rape and destroy. In place of the seeds of life, the false and hollow horse carries the forces of death.

Because Bly has been a busy student of America's history since deciding to "leap up into the psyche of the nation," he is probably well acquainted with *The Education of Henry Adams*. Adams's chapter on "The Virgin and the Dynamo," if not a source of influence, at least offers parallel perceptions about the American Temper. Adams himself feels the strong and almost mystical attraction Americans have for the dynamo and the wonders of science, and realizes that these represent for us the kind of force that the Virgin held for the builders of the Gothic cathedrals: "The force of the Virgin was still felt at Lourdes, and seemed to be as potent as X-rays; but in America neither Venus nor Virgin ever had value as force—at most as sentiment. No American had ever been truly afraid of either."[28]

Though "the Virgin had acted as the greatest force the Western world ever felt, and had drawn man's activities to herself more strongly than any other power, natural or supernatural, had ever done" (p. 388), "yet this energy was unknown to the American mind. An American Virgin would never dare command; and American Venus would never dare exist" (p. 385). St. Gaudens, a famous American sculptor in Paris at the time Adams wrote these words, could not appreciate the cathedral sculpture nor the power of the Virgin. "St. Gaudens' art was starved from birth, and Adams' instinct was blighted from babyhood. Each had but half of a nature, and when they came before the Virgin of Amiens they ought both to have felt in her the force that made them one; but it was not so" (p. 387). Instead Adams felt "the forty-foot dynamos as a moral force, much as the early Christians felt the Cross" (p. 380). As for the sculptor, "for a symbol of power, St. Gaudens instinctively preferred the horse, as was plain in his horse and Victory of the Sherman monument" (p. 388). The horse St. Gaudens "preferred" as a symbol of force was not just any horse, but a war-horse thrusting forward under the legs of the General in pursuit of the airy-winged female Victory. In St. Gauden's most representative work, "The Puritan," the male figure grasps a Bible to his chest with one hand and carries a heavy oak cudgel in the other, ready to conquer any evil, any frontier, and any feminine witchery.

Alongside the ghost of Locke and "The Puritan" one can, with some violence to the full truth, place the effigy of Plato. This it seems is Bly's intention, when after cataloguing the horrors of modern war in Vietnam, he tells us

> And Plato! Plato. . . . Plato wants to go backwards. . . .
> He wants to hurry back up the river of time, so he
>   can end as some blob of seaflesh rotting on an
>   Australian beach.
>
> (Teeth-Mother, p. 17)

Plato might want to go backward because he sees how men have fallen short of his vision, or he may be filled with revulsion at what his own teachings have brought. At first look, one cannot be sure whether Bly's attitude toward Plato here is positive or negative; but other lines of a parallel pattern afford the necessary clues: "The dams reverse themselves and want to go stand alone in the desert" ("Those Being Eaten by America," *Light,* p. 14). Plato, too, seems here to be experiencing a change of heart and would undo what he has done. Apparently, for Bly, Plato has been like the dam, holding back the stream of life and passion. There is, to be sure, a poetic Plato, a mystic Plato, a sensuous Plato, but these elements have been largely neglected and misunderstood by his less great-souled followers. The Plato that helped to shape the Western world is the Plato who saw material reality as a pale imitation of the pure ideas, art as a copy of a copy, and poetry as detrimental because it "feeds and waters the passions instead of drying them up" (*Republic,* Bk. 10). From this "copy" of the real Plato comes the definition of man as rational animal, the antipathy between mind and body, the emphasis on control and discipline of the lower nature, the hierarchical structures of governments, social classes, education, epistemology, and psychology. Plato was guilty, too, no doubt unforgivably so for Bly, of equating emotion with effeminancy. After witnessing the horrors of the Vietnam War—the evolutionary success of mind over emotion, of reason over instinct—Plato would supposedly flee backward in time away from mind, back to mindless primitive organism, senseless and rotting on a primeval beach.

For Plato the state was the individual writ large. There could be then no conflict between what was good for the state and what was good for the individual. (This can easily degenerate into the logic of fascism, communism, and capitalism—"what is good for General Motors. . . .") Plato thought the individual soul consisted of three qualities, each with a proper role and activity: Reason, Spirit, and Appetite, or wisdom, courage, and moderation (meaning obedience to reason), respectively. These were mirrored in the state by the three classes: Legislators, Warriors, and Tradesmen, who handled matters of government, defense, and production. Physiologically, whether in the individual or the imagined Leviathan of the state, the three qualities of the soul were located in the head, upper chest, and lower body; or more simply: head, heart, and genitals.

Alongside this threefold division there came to be a simpler twofold one—the spiritual and the material. Actually, Plato thought of courage (heart) as growing from the union of the spiritual and material souls, so that a familiar trinitarian pattern emerged—as in the Spirit generated between the Father and the Incarnation, or the love (or child) generated between male and female. So long as the heart belonged to neither reason nor appetite, and the warriors belonged to neither the legislators nor the people, but to both, all were joined in fruitful union instead of destructive conflict. But the middle term—spirit/courage/heart—became associated with reason and the "spiritual soul," while emotion and appetite remained alone in the "material soul." (Plato promoted that imbalance because his own will, volition, or "heart" was with reason and against appetite. Similarly, in his ideal state both of the "upper" classes were to enjoy communism so that they might avoid distraction with material concerns and could devote themselves to the spiritual, the abstract, the One; the "lower" class was not admitted to the communal scheme and was expected to engross itself with the material, the particular, the Many.)*

Thus the ideal three-part harmony where mind and matter were reconciled in heart became bifurcated lopsidedly into warring forces—'higher'' and "lower" natures. Women, who have never been logical, and, until modern Israel, seldom good warriors, were quite naturally associated with the appetite and the material body. "Emotion," too, belongs in that lowly company, for not only is it of the body, but, as Plato reminds us, it is by nature "effeminate." Physiologically, then, the twofold division cuts man along the dotted line at the waist. For women, who are neither intellectual nor courageous, the waist is located just a few inches above the top of the head. Reason and judgment take for themselves the task of repressing the "appetites," and within the state the rulers and their soldiery keep law and order among the workers, women, and "bleeding hearts."

The associations inherent in Plato's system from the first carried certain liabilities now made apparent in the modern experience and illuminated by the symbols of Bly's poetry. The diagram of a simplified and corrupted Plato given here adds new registrations to Robert Duncan's "swollen head of the nation" and Ginsberg's "college of the body." It especially clarifies the structure of Bly's work. The twofold division works naturally with Bly's use of juxtaposition and contrast, and the lopsided imbalance of forces accounts for the violence and sterility of modern life. Balanced, voluntary union is creative; coerced imbalance and submission are destructive. Bly's poetry gives the higher-lower, dominance-subjection pattern a spatial expression, and sets it reverberating on sexual, political, economic, physical, psychological, and philosophic levels: flexible tires under heavy machines, lake water pressed down by ice, vegetable walls destroyed by steel from the sky, burrowing animals killed

---

*Where does the heart belong? Plato of course was right originally: it belongs equally with both mind and body. But the modern split is typified in the slogan "Make Love, Not War." Each side makes us a dangerous syllogism of an either/or nature: "War goes with reason and the mind, 'love' with the body and the emotions. But reason and the mind are (good/bad); and body and emotions are (bad/good). Therefore it is good to make (war/love), but evil to make (love/war)."

by symbols dropped from helicopters by accountants, executives in cold skyscrapers or on icy mountainsides while the poor keep under or close to the ground. What is high is cold, hard, abstract, powerful, violent, oppressive, masculine; what is low is fluid, warm, damp, earthy, oppressed, feminine. In other poetry in other times rain may fall from the sky to impregnate the valley, the sun's rays may penetrate the soil to bring forth life, Sky may stir life in the Earth-Mother, and the masculine Logos may impregnate feminine Chaos; but in this poetry the interchange is coercive, unsatisfying, barren. Love has been replaced by rape, the stallion by the locomotive, and the Lover at the city gates by the Trojan Horse.

Bly's attitudes about the masculine/feminine forces are interestingly related to those of Robert Graves, who in *The White Goddess* argues the sanctity of the female, the moral force of matriarchy, and the goddess of love as the muse of true poetry originating in sacred matriarchal rites. In an interview in *Playboy* (December 1970, pp. 103–16), Graves further draws the lines along the "male/female" split involved in "Make Love, Not War." He implies that the poetry of love and of war are associated with the male and female: "Piracy and acts of violence—wars—are a male affair." True poetry should emphasize "the extreme dependence of man upon woman for her moral guidance and of woman upon man for his practical doing": "Patriarchal or Apollonian poetry started with ballads about war. Beowulf and the Icelandic sagas are examples. Such poems were enough for the men of the time when they sat together in a mead hall, throwing plates and bones at each other. But they lack lasting emotional value, because they are centered on war, not love. All poetry of value is matriarchal in its origin" (p. 114).

D. H. Lawrence, on the other hand, though he agreed with Bly and Graves about the nature of modern evils, tended to make somewhat different associations. His own life experience and consequent pathological suspicion and fear of women caused him to see the female and the Magna Mater not as a benevolent life-force, but as an anti-life-force that seeks to destroy true masculinity and Holy Spirit in the male. "Knowing" and mentalizing were not for him, as for Bly and Graves, masculine traits, but were feminine, and were embodied in such women as Edgar Allan Poe's Ligeia (see Lawrence's *Studies in Classical American Literature*). But many aspects of Lawrence's thinking are just what Bly would attack and see as evil. Lawrence would never "lose his leaves," never let himself float like a radish, never give himself to Whitman's democratic love (which he saw as a self-sacrifice, a death of self). Lawrencian thought is in some ways too masculine (certainly hierarchial, superior), too Apollonian (in spite of his campaigns for "blood-knowledge"), and tends to encourage the rise of Hitlers, violence, and war.*

Also interesting in connection with masculine/feminine images and associations are Frederick Karl's and Marvin Magalaner's remarks on James Joyce's novels:

> If a woman—or, at least, the Female principle—might be represented in Jungian psychology as a body of water (in *Finnegans Wake,* Anna Livia Plurabelle, the sparkling wife of Earwicker, is actually the river Liffey, as it flows through Dublin), then a smooth-flowing verbal stream, poured out with spontaneity and almost without check, might most effectively simulate the essence of Molly's being. Moreover, Molly's special type of femininity fits easily into the scheme. Lacking mind, missing the hardness and angularity which logic, reason, and judgment add to the total personality, Molly substitutes physical softness. Her amply-flowing curves are matched by the flimsiness and lack of definite structure of her thought processes. To approximate this liquid flow of emotional sensuousity, Joyce surrenders almost all punctuation. The monologue is an overwhelming continual outpouring. For the eye to attempt to separate the word groups into sentences is like trying to pick up a handful of water.
>
> (*Great Twentieth Century English Novels,* p. 229)

Mutatis mutandis, these same ideas say much about antiwar poetry's rejection of structure, its impetuous and free-flowing energies, its fascination with images of water and sea, its rebellion against logic and hardness.

---

*See John R. Harrison's *The Reactionaries: A Study of the Anti-Democratic Intelligentsia* [on Yeats, Lewis, Pound, Eliot, Lawrence] (New York: Schocken Books, 1967).

Bly's understanding of the history of ideas may not be minutely sophisticated, and his knowledge in many areas may by some criteria be dilettantish. But his pretensions are no greater than those of every other poet: he may venture into fields others avoid, but he makes no claim to professional expertise in any matter except poetry. As Robert Duncan has said, the goal of the poet and the poem "is to feel how things compose."[29] Bly does this. He stands with senses awake and takes the shape and measure of the forces impending on his body and spirit now, in this place. Whenever possible he has tried to let the language generate itself, adding what understanding his conscious mind could supply. *The Light Around the Body* is a book of many perceptions, and the larger unifying patterns are perhaps largely subconscious rather than calculated. But there is everywhere below the immediate surface of these poems a consistency, integrity, and *coherence* that makes them worthy of the National Book Award. In the award citation the judges, Theodore Weiss, Harvey Shapiro, and Donald Hall, wrote: "If we poets had to choose something that would be for us our Address on the State of the Nation, it would be this book."[30] Not only has he succeeded in giving us the psyche of the nation, but he has articulated what our individual psyches feel—our oppression, hysteria, and deep sadness have found a tongue.

IX

If all failures are failures of the imagination, certainly the greatest impediment to change is the failure to see the larger picture, or to envision how not just a part but the entire picture might be altered. New wine cannot be contained in old skins, and any desired new element in society will seem impossible and irrational in the old context. War indeed is the only "reasonable" possibility of action within the system of forces now at work. Those forces are of the outward man and are hollow travesties and brittle shells of the vital inner potencies they usurp. Bly not only helps us see the nature of this outward "giant," but also imagines a new human possibility. Wendell Berry, reviewing Lowenfels's *Where Is Vietnam?* claims it is a desperate book in spite of its new involvement; its poetry looks at the horror but is incapable of any alternative vision.[31] But what will satisfy us as an alternative vision? One senses that the only possible alternative is neither immediately acceptable nor even comprehensible to the Western mind. Though Bly's poetry is essentially wasteland poetry—his purposes are to give that landscape fuller expression—he does offer such an alternative. It seems at first a private and personal alternative, but it is open to every private person and thus ultimately to the society at large. Indeed, the great revolutionaries have understood that changes in individual consciousness are what is needed, and that changes in the outward political structures are otherwise irrelevant. Those structures are merely the body for which our attitudes are the spirit. Changes in consciousness are difficult, and, as Aeschylus and Sophocles and Shakespeare understood, are most often brought about by suffering sent from the gods. But changes of heart and consciousness can also to some degree be cultivated.

Bly believes the outward and the inward man can be brought again into communion, and envisions this in mystical/sexual images of rocks falling into water. In a poem significantly titled "A Journey with Women," he imagines us going

> . . . at night slowly into the tunnels of the tortoise's claws,
> Carrying chunks of the moon
> To light the tunnels,
> Listening for the sounds of rocks falling into the sea . . .
>
> (*Light*, p. 56)

These seem to be two *ways* to promote this reunion: one is to "give up desire," the formula of all spirituality; and the other is to accept the person as sacred. (These have some relation to the thunder-over-the-wasteland's *datta* (give) and *dayadhvam* (sympathize), though *damyata* (control) never sounds here; "control" is already momentarily in oversupply.)

The first "way" involves a "death" and a "defeat," for it is "in the deep fall, the body awakes." "The wind rises, the water is born" when "white tomb-clothes" are spread "on a rocky shore." If man is to become again the amphibian he properly is, the too-powerful shore must undergo some death so that the sea may rise again to fullness. "We did not come to remain whole. / We came to lose our leaves like the trees." Man must learn to lose, to spend less energy on being invulnerable and invincible, "And swim in the sea, / Not always walking on dry land" ("A Home in Dark Grass," *Light,* p. 44). The "leaves" we refuse to lose are strangely like scales that weight down the heavy body, "the body burdened down with leaves" (*Light,* p. 47). Leaves and scales were once perhaps needed when primitive man had to endure hardships of nature:

> Man cried out—like the mad hog, pierced, again,
> Again, by teeth-spears, who
> Grew his horny scales
> From sheer despair
> ("The Fire of Despair Has Been Our Saviour," *Light,* p. 48)

But the same "Fire of Despair" that formed the scales must now cause their shedding: "O holy trees, rejoicing ruin of leaves." It is no longer the Middle Ages ("iron ringing iron," "chill," "clatter," "stone") or the Ice Age (ice, "bone stacks," "snow," "snow-bound valley"), but "autumn" in man's history, a time for shedding of leaves, when the "spring coming in your black branches" is much easier to see. Yet man cannot find the road; and the monolithic Pentagon blocks our moving on beyond the drop of Indian blood and the military posture that at one time in man's history may have been a part of the way:

> Underneath all the cement of the Pentagon
> There is a drop of Indian blood preserved in snow:
> Preserved from a trail of blood that once led away
> From the stockade, over the snow, the trail now lost.
>> ("Hatred of Men with Black Hair," *Light,* p. 36)

The shell, the ossified outer protection must fall away, for we are all, like the State Department, becoming "exhausted crustaceans." Such symbols are Bly's own, though he occasionally expresses the same ideas with what seem borrowings from Zen Buddhism:

> The dying bull is bleeding on the mountain!
> But inside the mountain, untouched
> By the blood,
> There are antlers, bits of oak bark.
> Fire, herbs are thrown down.
>
> ("Moving Inward at Last," *Light,* p. 57)

Even as the bull, the outward man, the relative consciousness, dies, new life flames inside the mountain cave:

> The green leaves burst into flame,
> The air of night changes to dark water,
> The mountains alter and become the sea.
>
> (P. 57)

The second way to a new life is through the rediscovery of the awe-full, wonder-full person. The importance of the person was visible already in *Silence in the Snowy Fields*; in *The Light Around the Body* the value of humans "standing over against one another" (Buber's phrase) is emphasized in a number of poems. In "Evolution from the Fish" (*Light,* p. 59), we are reminded that man is, after all, the "grandson of fishes" and only the "nephew of snails"; and sometimes man still "lies naked on a bed / With a smiling woman." We still feel "What a joy to smell the flesh of a new child! / Like new grass!"

"Suddenly Turning Away" studies the sad truth that man's sensitivity, clarity, and gypsy joy are destroyed by fear and "not-love" (recall Ginsberg's "lack-love"). When someone "comes near," we close in, "the jaw / Tightens, bullheads bite / The snow," and the half-developed faculties of intimacy and communication are scarred again and again, "Half-evolved antennas of the sea snail / Sink to the ground."

"Looking into a Face" praises the spiritual warmth and strength that may be gained from intimate human contact

> . . . Opening
> The surfs of the body,
> Bringing fish up near the sun,
> And stiffening the backbones of the sea!
>
> (*Light,* p. 53)

To be noted are Bly's choice of "surfs," and the difference between backbones or endoskeletons and exoskeletons. Bly does
not advocate fleeing from all stiffness, all order, backward in
time to the jellyfish, but forward to a sense of the inner infinite,
to an order of personal volition. To be contrasted with these
images are those of the State Department crustaceans who are
also like confused squids in the heavy jellies near the bottom
("Hatred of Men with Black Hair," *Light,* p. 36), and the people
living under the shadow of the detective "Who sleep restlessly as
in an air raid in London; / Their backs become curved in the
sloping dark" ("Watching Television," *Light,* p. 6).

X

Hundreds of fascinating related images surface in Bly's work.
What is most amazing is that they *cohere.* Here, in a poet frequently accused of superficiality, dilettantism, and "theater," is
in fact a poetry that "grasps modern life as a lion grabs a dog,
and wraps it in heavy countless images, and holds it firm in a
terrifically dense texture." There is no way of telling whether
the unity of the images results from meticulous conscious effort,
or springs spontaneously from a deeper well where things are,
despite their seeming chaos, mysteriously orderly. But as the
reader draws closer to the poetry, he often discovers that what
seem arbitrary and random figures are either intentionally or
serendipitously full of significance. For example, in part 2 of *The
Teeth-Mother* Bly intends us to understand that the President lies
about everything and anything; but it seems strangely significant
that he should happen to have him lie about the date the mountains rose, the number of fish taken in the Arctic, the acreage of
the Everglades, and the composition of the amniotic fluid!

Bly's is a strange new poetry, more deeply involved, more
superficially raucous and polemical. It will not be readily em-
braced—the rocks on the shore do not easily submit to the sea. It
campaigns for a deeper, more spontaneous life, and follows its
own advice on its volatile and "uncivilized" subjective images.
And yet in the midst of its energy, it understands a tranquil
center, a letting go, so that at last, naked as a radish, "the
ocean . . . throws us into the ocean." The mountain has not yet

altered and become the sea, but partly perhaps because of Bly and other poets against the war, some rocks are falling.

NOTES

1. Robert Bly, "The Work of James Wright," *The Sixties* 8 (1966):77.

2. Cover blurb on back of Bly's *The Teeth-Mother Naked at Last* (San Francisco: City Lights, 1970).

3. Louis Simpson, "New Books of Poems," *Harper's,* August 1968, p. 75.

4. Denise Levertov, in Walter Sutton, "A Conversation with Denise Levertov," *Minnesota Review* 5 (1965):329.

5. Jonathan Williams, personal interview, February 25, 1971.

6. Robert Bly, *The Fifties* 1 (1958):39.

7. Ibid., p. 39.

8. Ibid., p. 38.

9. Robert Bly, "Some Thoughts on Lorca and René Char," *The Fifties* 3 (1959):8.

10. Robert Bly, "On Pablo Neruda," *Nation,* March 25, 1968, p. 414.

11. Robert Bly, *Silence in the Snowy Fields* (Middletown, Conn.: Wesleyan University Press, 1962).

12. Robert Bly, *The Light Around the Body* (New York: Harper & Row, 1967).

13. Robert Bly, "On Political Poetry," *Nation,* April 24, 1967, pp. 522–24.

14. Ibid., p. 522.

15. Martin Buber, *I and Thou,* trans. Ronald Gregor Smith (Edinburgh: T. & T. Clark, 1957), p. 52.

16. See Robert Bly, "On Political Poetry," *Nation,* April 24, 1967, and Bly's Preface to *Forty Poems Touching on Recent American History* (Boston: Beacon Press, 1970), which he edited.

17. Comments at a poetry reading for The Resistance, April 10, 1969, Lawrence, Kansas.

18. Robert Bly, "Crunk," *The Fifties* 2 (1959):11.

19. Louis Simpson, "The Inner Part," in Robert Bly and David Ray, eds., *A Poetry Reading Against the Vietnam War* (Madison, Minn.: The Sixties Press, 1966), p. 14.

20. Robert Bly, "Looking Backward," *Paris Review* 31 (1964):107.

21. Especially such essays as "Thoughts on War and Death," in

Sigmund Freud, *On War, Sex and Neurosis,* ed. Sander Katz (New York: Arts and Science Press, 1947).

22. Especially the lines on death in part 2. Personal interview with Duncan, May 9, 1969.

23. Robert Bly, "Lies," *Nation,* March 25, 1968, p. 417. [Cf. also the version in *Sleepers Joining Hands,* 1973.—ED.]

24. Michale Goldman, "Joyful in the Dark," *New York Times Book Review,* February 18, 1968, pp. 10, 12; and Louis Simpson, "New Books of Poems," *Harper's,* August 1968, pp. 73–77.

25. Louis Untermeyer, *Modern American Poetry* (New York: Harcourt, Brace & World, 1962), p. 288.

26. Robert Bly, "Murder as a Prudent Policy," Address before the National Book Award Committee, *Commonweal,* March 22, 1968, p. 17.

27. *Encyclopaedia Britannica,* 11th ed., s.v. "Locke."

28. Henry Adams, *The Education of Henry Adams: An Autobiography* (New York: The Book League, 1928), p. 383.

29. Personal interview with Duncan, May 9, 1969.

30. "National Book Awards," *Nation,* March 25, 1968, p. 414.

31. Wendell Berry, "Response to a War," *Nation,* April 24, 1967, pp. 527–28.

EKBERT FAAS

Robert Bly

An owl on the dark waters
And so many torches smoking
By mossy stone
And horses that are seen riderless on moonlit nights
A candle that flutters as a black hand
Reaches out
All of these mean
A man with coins on his eyes

The vast waters
The cry of seagulls

("Riderless Horses")[1]

Poetry such as this gives Robert Bly an almost unique position
in Anglo-American literature. With the possible exception of
Philip Lamantia, one has, I think, to go back to T. S. Eliot's *The
Waste Land* to find lines that capture the phantasmagories of the
subconscious with comparable convincingness and magic:

A woman drew her long black hair out tight
And fiddled whisper music on those strings
And bats with baby faces in the violet light
Whistled, and beat their wings
And crawled head downward down a blackened wall
And upside down in air were towers
Tolling reminiscent bells, that kept the hours
And voices singing out of empty cisterns and exhausted wells.

("What the Thunder Said")

Boundary 2 (1976): 707–25. Reprinted with permission.

Even in Eliot's work, however, *The Waste Land* stands out as a unique and mysterious creation. Not surprisingly, it grew more and more alien to the author, to the point where he felt called upon to deprecate the poem as a "structureless" "piece of rhythmical grumbling"[2] and a mere "relief of a personal and wholly insignificant grouse against life."[3] And there is little else in Anglo-American poetry which, like parts of *The Waste Land,* compares with the work of poets such as Éluard, Lorca, and Neruda.

Among the minor poets, David Gascoyne has (before Bly) made the most energetic attempt to launch a surrealist movement in the English-speaking world. But his poetry at best offers examples of the consciously manipulated dream-imagery that Breton himself had condemned as a pseudoform of automatic writing. And the theoretical position stated by the nineteen-year-old poet in his *Short Survey of Surrealism* (1935) was abandoned two years later in favor of the programmatic intent to narrate in poetry "the contemporary Zeitgeist of Europe."[4]

Among the major poets, Wallace Stevens welcomed "The Irrational Element in Poetry" and predicted its absorption into the mainstream of Western literature. But he was both too rational and too traditional a poet to contribute much to that tendency himself (Su, 309). William Carlos Williams praised the Surrealists as well as Gertrude Stein for their linguistic experiments, but he could hardly sympathize with their psycho-ideological claims and programs while propagating a philosophy of "no ideas but in things." Ezra Pound, whose interests after 1922 were increasingly absorbed by socioeconomic issues, was blind to the poetic and epistemological achievement of Surrealism and incensed by its later Communist orientation. In an ill-tempered diatribe he accused "The Coward Surrealists" (1936) of ideological escapism and compared their revolutionary stance with the "dim ditherings of the aesthetes in 1888" (Su, 185). If such party prejudice could do little to stop the influence of Surrealism in England and America, Eliot's well-informed controversy with its claims and theories, conducted over a period of several years, was considerably more successful along these lines.

After all, Eliot himself, while under psychiatric treatment in Lausanne, had produced, in a spurt of semi-automatic writing, some of the greatest and deservedly most famous Surrealist poetry in world literature. But *The Waste Land,* written after a serious nervous breakdown, was largely an efflux of that unconscious which Eliot, when in better control of his psyche, tried to exclude from poetic creativity. Poetry, as he stated as early as 1919, "is not a turning loose of emotion, but an escape from emotion; it is not the expression of personality, but an escape from personality."[5] After composing *The Waste Land,* he, of course, had to admit that there were periods in his life, mainly during "some forms of ill-health, debility or anaemia," when poetry had come to him like a mere "efflux . . . approaching the condition of automatic writing."[6] On principle, however, he had "no good word to say for the cultivation of automatic writing as the model of literary composition."[7] When asked whether he had ever felt the need for a new language to express the experience of his night mind, he answered with a definite *"no,"* and added: "I am not, as a matter of fact, particularly interested in my 'night-mind' " (Su, 213).

It is tantalizing to speculate what might have happened to the life and poetic career of Hart Crane if he had ever come into contact with the Surrealist poetry of France, Spain, or South America. Instead, it was *The Waste Land,* as seen through the distorting lens of its academic interpreters, which became the much admired model for *The Bridge* (1930), and it is tragically ironic how the critical dictates of its author, disseminated by the New Critics, came to cripple a creative impulse which came closer to Surrealism than that of any other of the major Anglo-American poets, with the possible exception of Dylan Thomas. Crane dreamt of a poetry that would "express its concepts in the . . . direct terms of physical-psychic experience,"[8] raising "the entire construction of the poem . . . on the organic principle of a 'logic of metaphor,' which antedates our so-called pure logic."[9] But despite the precedent of Whitman's *Leaves of Grass,* which, as Crane himself put it, was issued in a "number of editions, each incorporating further additions,"[10] he felt compelled to fit *The Bridge* into the procrustean bed of an obsolete unity concept. Analogously, his imagery and syntax, which occasional exercises in automatic writing could have infused with greater ease and naturalness, were all too often bogged down in the overelaborate convolutions of a self-conscious rhetoric and in a willful striving after symbolism, meaningfulness, and complexity.

It is with these examples in mind that Robert Bly had reason to claim, in *The Fifties,* that, unlike the poetries of Europe and South America, England and North America have practically "had no bold new poetry since the astounding daring of *The Waste Land,*" because the "other poetries have passed through surrealism; we have not." And in both Eliot and Pound "the mind won over the unconscious without too much struggle— the old Puritan victory." The result was that after the "rather dry flurry of leftist poetry in the thirties . . . poetry has been getting older and older every year" (F, 3, 7–9). According to Bly, a genuine rejuvenation of Anglo-American poetry must gain its impulse from the model of foreign poetries, from a return to the "fertile internationalism" of early Pound and Eliot[11] which their very followers among the New Critics had sacrificed to an "elegant isolationism" (Si, 6, 22). To be sure, Pound as well as Eliot, when drawing on the French tradition, had neglected the poetry with Surrealist elements (e.g., Rimbaud's "Le Bateau ivre") in favor of a more Objectivist kind of poem (e.g., Rimbaud's "Au Cabaret-Vert"). But it was their undeniable achievement to have drawn attention to poets such as Nerval, Lautréamont, Baudelaire, Rimbaud, and Laforgue, who were the first to adopt underground passages of association, to dare enter the "dark valley" of the unconscious and thus prepare the advent of a new imagination which finally, around 1910, began to appear "all over the world" (F, 1, 36). To Bly, this is the "jerky," "jumping," or "leaping" imagination, swiftly passing from the conscious to the unconscious and producing a poetry in which images become the very content of the poem. "It seems to me," he wrote in *The Fifties,* "that the greatest tradition of all modern poetry, and the *avant-garde* for a century has been the heavy use of images" (F, 2, 14). Bly tends to avoid the term "deep image," which Robert Kelly and Jerome Rothenberg coined in 1961 and which has since become the most common label for the kind of poetry written by himself and other poets under his infleunce. On the other hand, there is little in his critical writings which yields a clearer and more accurate description of the term "image." We can only guess that Bly may mean something like the "expression of psychic force which suddenly becomes language" (Gaston Bachelard), which thinks for the poet (Paul Éluard) (Su, 49), and which is close "to the psychological archetype of Jungian analysis" (Robert Duncan).[12] Bly himself has repeatedly referred to Freud and Jung as the fountainheads of the new imagination and has criticized Imagism for its lack of psychological depth: "The Imagists were misnamed," he wrote in *The Fifties,* because "they did not write in images from the unconscious" (F, 3, 8). An image such as Pound's "petals on a wet, black bough" is a mere picture, whereas true images like Lorca's "death on the deep roads of the guitar" (F, 1, 37–38) bring "together different thoughts by inexplicable means" (Si, 5, 81).

Even if Bly was right in claiming that American poetry had failed to traverse the "dark valley" of the unconscious, there was little in his first volume to suggest that he would make this journey himself. Granted, the poems in *Silence in the Snowy Fields* (1962) frequently mention the wind with its numinous afflatus, or death and darkness in which man has to immerse himself for his psychic rejuvenation; and there are the ubiquitous assertions that we "want to go back, to return to the sea," dive "into the sea of death," "go back among the dark roots," that we are "returning now to . . . the depth of the darkness," or are "falling into the open mouths of darkness." But such language is at best reminiscent of D. H. Lawrence, whereas the imagery which poets like Lorca and Neruda have gathered from these archetypal depths hardly disturbs the almost idyllic *Silence in the Snowy Fields.* Instead, there are similes such as "the bare trees more dignified than ever, / Like a fierce man on his deathbed"; images which tell a little story or fairy tale (e.g., the snowflakes "like jewels of a murdered Gothic prince / Which were lost centuries ago during a battle"); or, even more elaborate, the conceitlike expansion of an initial image that determines the structure and meaning of an entire poem, such as "Waking from Sleep":

Inside the veins there are navies setting forth,
Tiny explosions at the water lines,
And seagulls weaving in the wind of the salty blood.

It is the morning. The country has slept the whole winter.
Window seats were covered with fur skins, the yard was full
Of stiff dogs, and hands that clumsily held heavy books.

Now we wake, and rise from bed, and eat breakfast!—
Shouts rise from the harbor of the blood,
Mist, and masts rising, the knock of wooden tackle in the sunlight.

Now we sing, and do tiny dances on the kitchen floor.
Our whole body is like a harbor at dawn;
We know that our master has left us for the day.

(S, 13)

This is not to deny the aptness, beauty, and vividness of some of these images, or the mythopoeic power of a stanza like the following:

> The strong leaves of the box-elder tree,
> Plunging in the wind, call us to disappear
> Into the wilds of the universe,
> Where we shall sit at the foot of a plant,
> And live forever, like the dust.
>
> ("Poem in Three Parts," S, 21)

However, there is little that is genuinely surrealistic here, and even where Bly comes close to it, he is reminiscent less of Dali's minutely detailed hallucinatory psychographs than of Arnold Böcklin's late nineteenth-century Romanticism with its weird, apocalyptic animals and statuesque mythic creatures inhabiting a crepuscular landscape of death:

> I know these cold shadows are falling for hundreds of miles,
> Crossing lawns in tiny towns, and the doors of Catholic churches;
> I know the horse of darkness is riding fast to the east,
> Carrying a thin man with no coat.
>
> ("The Clear Air of October," S, 52)

This seems like the world of a man in love with death, and indeed no other theme is more central to the poet's early work.

However, there is none of Bocklin's sickly fascination with a death that is terrifying, but instead an almost Zen-like acquiescence to death as an inevitable part of life which the poet has learned to fear and love as much as life itself. "Through our dark lives," we read in one of his poems, "Like those before, we move to the death we love" (S, 32). What at first seems full of darkness and gloom is finally revealed as a world of serene happiness which Bly expresses in the most direct and simple terms. For at its basis lies the conviction that our human life is embedded in the larger life around us, and that despite death, it will continue there:

> Oh, on an early morning I think I shall live forever!
> I am wrapped in my joyful flesh,
> As the grass is wrapped in its clouds of green.
> ("Poem in Three Parts," S, 21)

The final aim of Surrealism was a heightened level of consciousness from which "life and death," as Breton put it in the *Second manifeste du surréalisme* (1930), "le réel et l'imaginaire, le passé et le futur . . . cessent d'être perçus contradictoirement."[13] The French Surrealists never reached that goal themselves. But they hewed a path through the obscure psychic woods of the Western subconscious from which later artists such as Jackson Pollock, Charles Olson, and John Cage have been able to emerge toward a new understanding of reality similar to that which Buddhist artists, for instance, have for centuries embodied in their music, painting, and poetry.

Before he began to publish his poetry, Bly spent several years in solitary self-confinement and analysis, a time he frequently remembers in his interviews and more recent poetry: "When I was alone, for three years, alone . . ." (Sl, 58), "in New York, in that great room / reading Rilke in the womanless loneliness" (Sl, 59). It was here that he first found "the inward path I still walk on," and where one day he lost himself in the "curved energy" of an all-pervasive Godhead which "makes grass grow," "gives food to the dark cattle of the sea," or, as a kind of double, frequently invoked in Bly's poetry, shares the poet's own personality:

There is another being living inside me.
He is looking out of my eyes.
I hear him
in the wind through the bare trees.
                    ("Water Drawn Up Into the Head," Sl, 65)

Bly's first volume, *Silence in the Snowy Fields,* seems to show the
poet emerging, as if from a shamanistic journey, into the light of
this new, joyful consciousness. However, one poem, entitled
"Unrest," stands out from the rest like an open wound, fore-
shadowing the world of Bly's future poetry. Here we have his
first vision of the "strange unrest [hovering] over the nation"
that was to become the central theme of his second volume, and
which led him in 1967 to found, with David Ray, "American
Poets Against the Vietnam War." And here, for the first time, in
a poem about his nation's society and politics, we find the surrealist imagery absent in the poems about himself. Viewing the
psycho-political disorder around him, the poet retreats into the
selva oscura of the unconscious he was personally about to leave
behind.

A strange unrest hovers over the nation:
This is the last dance, the wild tossing of Morgan's seas,
The division of spoils. A lassitude
Enters into the diamonds of the body.
In high school the explosion begins, the child is partly killed,
When the fight is over, and the land and the sea ruined,
Two shapes inside us rise, and move away.

But the baboon whistles on the shores of death—
Climbing and falling, tossing nuts and stones,
He gambols by the tree
Whose branches hold the expanses of cold,
The planets whirling and the black sun,
The cries of insects, and the tiny slaves
In the prisons of bark:
Charlemagne, we are approaching your islands!

We are returning now to the snowy trees,
And the depth of the darkness buried in snow, through
    which you rode all night
With stiff hands; now the darkness is falling
In which we sleep and awake—a darkness in which
Thieves shudder, and the insane have a hunger for snow,
In which bankers dream of being buried by black stones,
And businessmen fall on their knees in the dungeons of
    sleep.

(S, 25)

In using such images while writing about the outer world rather than about himself, Bly seems to depart from the original Surrealist impulse. And indeed, he has little interest in automatic writing. Breton's or Aragon's poetry appears to him "drab and squeaky" beside that of Lorca or Neruda, whose *Residencia en la tierra* he considers the "greatest surrealist poems yet written in a Western language." For Aragon and Breton "are poets of reason, who occasionally throw themselves backward into the unconscious, but Neruda, like a deep-sea crab, all claws and shell, is able to breathe in the heavy substances that lie beneath the daylight consciousness,"[14] and at the same time he never loses his hold on concrete reality.

Bly himself heavily revises his own poetry, claiming that the approximately 1,000 lines of a recently published book, for instance, are based on about 100,000 actually written.[15] Such conscious sifting and correcting, he is convinced, can probe deeper into the subconscious than any direct outpourings of the ego, while the process of creativity remains as open and unpredictable as in automatic writing. As he said in an interview, he often starts with a somehow striking line, "and then the unconscious keeps putting things in one after another that you were not quite aware of and at the end of the poem you feel amazed" (I, 63).

This process is reflected in the halting staccato of surrealist images which in Bly's second volume, *The Light Around the Body* (1967), provide us with a nightmare vision of the American psyche. The fairy-tale world of his earlier work with its Arthur Rackham-like lyricism, romantic oddity, and occasional cuteness (for example: "This new snow seems to speak of virgins / With frail clothes made of gold, / Just as the old snow shall whisper / Of concierges in France" [S, 16]) has been transmogrified into the schizophrenic phantasmagories of a painter like Richard Dadd. The bankers and businessmen who made their first appearance in "Unrest" are now part of a proliferating host of famous political figures, of types and characters from all walks of modern life, inhabiting a world of grotesque disfiguration, horror, and death, side by side with "strange plants," "curious many-eyed creatures," and other monsters. And all this is portrayed with such graphic precision and vivid plasticity that it evokes the illusion of a surrealist wax-figure cabinet.

Bly obviously had to sacrifice his hard-won personal serenity to achieve this vision. As he claims in a programmatic essay "On Political Poetry" (*Nation*, April 24, 1967), the "life of a country can be imagined as a psyche larger than the psyche of anyone living," yet only the poet who has "such a grasp of his own concerns that he can leave them for awhile" is able to penetrate into this sociopolitical unconscious and come back with a truly political poetry which (like Yeats's or Neruda's) transcends the mere versification of political opinions found in, for example, the works of Kenneth Fearing or Edwin Rolfe. As in "The Great Society," this surrealist vision of contemporary life and politics ironically inverts the accepted image of that society, thus offering a critique of its actualities as powerful as any poetry of a directly polemical and propagandist orientation:

Dentists continue to water their lawns even in the rain;
Hands developed with terrible labor by apes
Hang from the sleeves of evangelists;
There are murdered kings in the light-bulbs outside movie theaters;
The coffins of the poor are hibernating in piles of new tires.

The janitor sits troubled by the boiler,
And the hotel keeper shuffles the cards of insanity.
The President dreams of invading Cuba.
Bushes are growing over the outdoor grills,
Vines over the yachts and the leather seats.

The city broods over ash cans and darkening mortar.
On the far shore, at Coney Island, dark children
Play on the chilling beach: a sprig of black seaweed,
Shells, a skyful of birds,
While the mayor sits with his head in his hands.

(L, 17)

Of course, a poem like "The Great Society," except for the irony of its title, is not political in any exclusive sense. That aim is part of the much larger attempt to change the general bourgeois consciousness which Bly, not unlike the French Surrealists, holds responsible for our destructive politics and general life-style. Just as the establishment culture is dominated by hypocritical moralizing, pragmatic reasoning, and future-oriented ideology, the new consciousness and the poetry which is its medium should be characterized by an amoral, prerational, and ateleological outlook.

It was in this sense that Bly defended his friend James Wright against the attacks leveled at *The Branch Will Not Break* (1963) (Si, 8, 59 ff.). Thom Gunn had criticized Wright for deliberately excluding "the operation of the discursive reason," and Larry Rubin had attacked his "willful refusal to enter into the business of interpreting experience . . . and attempting to show relationships." In his retort, Bly simply questioned the validity of these criteria. What Gunn and Rubin posit as absolutes, he argued, boils down to the demand that Wright should "relate what he is describing to the great ideas of the Western World." "This is called 'giving meanings'" whereas the demand for "discursive reasoning" in poetry more often than not results in the handling of "accepted ideas" and "moral platitudes." Such "poetry of 'relationships'" may still dominate the English-speaking world, yet Wright and himself, Bly argued, are far from alone in their refusal to impose rational order and meaning on reality. After all, Chinese poets have written in this way for three thousand years, and amongst his contemporaries there is "the generation of '62 . . . Creeley, Wright, Snyder, etc. [which] represents a watershed in American poetry."

The fact that James Dickey, whom shortly before Bly had

hailed as a fellow traveler and the "exact opposite of the fashionable 'my healthy limitations school'" (Si, 7, 55), is not mentioned as a member of this group, was a portent of what was to follow. For only one year after his article on Wright, Bly launched a blistering attack against *Buckdancer's Choice* (1965) (Si, 9, 70–79), whose author he called "a huge, blubbery poet, pulling out Southern language in long strings, like taffy, a toady to the government, supporting all movements toward Empire, a sort of Georgia cracker Kipling." For a man pretending to advocate a poetry free from the platitudes of Western ideology and moralizing, the attack seems curiously self-defeating.

Echoing his article on Wright, Bly grants that "a true work of art . . . moves into deep and painful regions of the memory, to areas most people cannot visit without wincing." When Dickey, in "The Firebombing" and "Slave Quarters," portrays feelings of self-protective apathy and gloating joy over Western racial superiority and the destructive power provided by our technology, he not only, it seems to me, fulfills that function but extends it into the realm of his nation's psyche. And though his method is nonsurrealistic, it is no less truthful than Bly's in poems such as "Unrest" and "The Great Society." Bly criticizes Dickey's poetry for its "easy acceptance of brutality" and concomitant repulsiveness. Yet how could Dickey's poems be considered more repulsive than Bly's? And where in "Unrest" or "The Great Society" do we find "the real grief . . . [the] masculine and adult sorrow" which, according to Bly, can alone redeem that repulsiveness? It is the very absence of any such philanthropic attitudinizing which saves these poems from the "kitsch" Bly has attributed to "Slave Quarters," and which gives them the terrifying and cathartic power they possess.

The issues at stake here are as old as the genre in which Dickey's poems are composed. It is true that the speakers in "Slave Quarters" and "The Firebombing" are not as clearly individualized as the personae of Robert Browning, and that it is often difficult to dissociate them from the author. Yet even Victorian dramatic monologues, as nineteenth-century critics were the first to realize, are characterized by a strange amalgam of "subjective objectivity." Just as the most confessional of poets has to resort to some "oblique, objective, or dramatic way of expression,"[16] so Browning, giving words to a murderer and sexual psychopath like Porphyria's Lover, could only do so by transmogrifying, through his empathetic imagination, what was part of himself into the character of his poem. And although he was far more concerned than Dickey to invest his personae with all the trappings of an autonomous individuality, there were enough critics who identified these characters with the author and accused him of the cynicism of Bishop Blougram or the dissoluteness of Fra Lippo Lippi.

The confusion persists, and Bly, while making fun of the "jabber about 'personae,' " hardly clarifies the issue by declaring that in "Slave Quarters" "the umbilical cord [between author and speaker] has not been cut. Mr. Dickey is not standing outside the poem." It is far more convincing when Dickey, in an indirect answer to these charges, points out that

> every poem written—and particularly those which make use of a figure designated in the poem as "I"—is both an exploration and an invention of identity. . . . A true poet can write with utter convincingness about "his" career as a sex murderer, and then in the next poem with equal conviction about tenderness and children and self-sacrifice. As Keats says, it is simply that the poet "has no personality." I would say, rather, that he has a personality large enough to encompass and explore each of the separate, sometimes related, sometimes unrelated, personalities that inhabit him, as they inhabit us all.[17]

To be sure, Bly's criticism, if taken *cum grano salis,* is not entirely irrelevant. For a poet using personae without the techniques of multiperspective fragmentation developed by Pound, Eliot, and Williams, or without the self-transcendence achieved by D. H. Lawrence, somehow remains caught within a closed ego system. In other words, it seems doubtful whether anybody writing in the second half of this century can adopt a genre as obsolete as the dramatic monologue without falling into patterns, clichés, and sentiments of a previous age and alien to our literary sensibility as well as to our understanding of man in our time. And indeed, if poems such as "Slave Quarters" avoid these pitfalls by the compelling urgency of their subject and sheer technical brilliance, there are other poems by Dickey which sound like unintentional parodies of Browning. Keats's prophetic notion of the "chameleon poet" without a personality found an embodiment, appropriate for its time, in the Victorian poet and the proliferating multitude of "men and women" he projected in his dramatic lyrics. But modern man has learned to see his ego as immersed in Jung's collective unconscious, as only another object or event in Whitehead's open-ended universe of interrelated forces, or even as the final Emptiness of Eastern philosophy. And it is possible that no great poetry can be written now which precludes an awareness of such insights.

In "The Teeth Mother Nakes at Last" from his most recent volume of verse, *Sleepers Joining Hands* (1974), Bly attempted a solution for some of these problems. A combination of Neruda's surrealism with Ginsberg's Whitmanesque rhetoric and Pound's techniques of fragmentation, the poem in its indictment of the Vietnam war reads like an indirect answer to "The Firebombing" and its "easy acceptance of brutality." "The Firebombing," Bly had written, "has no real anguish. If the anguish were real . . . we would stop what we were doing, we would break the television set with an axe, we would throw ourselves on the ground sobbing" (Si, 9, 74). Yet it is exactly where it translates these gestures into verse that "The Teeth Mother" has the least effect on the reader:

> If a child came by burning, you would dance on a lawn,
> trying to leap into the air, digging into your cheeks,
> you would ram your head against the wall of your bedroom
> like a bull penned too long in his moody pen—
>
> If one of those children came toward me with both hands
> in the air, fire rising along both elbows,
> I would suddenly go back to my animal brain,
> I would drop on all fours, screaming,
> my vocal chords would turn blue, so would yours,
> it would be two days before I could play with my own children
>   again.
>
> (Sl, 25)

My anguish is far more real when I consider the diabolic destructiveness in the following lines from "The Firebombing," regardless of whether the speaker voices the poet's own feelings or
not. For if he does, it is only to Dickey's credit that he portrayed
himself with the unflinching objectivity even poets frequently
reserve for the more attractive aspects of their personality:

> All leashes of dogs
> Break under the first bomb, around those
> In bed, or late in the public baths: around those
> Who inch forward on their hands
> Into medicinal waters.
> Their heads come up with a roar
> Come up with the carp pond showing
> The bathhouse upside down,
> Standing stiller to show it more
> As I sail artistically over
> The resort town followed by farms,
> Singing and twisting
> All the handles in heaven   kicking
> The small cattle off their feet
> In a red costly blast
> Flinging jelly over the walls
> As in a chemical war-
> fare field demonstration.
> With fire of mine like a cat
>
> Holding onto another man's walls,
> My hat should crawl on my head
> In streetcars, thinking of it,
> The fat on my body should pale.[18]

Bly must have come to recognize some of the contradictions
pointed out when he declared, in 1972, that he "didn't criticize
[Dickey] on moral grounds," and granted him the rank of an
"extraordinary man, almost a genius" with "this quality of
thinking about these negative things and trying to write about
them." And it is easier to agree with Bly when he limits his
criticism to the fact that Dickey's "imaginative form starts to

collapse" and that "in terms of metaphor and action [he] has stopped going through the skin," which, according to Bly, separates Western man from his inner spiritual life (I, 59–60).

This change may partly be due to Bly's increasing immersion in Buddhist philosophy, which largely confirmed, but also deepened and modified the beliefs he had held from the very beginnings of his poetic career. "In the last eight or nine, ten years," he confessed in 1972, "the thinking I've learned most from has been Buddhist" (I, 50). Buddhism also seems to have given him a maturity which is reflected not only in the softening of his attitude toward Dickey and others but in the greater complexity of his more recent poetry. Bly sounded convincing enough when in his earliest collection he wrote lines such as

> through our dark lives
> Like those before, we move to the death we love
>
> (S, 32)

And his acceptance of death as well as the Zen Buddhist-like serenity derived from it may well have evolved from a long spiritual struggle. It is all the more admirable that Bly was ready to repeat, on the level of our sociopolitical consciousness, the journey through the "dark valley" of the subconscious, which he had personally already brought to a resolution. And the results speak for themselves. In lines like the following, which, in a fusion of his early and middle styles, seem to expose his hard-won serenity to the horror and suffering of the world around him, a new tone of harrassing self-analysis and genuine sorrow emerges:

I decide that death is friendly.
Finally death seeps up through the tiniest capillaries of my toes.
I fall into my own hands,
     fences break down under horses,
cities starve, whole towns of singing women carrying to the burial
    fields
     the look I saw on my father's face,
I sit down again, I hit my own body,

I shout at myself, I see what I have betrayed.
What I have written is not good enough.
Who does it help?
I am ashamed sitting on the edge of my bed.

> ("The Night Journey in the Cooking Pot," Sl, 62–63)

Buddhism also must have brought Bly a clearer understanding of his own philosophical and poetical position and to some extent transformed his attitude to those American poets who are engaged in a similar quest. In the past, for instance, he has often reprimanded Ginsberg for his obscenity, "unkindness," and "fear of the unconscious," or for giving up "all hope of imaginative precision and delicacy" (Si, 4, 38; 5, 70; 6, 40). But, more recently, he has hailed him as "the rebirth of a very powerful spiritual man" and as a fellow traveler in a common pursuit who, unlike Gary Snyder and himself, has gained his access to a new consciousness "not through the Tibetans and Japanese—but through the Hindus." With obvious approval Bly quotes Ginsberg's remarks about the psycho-physiological basis of poetic language, that "as soon as you have a new syntax," for instance, "you have a new way of breathing and as soon as you have that you have a new consciousness" (I, 54, 59).

These, of course, are insights closely akin to, if not inspired by, Olson. Yet, ironically, it is the latter's position, above all, which seems to have eluded Bly in his search for a new poetry and poetics. Bly's accusation that Olson embodies the "formalist obsession" of American poetry hardly needs refuting, while his contention that both form and content are "expressions of a certain rebellious energy rising in the psyche"[19] is not too far a cry from Olson's (or rather Creeley's) famous dictum that "form is never more than an extension of content" or that "if one taps, via psyche, plus a 'true' adherence of Muse, one does reveal 'Form.'"[20] And in the light of Buddhist philosophy it should be easy to understand that Olson's Objectism does not imply a positivist approach to nature or an evasion of self, but a quest complementary rather than opposed to that of Bly or Surrealism generally.

To Bly, however, Objectivism is no more than the theoretical formula for a failing more widespread than any other in American poetry—for the absorption in things which, as he wrote in *The Sixties,* "is shared by almost all the poets in America to-day. . . . It is the quality that the poetry of Lowell and of Merwin has in common with that of the Beats, as well as with the poetry of the *Black Mountain* group, who after Charles Olson and William Carlos Williams emphasize 'objects' and 'objectivism'" (Si, 4, 39). All this may be true, though even Williams, the most famous and uncompromising practitioner of such thingyness in verse, at least *strove* for the inwardness Bly finds lacking in his poetry. "A life that is here and now is timeless," he wrote in 1939. "That is the universal I am seeking: to embody that in a work of art, a new world that is always 'real.'"[21] Such timelessness reached by an absorption in the *hic et nunc* has, of course, been the universal aim of mystics of all traditions and is a notion central to most Eastern philosophies. The Zen Buddhists, for instance, call it *ekakṣaṇa,* which in Suzuki's paraphrase is the "eternal Now" or "absolute present"[22] reflected in the "momentariness of *sumi* paintings and *haiku*"[23] as well as of most Sino-Japanese art and poetry. In this way the famous Chinese poet Tu Fu, whom Bly quotes as a model for real inwardness (Si, 4, 39), might well have preferred Williams's poetics to the Surrealist manifestoes or to Rimbaud's plea that the poet should "par un long, immense et raisonné *dérèglement* de *tous les sens*" try to immerse himself into the unknown of "l'âme universelle."[24] And where, one might ask, does a lyric like the following by Tu Fu differ markedly from any of Williams's shorter "Objectivist" poems?

> The catkins line the lanes,
> > making white carpets,
> And leaves on lotus streams
> > spread like green money:

> Pheasants root bamboo shoots,
> > nobody looking,
> While ducklings on the sands
> > sleep by their mothers.[25]

Yet, granting the ultimately mystical orientation of Williams's poetic aims, there remains the more serious question of whether he or any of his Western peers can, like some Eastern poets, reach this goal by a mere empathetic immersion in objective reality. It is the very model of Zen Buddhism which has led many of his followers to the erroneous belief that such a shortcut to a new consciousness is generally accessible.

Zen teaches its disciples to ignore and avoid hallucinations and dreams and instead to focus on the preconceptual suchness of reality. Yet such a seeming rejection of the unconscious is the outcome of a struggle that lasted more than two millennia, so that the "participation mystique" (Lévy-Bruhl) with the sub-conscious, which may be a matter of painful and strenuous therapeutic effort for a Westerner, has long been a readily available experience for the Buddhist. And even Suzuki, a more recent exponent of the doctrine, defines *ekakṣaṇa* as "the awakening of consciousness out of the darkest recesses of the unconscious";[26] while the pre-Christian *Lankavatara Scripture,* the most important of the sutras for the evolution of Zen Buddhism, reads like a running commentary on what, in Jungian terms, we would now call the collective unconscious—that "memory of . . . discriminations, desires, attachments and deeds [which] is stored in Universal Mind since beginningless time, and is still being accumulated," that "habit-energy" which "like a magician . . . causes phantom things and people to appear and move about."[27] The "intuitive-mind" which is able to penetrate beyond the conscious and unconscious world helps us understand the dreamlike emptiness of both: "The discriminating-mind is a dancer and a magician with the objective world as his stage. Intuitive-mind is the wise jester who travels with the magician and reflects upon his emptiness and transiency. Universal Mind keeps the record and knows what must be and what may be." Yet, again and again, it is emphasized that the final insight into the unruffled quietude of Universal Mind can only be reached by traversing the unconscious to the point of a sudden "'turning about' at the deepest seat of consciousness."

It is only beyond this stage that all dichotomies of good and evil, past and future, inward and outward, and, above all, the duality of subject and object cease to be seen as opposites—not, however, by an extinction of the mind but by its tranquilization. Just as the "old body" continues to operate, so the "mind-system, because of its accumulated habit-energy, goes on functioning." To talk of the egolessness of either the self or the nonself would therefore be as pointless as to assert their essentiality. Both are "neither real nor unreal," so that their relationship, as one Zen expert puts it, "becomes a real relationship, a mutuality in which the subject creates the object just as much as the object creates the subject. The knower no longer feels himself to be independent of the known; the experiencer no longer feels himself to stand apart from the experience."[28]

Modern quantum mechanics teaches a similar lesson, and it was from its combination with the Eastern philosophy he knew through reading Jung that Olson derived his theory of Objectism. According to Heisenberg's Indeterminacy Principle, which the poet repeatedly invokes in his writings, "it is impossible to measure the simultaneous place and speed of a nuclear particle with absolute exactitude,"[29] for (in Olson's paraphrase) "a thing can be measured in its mass only by arbitrarily assuming a stopping of its motion, or in its motion only by neglecting, for the moment of measuring, its mass."[30] As Heisenberg points out in more general terms, we can only gather knowledge about our relationship to nature, never about nature as separate from the observer, so that rigid dichotomies such as internal versus external, soul versus body, and subject versus object lose their validity. Objectism, which in his "Projective Verse" essay of 1950 Olson defined as "the getting rid of the lyrical interference of the individual as ego, of the 'subject' and his soul," is a reinterpretation of Williams's and Zukofsky's "objectivism" in the light of these insights. In contrast to Objectivism, Objectism is not conceived of as the opposite of subjectivism, nor is man seen in contrast to nature. For man, as Olson says, "is himself an object."[31]

Despite this clarifying afterthought, Robert Creeley, long before Bly, felt called upon to wage a "battle against objectivism."[32] What he advocated instead was the "*subjective* in a more basic character." For, as he explained in a marginal comment to his "Note on the Objective" (1951), sent to his friend

Olson shortly before its publication, "to be *objective,* as far as I can see, MEANS to be so *subjective* that the possession of content . . . is complete enough for the poet to hand over."[33] But Creeley soon realized that his notion of the *"subjective* in a more basic character" was merely, as it were, the photographic negative of Olson's Objectism; or in other words that "subjective" and "objective" are both misleading and obsolete concepts in a description of the new consciousness. As Creeley concluded in the final paragraph of his "Note," it therefore is "perhaps best to junk both terms" and to replace them with a more neutral and monistic vocabulary: "a man and his objects must both be presences in this field of force we call a poem."[34]

Analogously, Bly may come to recognize that Olson, in his lifelong concern with the poetic image, held a position not at all unlike his own. Needless to say, Olson opposed "the suck of [the] symbol which has increased and increased since the great Greeks first promoted the idea of a transcendent world of forms,"[35] and he tried to limit the use of that term to what he believed to be its original meaning: "Greek *symbolon,* 'a sign by which one knows or infers a thing.' "[36] In this way, Olson was fond of quoting a slightly altered sentence from the Taoist treatise *The Secret of the Golden Flower* as the sum total of what he "had to offer": "That which exists through itself, is what is called meaning" (originally: "the Way [Tao]").[37] Meaning, in other words, is identical with, not referential to, preconceptual reality or suchness—identical with things viewed (as Shao Yung, another Taoist put it) "not subjectively but from the viewpoint of things."[38] A Western poet in search of such reality, however, must first traverse the "dark valley" of the unconscious, and then, in the attempt to express himself, contend with the final incommunicability of such insight.

Olson, albeit vaguely, seems to have been aware of both these problems. He knew that it was only by using images, and avoiding allegory, symbolism, and discursive logic, that the poet could stay close to the suchness of things, and that his images, in order to express this "meaning," have to be imbued with both the world of the conscious and of the unconscious. This, I think, is the meaning of a cryptic note Olson jotted down in 1955: "An image is truth, not image, except as without image it is impossible to present truth (An image may be defined as any proximate object to which there is a flow of feeling) The conversion of archetypes to working images."[39] In insisting on the fluidity and dynamism of such imagery, Olson again almost seems to anticipate Bly's plea for a poetry that evokes "that swift movement all over the psyche, from conscious to unconscious, from a pine table to mad inward desires."[40] To Olson an image should not be a static picture, but a "vector." "As the Master said to me in the dream, of rhythm is image / of image is knowing / of knowing there is / a construct."[41]

Of course, it is one thing to explicate Olson's poetics and another to evaluate its general influence. And no doubt it was the latter which inspired and, to a degree, justified Robert Bly's criticisms. In this way, his single-minded and sometimes over-aggressive attacks on Olson and the "elegant isolationism" (Si, 6, 22) of American poets generally, has performed a salutary function. The image of Bly as the surrealist opponent to Objectivism may therefore soon come to be replaced by that of the poet who helped relate American open form poetics back to some of its European origins.

NOTES

1. The *Light Around the Body* (New York: Harper & Row, 1967), p. 58; further references will be abbreviated as L. The following abbreviations will be employed for Bly's writings: *The Fifties* and *The Sixties* (a literary journal edited by the poet and now continued as *The Seventies*) as (F *or* Si, number, page); "An Interview with Robert Bly," *The Lamp in the Spine* 3 (Winter 1972): 50–65, as I; *Silence in the Snowy Fields* (Middletown, Conn.: Wesleyan University Press, 1962), as S; *Sleepers Joining Hands* (New York: Harper & Row, 1974), as Sl.

2. *The Paris Review* 6 (Spring–Summer 1959): 54.

3. Valerie Eliot, ed., *The Waste Land: A Facsimile and Transcript of the Original Drafts, Including the Annotations of Ezra Pound* (London: Faber and Faber, 1971). p. 1.

4. P. C. Ray, *The Surrealist Movement in England* (London: Cornell University Press, 1971), pp. 167 ff.: further references will be abbreviated as Su.

5. T. S. Eliot, *Selected Essays* (London: Faber and Faber, 1966), p. 21.

6. Eliot, *The Use of Poetry and the Use of Criticism* (London: Faber and Faber, 1967), p. 144.

7. Eliot, *Selected Essays,* p. 405.

8. Hart Crane, *The Letters,* ed. Brom Weber (Berkeley: University of California Press, 1965), p. 239.

9. Hart Crane, *The Complete Poems and Selected Letters and Prose,* ed. Brom Weber (London: Oxford University Press, 1968), p. 221.

10. John Unterecker, *Voyager: A Life of Hart Crane* (New York: Farrar, Straus and Giroux, 1969), p. 590.

11. See "An Interview with Robert Bly," *Tennessee Poetry Journal* 2, no. 2 (Winter 1969): 29–38, esp. 38.

12. Robert Duncan, "The H. D. Book: Part II, Chapter 4," *Caterpillar,* 7 (April 1969): 29.

13. André Breton, *Manifestes du surréalisme* (Paris: Gallimard, 1972), pp. 76–77.

14. *Neruda and Vallejo: Selected Poems,* ed. Robert Bly (Boston: Beacon Press, 1971), p. 3.

15. *Tennessee Poetry Journal* 4, no. 3 (Spring 1971): 30.

16. See Ekbert Faas, *Poesie als Psychogramm* (Munich: W. Fink, 1974), pp. 11, 143 ff.

17. James Dickey, *Sorties* (Garden City, N.Y.: Doubleday, 1971), pp. 155, 161.

18. Dickey, *Poems 1957–1967* (New York: Collier Books, 1967), pp. 184–85.

19. *Naked Poetry: Recent American Poetry in Open Forms,* ed. Stephen Berg and Robert Mezey (New York: Bobbs-Merrill, 1969), pp. 163–64.

20. Charles Olson, *Selected Writings,* ed. Robert Creeley (New York: New Directions, 1966), pp. 16, 29.

21. William Carlos Williams, *Selected Essays* (New York: New Directions, 1969), p. 196.

22. *Zen Buddhism: Selected Writings of D. T. Suzuki,* ed. William Barrett (Garden City. N.Y.: Doubleday, 1956), p. 268.

23. Alan W. Watts, *The Way of Zen* (New York: Vintage Books, 1957), p. 199.

24. Arthur Rimbaud, *Poésie complètes* (Paris: Gallimard, 1963), pp. 220–21.

25. "Wandering Breezes: 8," *Li Po and Tu Fu,* ed. A. Cooper (Harmondsworth: Penguin, 1973), p. 205.

26. Barrett, ed., *Zen Buddhism,* p. 268.

27. *A Buddhist Bible,* ed. Dwight Goddard (Boston: Beacon Press, 1970), pp. 300 ff.

28. Watts, *The Way of Zen* p. 120.

29. Werner Heisenberg, *Das Naturbild der heutigen Physik* (Hamburg: Rowohlt, 1972), pp. 18, 28.

30. Charles Olson, *Selected Writings,* p. 61.

31. Olson, *Selected Writings,* p. 24.

32. Geraldine Mary Novik, "Robert Creeley: A Writing Biography and Inventory," (Diss. University of British Columbia, 1973), pp. 37 f.

33. Robert Creeley, *A Quick Graph: Collected Notes and Essays,* ed. Donald Allen (San Francisco: Four Seasons Foundation, 1970), pp. 18–19.

34. Creeley, *A Quick Graph,* p. 19.

35. Olson, *Selected Writings,* p. 61.

36. Maps No. 4, featuring Charles Olson (1971), p. 11.

37. *Poetry and Truth: The Beloit Lectures and Poems,* ed. G. F. Butterick (San Francisco: Four Seasons Foundation, 1971), p. 61; see also *The Secret of the Golden Flower,* ed. Richard Wilhelm (London: Routledge and Kegan Paul, 1972), p. 21.

38. *Classics in Chinese Philosophy,* ed. Wade Baskin (Totowa, N.J.: Littlefield, Adams, & Co., 1974), p. 451.

39. Quoted by R. von Hallberg, "Olson, Whitehead and the Objectivists," *Boundary 2* 2 (Fall 1973–Winter 1974): 107.

40. Berg and Mezey, eds., *Naked Poetry,* p. 163.

41. *Human Universe and Other Essays,* ed. Donald Allen (New York: Grove Press, 1967), p. 121.

CHARLES ALTIERI

Varieties of Immanentist Experience
Robert Bly

I

To reject one poetic for another requires some implicit set of standards, or at the very least a complex of needs not satisfied by the current orthodoxy. [Elsewhere] I have shown how the New Critical aesthetic could not satisfy [Robert] Lowell after his loss of faith in the symbolic, form-creating imagination, so that Lowell's existential crisis also entailed a poetic one. Now I shall attempt to explore why Lowell's solutions did not satisfy other poets similarly disaffected from the epistemological and cultural implications of the New Critical aesthetic. The various forms this disaffection took can be clarified by describing three basic self-consciously postmodern positions—those of Robert Bly, Charles Olson, and Frank O'Hara.

Those three positions are united by a single theme—an emphasis on what I call *radical presence,* the insistence that the moment immediately and intensely experienced can restore one to harmony with the world and provide ethical and psychological renewal. The term *presence* is dangerously abstract and requires further definition, but that definition will best emerge in the process of my treating the specific forms of presence elaborated by the poets. One way of beginning to define presence is by its opposite—by the idea of *absence*—and here Lowell's poetry plays an important role, for it is the constant pressure of loss and

Enlarging the Temple (Lewisburg, Pa.: Bucknell University Press, 1979), pp. 78–93. Reprinted with permission from Associated University Presses.

separation in his poetry that leads contemporaries to reject his work as a useful model.

In *Life Studies,* for example, the culminating crisis is a moment of intense emptiness—"I myself am hell; / nobody's here." Lowell richly combines two versions of hell, Satan's absolute individualism and the modern sense of complete inner emptiness, a collocation that provides an excellent gloss on the spiritual problems involved in confessional poetry. Beginning with his realization that traditional value structures are no longer operable, Lowell in *Life Studies* seeks to make present and possess at least his own psychic reality. However, the quest for self-possession without any trustworthy reference points outside the self generates only a despairing awareness of how empty, how fictive and self-generated, the isolated individual is. At the volume's most intense moment of self-conscious presence ("I myself am hell"), there emerges also the deepest sense of inner emptiness. The individual consciousness threatens always to become what Sartre calls a principle of sheer negation, unless it recognizes processes it shares with other modes of life. The poem "Skunk Hour" does manage to survive this crisis by discovering a principle of continuity with the natural instincts of other living beings, but one sense of absence will soon be replaced by others. In Lowell's later contemplative poems there remains a constant pressure of loss and anxiety that at times mocks and at times—in the tragic poems—intensifies whatever the present affords. There is in Lowell the constant pressure of memory, of the mind seeking to be free of its involvement in material processes that are quite sufficient without it and finally of the separation of his particular self from the society and from others. Finally Lowell's ultimate values stem from culture, not nature, and are thus doubly removed—first from the present as immediate experience and then from the perverse and distorted contemporary culture so different from the imaginative ideals he envisions as a true culture. And despite his alienation from American culture, Lowell here presents a form of what may well be its basic experience of absence, for there is a pervasive sense that contemporary culture is a dying and inadequate one, wasting even the potential it has for improving the quality of the lives it controls. Instead of living confidently within it, man finds himself continually denying his cultural role in nostalgic dreams of happier pasts or wishful fantasies of a better future.

For many postmodern poets, then, one needs what Wallace Stevens called "a cure of the ground / or a cure of ourselves that is equal to a cure / of the ground." Even imagining a cure, the poets feel, will entail changing one's fundamental perspectives on experience. Where humanist cultural ideals were, there some form of immediate contact with natural energies must be restored. But this restoration cannot follow even the example of Romantic nature poetry, for Romantic views of a purposive and numinous force immanent in nature are derived from a renewal and reinterpretation of Christianity. Now the challenge is to imagine non-Christian sources of immanent value . . . and . . . to show how postmodern poets articulate states of mind exemplifying ways these values can be apprehended and can dispose one to action.

Bly, Olson, and O'Hara represent three distinct typical postmodern modes for articulating these states of mind. None of these poets approaches canonical status among his peers, but they do take up and reflect abstractly upon positions that others adapt and experiment with. In fact, one could, without much distortion, define most of the poetry of the sixties that is neither "academic" nor confessional by mapping its relationship to coordinates provided by Bly's poetics of the deep image, Olson's Objectivist or projectivist aesthetic, and the New York school that O'Hara most fully represents. And because these poets have roots in marginal aspects of modernism—Bly in theosophically inspired poetry and Surrealism, Olson in Williams and Objectivism, and O'Hara in Dada, Surrealism, and Expressionist painting—they help make clear how contemporary poetics flowers from earlier seeds never really central to modernist English and American poetry.

Intellectually, postmodern poetics derives from Romanticism, but equally important is the characteristically American quality of its search for authority in modes of immediate presence. As one explores the ways poets of the sixties seek to go beyond Lowell, it will be useful to keep in mind how closely the entire process re-enacts what D. H. Lawrence has described as the recurrent form of classic American literature—both for its cultural interest and because Lawrence used America to define his own highly influential vision of presence as a source or value dependent neither on romantic theology nor on Paterian aestheticism. Lawrence sees the central American experience as a flight from the spiritual authority of Europe—an authority characterized by doctrines of eternal truth only partially within experience and by reliance on hierarchical structures of value. American literature, then, continually enacts a process of negation, and negation is frightening because it casts man into a void. Without masters it can accept, American literature vacillates continually between submission to the land and a retreat to even more extreme and destructive embodiments of the European ideals. Only with Whitman does the destructive journey end. And the two stages Lawrence sees in Whitman's career nicely parallel the movement from Lowell to Bly, Olson, and O'Hara. Whitman first explores a radical possibility for retaining the dream that consciousness and the human ego can create forms nature obeys. He tries to make his ego in all-embracing consciousness, possessing all beings and possessed by them. (Lowell's ego exhibits, of course, a more limited and ironic version of the same strategy.) But he soon comes to see that the desire to identify with all that lives is the equivalent of a desire to die and to merge with an infinite emptiness. Through his imaginative experience of death, however, Whitman emerges reborn with a radically new vision, the vision of the "Open Road." The "Open Road" is for Lawrence the way of presence, and he carefully distinguishes it from any vision of experience that seeks to define value by relating experience to the universal categories of individual or collective consciousness:

> It is a new great doctrine. A doctrine of life. A new great morality of actual living, not of salvation . . . [Whitman's] morality was no morality of salvation. His was a morality of the soul living her life, not saving herself.
> The Open Road. The great home of the Soul is the open road. Not heaven, not paradise. Not "above." Not even "within." . . . The journey itself, down the open road. Exposed to full contact. . . . Towards no goal. Always the open road.

> It is not I who guide my soul to heaven. It is I who am
> guided by my own soul along the open road.

The morality of ends require a conscious ego determining the meaning of experiences by referring them to phenomena not immediately present—for example, to schemes of salvation, or even to social and philosophical systems. (Kant's categorical imperative is a perfect model for the morality of ends.) Authority, then, is not immediately within the energies of experience. The morality of the open road, on the other hand, allows no absolute; morality, or authentic action, depends on a constant adjustment of the ego to the energies of the moment—in nature or in forces exerted by the human beings with whom one comes into contact. Consequently, there is little sense in ethical or poetic visions that perpetuate the Victorian dream of improving society by creating imaginative models of ideal behavior or appealing to men's sense of duty and self-regard. Perception and not reflection is the primary means for developing a man's capacities for an authentic life. The second aspect then follows logically; if perception is primary there must be something humanly significant to be perceived. Some principle of authority must be conceived as residing in the energies of the moment, so even if one seeking a philosophy of presence rejects Lawrence's theories about the gods, he must describe ways in which the present is numinous and something more than simply intense energy. That energy must have some kind of purposiveness, some way of influencing behavior and determining authentic modes of interrelationship between an individual, his environment, and other men. By exploring the various ways in which presence can be adapted to these axiological needs, the poets of the sixties in effect break with an immediate past only to recover what may be the true American heritage.

II

The heirs of Whitman, of course, are Roethke and Williams, both of whom can be considered spiritual fathers of the poets I am studying. But it is to those writers heavily influenced by them, to Robert Bly and Charles Olson, one must turn if one wishes to see how their visions are carried over into postmodern poetics. Bly is a particularly fruitful figure with whom to begin because so much of his critical theorizing is an explicit attack on Lowell and on the reasons why Lowell can express the death of a poetic tradition but not break through that death to a new life. Moreover, Bly's poetic is outspokenly, almost simple-mindedly, moral and ontological; it begins with the opposition between absence and presence, between a world of dead facts and one of numinous realities, and goes on to explore ways one can recover a suprahuman ground for establishing a basis for value at once immanent and public.

Lowell's poetry is for Bly a perfect example of the absence or emptiness that plagues so much contemporary experience. Lowell's very attempts to intensify the present moment, both in his choice of poetic detail and in his presentation of emotional experience, only call attention to how dead a world even the best poets are forced to inhabit. Like the body of Charles Bovary at the end of Flaubert's novel, Lowell's poems offer the appearance of vital life only to yield up, on investigation, a horrifying glimpse of how empty is the world as one now normally experiences it. Lowell's poems, Bly argues, have no poetic center, no radiating presence that gathers and gives an appropriate relevance to the specific details; instead they include facts simply because they happened: "A flood of objects comes and buries the poem's project of living inside a certain emotion." Facts are separate from emotion in Lowell because he has no way of conceiving the unity of man and nature, no way of opening himself to see how the facts can speak to and call for the human emotions which might complete them. Lowell's only intensity is psychological; he pretends "to have a poetic excitement when all he has to offer is nervous excitement" ("Robert Lowell's *For the Union Dead*," p. 96).* "Poetic" to Bly means a sensitive awareness of the "soft ground" of experience and is radically opposed to the elaborate dramatic and psychological sensationalism Lowell requires to give his details any resonance at all:

---

*Full citations for all parenthetical notes appear in the bibliography, part I, the articles section—ED.

For the confessional poet anything less than an abortion or a cancer operation really doesn't justify the machinery. A poem becomes a tank that can't maneuver on soft ground without destroying it. ("The Dead World and the Live World," p. 6)

For Bly genuine poetic excitement depends on the union of poetic feeling with some deeper, nonsubjective reality. Lowell's failure ultimately stems from an existential crisis—he cannot link the aesthetic with the ontological, experience with its ground, or intense moments with secure bases for value. His poetry vacillates between the prosaic and the sensational because it is exclusively centered in man and in the individual ego: "The human being is not studied in relation to non-human lives" (*DW*, p. 4). In true emotional experience man feels in himself the "*Gott-natur*" (a term taken from Georg Groddeck) and "senses the interdependence of all things alive, and looks to bring them all inside the work of art" (*DW*, p. 3). Authentic experience, then, is concentrative (cf. "A Wrong Turning in American Poetry," pp. 33–34; *DW*, p. 6); it draws together events in the unity of emotion. The psychological emphases of the confessionals, on the other hand, create a diffusive, fragmenting effect. Caught in the flux of isolated subjectivity, and feeding off the most problematic aspects of that selfhood to create poetry, the confessional poet flirts always with complete "disintegration of [the] personality" he or she so desperately seeks to understand (*WT*, pp. 41–42).

Bly's opposition to the homocentric universe as the mere residue of a world once resonant with ontological depth leads one to the central quest in Bly's own work. His poetic theory concentrates on the possibility of the poem recovering that resonance by once again putting readers in touch with the *Gott-natur* and restoring their awareness of the life man and objects share. His central strategy is to define a theory of imagination that demonstrates how the Romantic organicist poem makes visible latent orders of being where nature and consciousness, existential facts and the metaphor or poetic image, share the vital life. There are some parallels here to Coleridge's faith that the creative imagination participates in a level of reality beneath that of mere appearances. But, as I shall soon show, Bly remains radically postmodern by insisting on the imaginative act as a denial of the ego and by pointing to the immediate act of sympathetic perception as the source of one's participation in this deeper life. The poetic imagination does not create unity but finds attitudes or modes of attention that station the mind in levels of reality deeper and more organically unified than those which conscious art can create.

Bly works out his idea of the imagination by developing two corollary terms—*intuition* and *image*. *Intuition* is the creative faculty that can generate the poem once it learns how to inhabit its experiences, and *image* is Bly's term for the resultant work. Both terms are carefully chosen to combine the art of making with the art of seeing, and both allow Bly to adapt the organicist tradition without subjecting himself to a New Critical interpretation of it. Thus *image* refers to the poem as an organic entity, yet the term calls attention to the work not as artifact but as a specific way of seeing or of participating in experience. In a similar way, *intuition* is often used by aesthetic critics like Croce, but Bly's own insistence on the metaphysical implications of the term brings him closer to the Thomism of Maritain. *Intuition* is by definition the creative union of emotion and its ground in the *Gott-natur* (cf. *WT*, p. 34). Neither psychology nor nature by itself can save man from despair and its corollary violence; there is needed instead "a poetry that goes deep into the human being, much deeper than the ego, and at the same time is aware of many other beings" (*DW*, p. 6). Poetic intuition then allows consciousness to enter a "field" (analogous to Olson's) where reside the secrets man and objects share:

> In the poems of Neruda, Vallejo, Jiminez, Machado, Rilke, the poem is an extension of the substance of the man, no different from his skin or hands. The substance of the man who wrote the poem reaches far out into the darkness and the poem is his whole body, seeing with his ears and his fingers and his hair. Impersonal poets construct; great poets merely are sensitive. (*WT*, p. 38)

To enter this condition of experience, intuition must penetrate the merely factual truths of experience in the "outer world." Thus Bly's *image* responds to very different needs from those met by Imagism:

> Imagism was largely "Picturism." An image and a picture differ in that the image, being the natural speech of the imagination, cannot be drawn from or inserted back into the real world. It is an animal native to the imagination. (*WT*, p. 40)

The true image, then, is a concentration of outer and inner energies into a single intense state of feeling whereby the poem (and, by implication, the audience) "is released from imprisonment among objects" (*WT*, p. 47).

Bly's poetic treads a delicate and often shifting boundary line between traditional Romanticism and the more secular ontological strategies of other postmodern poets. To combat the split between value and fact, between the isolated human consciousness and more universal energies that might serve as a source of value. Bly returns once more to a series of oppositions that plagued the Romantics. Bly often seeks to separate and then integrate notions of the artist as maker and the artist as seer, of outer and inner experience, of a sense of one's mere facticity and a sense that one feels his interdependence with the universe. And all these oppositions come into play with respect to his central polarity—that of the ordinary public language and a true visionary language. He is nowhere so Romantic as in the epigraphs from Boehme he gave to his two most influential volumes in the sixties:

> We are all asleep in the outward man. (*Silence in the Snowy Fields*)

> For according to the outward man, we are in this world, and according to the inward man, we are in the inward world. . . . Since then we are generated out of both worlds, we speak in two languages, and we must be understood also by two languages. (*The Light Around the Body*)

In so distinguishing inner and outer worlds as the basis for his theory of poetic and public languages, Bly comes dangerously

133

close to the most naive Romantic and Symbolist restatements of Christian theology. But without such an insistence, Bly could find himself trapped in T. E. Hulme's Bergsonian version of the two-language theory, which authorized the Imagist poetic Bly despises. And at his best, Bly adapts his theological model in thoroughly secular terms; the grounds for a language of the inner life can be discovered in familiar processes if one learns to look beneath manifest appearances: "A human body, just dead, is very like a living body except that it no longer contains something which was invisible anyway" (*WT,* p. 46). This force, because invisible, can only be known by the imagination, but it is not therefore outside of nature. Furthermore, since this force is both shared by all beings and life-enhancing, it has a moral function; it makes man aware of what he shares with all life, and thus it can help combat the egocentric violence of American culture. The unconscious, then, that the *deep image* brings into play is as much an ontological as it is a psychological entity. It is man's way of experiencing the nonsubjective depths of his own being alive, and thus is the manifestation in man of the *Gott-natur.*

Bly's poetry functions in terms of the same basic oppositions as his poetic. His characteristic themes and stylistic strategies come back again and again to the tension between dead and live worlds, public versus visionary language. And these oppositions in turn generate his two basic lyric modes—a satiric one when the dead world dominates and a surreal one expressing momentary breakthrough into the interpenetrating energies of psyche and landscape. The satiric mode concentrates on the blindness and moral failings that follow from trusting public rational models of thinking. Here the poems concentrate on the blocking aspects of paternal authority whose ultimate prop is the reality principle. The second mode is a poetry of metamorphosis—not from object to object but from one level of being to another. These poems gradually subvert the authority of a public descriptive language and "slip suddenly inward" to a version of Lowell's "downward and vegetating Kingdom" that Bly envisions as the dark, soft, feminine ground of the true imaginative life. The poems begin with a casual event like walking through a field and then dramatize the imagination transforming the scene into a mysterious and evocative presence. The goal is to achieve a point where the radiant present abolishes all distinctions between imaginary and real, metaphor and fact, so that the reader is led to inhabit a world where aesthetic awareness blends with a sense of ontological resonance.

For Bly, then, the poet's role is to absorb the limited public language and leave the reader with a new level of awareness. To do so he repeats the characteristic movement of individual poems in the structure of his volumes by gradually moving from satiric to visionary modes. *The Light Around the Body,* for example, develops like a five-act drama, moving from a survey of the paralysis afflicting those caught in the public language, through the war in Vietnam as a summary exemplum of the effects of a culture's depending on that outer life, to a third part devoted to surrealistic explorations of the psychological pains created by those events. Through suffering, one learns in the fourth part to participate imaginatively in death and realizes by that participation a sense of the unity of all that lives. Then in the last section the speaker becomes secure in what Bly elsewhere calls "the masculine sadness of true poetry" ("Prose Versus Poetry," p. 70) and learns the stance that allows a poem after poem to slip inward to a vision of *Gott-natur*. Three poems from that volume—the first central to the crisis in public life and the other two illustrating two different strategies of metamorphosis possible once one can move to visionary language—should suffice to illustrate the kinds of imaginative strategies and experiences of value made possible by Bly's poetic.

"Counting Small-Boned Bodies" is Bly's finest poem in the satiric mode:

Let's count the bodies over again.

If we could only make the bodies smaller,
The size of skulls,
We could make a whole plain white with skulls in the moonlight!

If we could only make the bodies smaller,
Maybe we could get
A whole year's kill in front of us on a desk!

If we could only make the bodies smaller,
We could fit
A body into a finger-ring, for a keepsake forever.

(*Light,* p. 32)

One notices first of all how Bly's sense of collective consciousness allows him readily to assume the voice of a whole
culture, and his secure sense of values justifies a biting criticism
of that culture, not only for its actions (as in Lowell) but for the
modes of consciousness that support those actions. Three specific aspects of the public consciousness are dramatized in the
poem. First Bly plays on the idea that counting, the manipulation of elements in the outer world, can ever be an adequate
measure of events. (The history of body counts provides adequate empirical data to support Bly here.) Counting then leads
to a second empty form of public measurement: the poem's tone
and grammatical mood express a technological fantasy inspired
by the false language of advertising. Finally, the concluding line
allies the violence of war with perverted and simplified visions
of love. It establishes and casts back over the rest of the poem a
purposive role for the irony as intensifying the gap between
public desire and the lack of a true inwardness that might define
and direct that desire. These distortions then combine to present
an inverted version of Bly's typical concentrative movement.
The more compressed the bodies become the more the reader
approaches the ring, the central unifying symbol of the horror
involved in this exercise of perverted love. And the horror is
deepened by the fact that advertising's words for this particular
union are literally true, though of course in an unexpected sense:
those dead bodies will remain intimately involved with our lives
for a terribly long time.

   The other poems present Bly's two most significant ways of
embodying his sense of the true vision of inner man—one dramatizing the process of expansion through concentration and the
other the process of interpenetration or, in rhetorical terms,
analogy. Visionary concentration in Bly's work serves as a
structural response to some of his deepest fears. Not only are
there moments of ironic concentration in poems like "Counting
Small-Boned Bodies," but the radical splits of inner and outer

man continually threaten Bly with disintegration. One need only consider the images of explosion and fragmentation that permeate *Light Around the Body*. But beyond, and probably through, the tension there are moments of exquisite union. Take for example "Looking into a Face":

> Conversation brings us so close! Opening
> The surfs of the body,
> Bringing fish up near the sun,
> And stiffening the backbones of the sea!
>
> I have wandered in a face, for hours,
> Passing through dark fires.
> I have risen to a body
> Not yet born,
> Existing like a light around the body,
> Through which the body moves like a sliding moon.

(Light, p. 53)

Through conversation here the speaker experiences at once an intense union with the other and an "opening" into a larger reality (one can look "into" and not "at" a face). In the natural context of the first stanza the other person functions as a sun drawing toward itself the submerged, cold parts of the poet, while in the second the containing force of the intense union becomes the contained as the mysterious forces of the moon control, define, and illuminate the existential body in a space at once cosmic and human. Bly's own act of concentration in the poem combines the expansive depth of spirit sought by so many in the mystical and Romantic traditions with a sense of security and equilibrium achieved by very few. Psychic depth and cosmic force, the Romantic dream of the redeemed human body and the contemporary quest for a vision of cosmic harmony based on natural law, interpenetrate and reinforce one another.

This union of psychic and cosmic energy is realized most frequently through a rhetoric of analogy. Bly quietly builds the poem through a series of muted analogies between psyche and world to a final moment where an image or series of images express and insist that the reader attend to the completely realized interpenetration now blossoming forth. In other words, Bly the poet slips inward before he asks the same slip of the reader, and the sustained analogy then gives depth and a sense of secure grounding to the moment of insight. This preparation, I think, is the key to the remarkable sense of illumination and peace one experiences at the close of Bly's best poems. There is neither the shattering disharmony felt in Lowell's epigrammatic insights nor the forced discovery found in Bly's less successful poems or in his many imitators. Even soft ground requires an elaborate foundation.

"A Home in Dark Grass" illustrates the processes I've been discussing:

> In the deep fall, the body awakes,
> And we find lions on the seashore—
> Nothing to fear.
> The wind rises, the water is born,
> Spreading white tomb-clothes on a rocky shore,
> Drawing us up
> From the bed of the land.
>
> We did not come to remain whole.
> We came to lose our leaves like the trees,
> The trees that are broken
> And start again, drawing up from the great roots;
> Like mad poets captured by the Moors,
> Men who live out
> A second live.
>
> That we should learn of poverty and rags,
> That we should taste the weed of Dillinger,
> And swim in the sea,
> Not always walking on dry land,
> And, dancing, find in the trees a saviour,
> A home in dark grass,
> And nourishment in death.

(*Light,* p. 44)

The poem derives its energy from a complex synthesis of the human and the natural leading to a concluding paradox that embodies the significance of those relationships. The first two stanzas dramatize man and nature exchanging roles; in the first nature is seen in human terms—perhaps the reason that there is nothing to fear—while in the second the speaker is naturalized in the metaphor of the trees. The third stanza, with its shift to the subjunctive, presents the condition of desire generated by the speaker's awareness of the relationship in the first two, a desire culminating with the slip to a new generalized sense of inwardness in the last line. The last three lines frame that shift of levels with a marvelously complex restatement of nature and man. Three natural terms (trees, grass, and, in context of the preceding two, death) are posed as possible satisfactions for three human needs, and the penultimate lines further emphasize the relationships by arranging them in a chiasmus (trees saviour) (home grass). The last line then progresses a step further. While death completes the series of natural terms satisfying human needs, it is itself a general condition in which man shares. At the same time "nourishment" is a human need shared by natural life. "Nourishment in death" is dangerously close to cliché, but the poem by now has established a basis of exchange in which the phrase (at best, initially a paradox) is sustained on several literal levels—from the level of natural cycles to one where consciousness can see all being participate in "the impersonal stillness in things." To develop further the implications of these metaphors of exchange, the poem presents opposite progressions in the two categories: the natural terms grow more general and symbolic or psychological (between trees and death, "dark grass" appears both more extensive than trees as a natural phenomenon and, with the adjective, clearly more suggestive), while the human ones grow more specific and closer to those needs man shares with all of life (a "saviour" fills a mythic need; nourishment, a universal physical one). By the last line there is again intense concentration as the human and natural meet at the point of death and, through that concentration, a sense of expansive opening into another realm of being shared by death. As all natural beings come together in death, all human needs return to the natural where they enable one to imagine the secure ground shared by all life.

Bly's analogical method demands a use of metaphor very

different from Richard Wilbur's. Bly's poems are at least as metaphoric; without metaphor one is left with only the outer realities of objectivism. The structure of analogy, in fact, often borders on the conceit, but attention is not focused on metaphor as a verbal act. Instead the metaphors frequently ask to be taken as literally true relationships. The links between man and trees and grass and death appear not fictive but natural. The metaphysical conceit suggests wonder at the powers of mind and its playful creative ways of illuminating events and their meanings, a wonder John Crowe Ransom tried to describe with the term *miraculism*. In Bly, on the other hand, the extended analogues focus on the miraculism of natural processes or the *Gott-natur*, which creates and sustains the relationships. Nature is "that synthetic and magical power" which "blends, and (as it were) fuses, 'each into each.'" The poet then need not strive to unify opposites; he need only open himself to that second language of imaginative vision which places man in the condition where unity is the basic ontological reality.

The relevance of the term *miraculism* to Bly's work, however, raises a crucial question: can an ontology based in the soft ground of imaginative association provide also the secure base in nonfictive reality needed so desperately by Lowell and others? Can so special a form of vision, "released from imprisonment among" the objects of the prose world (*WT*, p. 47), claim truth for itself within that world? Might not Bly in his claims for the truth of his poetic visions be confusing art and life, taking the unity of art as symbol for nature, and treating as experiences of ontological value what are really responses of the aesthetic faculty to human creations? How separate are the two languages of outer reality and inner vision? These questions become more pressing when analysis shows how skillfully Bly's analogical rhetoric sustains his moments of vision. Are will and imagination doing for Bly the work best reserved for perception and analysis?

The questions, of course, do not admit of "yes" and "no" answers. For one thing, they beg other questions like the relationship of aesthetic experience to the possible ways one's sense, if not his conceptual grasp, of values realized within art can be operable outside it. But the questions do, nonetheless, enable one to see why many poets cannot be content with Bly's articulation of value and, fearing that soft ground may also be quicksand, insist on more objectivist, less privileged moments of experience as the necessary poetic base for a believable value frame. Moreover, these questions demand that one try to be more precise about the ontological status of poetry like Bly's. Such precision is possible, I think, by adapting some of the argument of Maurice-Jean Lefèbre's *L'Image Fascinante et Le Surreel*. (I say "adapt" because Lefèbre tries to explain only the fascination of images and not the additional qualities in Bly of serenity and the sense of cosmic unity—qualities I think also explicable in Lefèbre's terms.) Following Sartre, he argues that the image is by definition never a present reality but the construct of imagination, precisely because it *is* the making present in the mind what is absent in perception. The image, in other words, is by its nature free "from imprisonment among" objects, and this condition, Lefèbre continues, is the reason why images seem to fascinate readers and project an infinite mystery. This image at once absent and present evokes in one an ambivalent state toward the world known as real. The more one attends to the image, the more one is dissatisfied with the real world that does not include it and the more one tries to see what the image might mean were it real and filling the gap it has created in one's sense of the real. In Bly's dichotomy between the two languages, the image mocks the self-sufficiency of the "outer world," yet the second language containing the image cannot so much replace the language of the outer world as trouble it and provoke the reader's desire to go beyond it. Perhaps the image in Bly's sense so fascinates one because it occupies a mental space on the horizon of experience—always offering a full presence but, when one seeks to grasp it, evaporating into a silent void. Lefèbre offers as the nearest analogue to the image the discipline of metaphysics, for it too is based on one's fascination with entities that are in fact absent but that, once created, trouble the reader with a sense of the insufficiency of the world of facts. One comes more and more to dwell on the absent and hopes to find through it ways of extending the unsatisfactory reality. But where metaphysics tries to deny absence and claim its projection as real, the poetic image is content to revel in its own ambiguity; the image "n'est pas le repos dans une verité, c'est une passion," "la meta-physique du coeur."

Bly, of course, would accept neither Lefèbre's characteristic French dualism nor his academic's realist insistence that poetry is only "la metaphysique du coeur" and not "la verité, revelé dans le coeur." Like so many contemporary poets, he must try with images to do the work of metaphysics, even if his poems stagger under this burden. In Bly's particular case, the quarrel with those willing to resign poetry to the heart may also have deeper significance. Lefèbre defines problem that helps clarify both Bly's contribution to contemporary poetry and his two basic weaknesses—a terribly small range of subject matter and at-titudes and a recurrent insistence that value can only be recog-nized by one metaphorically at the point of death. (This second characteristic is, of course, justifiable as a metaphor, but its re-currence seems almost pathological; at best it manifests an at-titude surprisingly alien from the activist voice of Bly's prose.) Both these weaknesses stem from Bly's attempt to have his poems occupy the space Lefèbre defines as the place of the im-age, but at the same time, to insist that the interpenetrations glimpsed and the mystery realized are actually present within experience for one who has learned to see with the vision of the inner man. Very few experiences, and an even smaller range of attitudes, can consistently occupy this space without pushing the material into either conscious artifice or ironic interplay with an inadequate reality.

The one human experience, in fact, that most obviously exists in the space between simple reality and an absent, mysterious stillness of things is death. For death is at once an undeniably real experience and the entrance into a state of being eternally in-volved in the continual processes and energies of life. Only when nourished by death can one both possess his own real being and feel himself surrendering to a merger with the univer-sal condition never experienced among the brute particulars and fragments of normal experience.

Death is a state of absence, a state calling forth images that can only fascinate and never be tested for their truth. Yet . . . death is also probably the most absolutely real and present phe-nomenon man is acquainted with, since all animate life is subject to its power. Death, like the poetic image, occupies a threshold space between absence and presence, calling man beyond his empirical sense of facts but only famishing the craving it creates for deeper, more intense forms of knowledge.

Bly's work, then, seeks to preserve two basic aspects of Whitman's vision. It images an ideal state of consciousness as one in which the ego merges in all being by meditating its death, and it takes that mode of awareness as grounding the understanding and the confidence necessary to appreciate life as a journey along the open road. But because he becomes so obsessed with the means for attaining this vision, one must turn to other poets if one wishes to appreciate what the actual journey might be like.

CHARLES MOLESWORTH

"Rejoice in the Gathering Dark"
The Poetry of Robert Bly

I

Since *Silence in the Snowy Fields* appeared over fifteen years ago, Robert Bly has steadily accumulated a poetry of secrecy and exultation, that most difficult of combinations. While excoriating the destructiveness of false public values, he insists on a silencing solitude as the primary poetic discipline. Diving into the stillest mythical recesses, he resurfaces with thrashing energy, intensely unwilling to settle for any but the most blinding light. His body of work is relatively small—certainly smaller than that of others of his generation such as Levertov, Snyder, and Ashbery—and this sharpens the sense of a patient accumulation. In describing his contemporary Robert Creeley, Bly uses the prose poem to simultaneously heroize, domesticate, and totemize:

> The beak is a crow beak, and the sideways look he gives, the head shoved slightly to the side by the bad eye, finishes it. And I suppose his language in poems is crow language—no long open vowels, like the owl, no howls like the wolf, but instead short, faintly hollow, harsh sounds, that all together make something genuine, crow speech coming up from every feather, every source of that crow body and crow life.
>
> The crows take very good care of their children, and are the most intelligent of birds, and wary of human company, though when two or three fly over the countryside together, they look almost happy.

From *The Fierce Embrace: A Study of Contemporary American Poetry* by Charles Molesworth by permission of the University of Missouri Press. Copyright 1979 by the Curators of the University of Missouri.

Though not the total picture, this offers a good grounding in Bly's poetics. For him, authentic language arises out of a depth, "coming up from . . . every source," and is never to be thought of as floating or being passed around aimlessly. All artistic intuition is body centered, all "thou-saying" becomes a way of being-in-the-world. Articulations of the tongue are simply higher forms of the organism's exploration and control of the environment: adjustments, like the tilt of the head, to assure the proper perceptual thrust. But physical harmony provides for moral equilibrium, and we have a moral obligation to be intelligent for the sake of the species. We ought not to seek to illumine nature so much as to make her dark energies the source of our own. The health of the individual's interior life measures the higher truths, for if we are concealed from ourselves, we will destroy everything that doesn't blend with our own ego.

You will notice, of course, how the poetics have become an ethic. But the highest virtue, aesthetically and morally, is patience:

> Beneath the waters, since I was a boy,
> I have dreamt of strange and dark treasures,
> Not of gold, or strange stones, but the true
> Gift, beneath the pale lakes of Minnesota.
>
> This morning also, drifting in the dawn wind,
> I sense my hands, and my shoes, and this ink—
> Drifting, as all of this body drifts,
> Above the clouds of the flesh and the stone.
>
> A few friendships, a few dawns, a few glimpses of grass,
> A few oars weathered by the snow and the heat,
> So we drift toward shore, over cold waters,
> No longer caring if we drift or go straight.
>
> ("After Drinking All Night . . .")

It may seem odd to think of patience in connection with Robert Bly, when for many he remains a master polemicist, a "self-advertising" publicist (Allen Tate's view), or an intemperate dissenter. Bly has touched and often irritated virtually every poet and every issue in contemporary poetry in at least one of his roles: editor, satirist, theorizer, organizer, translator, regionalist, prizewinner, and iconoclast. One might well say, as Eliot said of Pound and Chinese poetry, that Bly has invented South American poetry for our time. No literary history of the last twenty years would be complete without reference to Bly's magazine, *The Sixties*. And few social aestheticians would ignore Bly's acceptance speech at the 1968 National Book Awards ceremony: "I know I am speaking for many, many American poets when I ask this question: since we are murdering a culture in Vietnam at least as fine as our own, have we the right to congratulate ourselves on our cultural magnificence? Isn't that out of place?"[1]

As a critic and as a poetic theorist, Bly has contributed much to the recent shift from a tightly ordered, highly structured verse, with irony as its dominant mode, toward a poetry more open in form, associative in structure, and ecstatic in intention. When people attempt a balanced assessment of his accomplishments, though, his criticism all too often outweighs his poetry. It has become almost necessary to right this situation and concentrate for a while on Bly's poetry, placing, where possible, his criticism in relation to *it* rather than picking at the poems through the grid of the polemics. What follows is an attempt to do just that; but before proceeding, it will be useful to have before us at least two of Bly's critical assumptions, assumptions unavoidably central to his work and almost invisibly dispersed throughout it. The first, from a review of David Ignatow's poetry, argues for a proper sense of the position of ideas in poetry:

> In the most nourishing prose or poetry, I think, we always find ideas. But an essay and a poem are different in the way an idea lies inside them. In an essay, obviously, the idea must be clear—every inch of the idea's skin should be visible. The idea should be laid out flat—like the skin of a goat—we should be able to walk around it, tell the head from the tail. Ideas in poems don't appear that way—in poems ideas lie curled under tree roots, only a strong odor of fur indicating anything is there. . . . To learn to read poetry in fact we have to learn to reach in and uncover ideas, which actually are so much fresher than the ideas in prose precisely because they have been lying curled.

As several people have pointed out, William Carlos Williams did not say "no ideas, only things," but rather "no ideas but in things." Likewise, Bly doesn't exclude ideas or choke them into submission or dilute them into mere fancies when he writes his poems. Instead, he places himself differently in relation to the idea, approaches it differently, than would a writer of expository prose or more traditional poetry. Ideas lie close to the source of nourishment and support in his poems, but they must work their way in almost by stealth. Bly's use of animal imagery, his emphasis on olfactory and kinesthetic sensation, tells us more about his "thinking" than any paraphrase can. His thought aspires to a form in which gesture and intention are the same, to an integrity that ties together perception and conception, object and subject. His psychology and epistemology are clearly much closer to those of the phenomenologists (such as Merleau-Ponty) than those of the classical materialists or idealists.

The other principle in Bly's poetics creates more heat than light in his polemics but vitalizes his poetry in ways that are very important: it claims that technique is the work of rationality, ego, and hence suffocation:

> I refuse to say anything at all about prosody. What an ugly word it is! In the true poem, both the form and the content rise from the same place; they have the same swiftness and darkness. Both are expressions of a certain rebellious energy rising in the psyche: they are what Boehme calls "the shooting up of life from nature to spirit." What is important is this rebellious energy, not technique. If I write a bad poem it is because I have somehow taken the thought from someone else—I haven't really lived it: it isn't my energy. Technique is beside the point in this matter.

Such a doctrine, in the hands of unskilled enthusiasts (critics as well as poets), might easily spell bathos. But the theories of Eliot and Pound had begun to do the same when Bly wrote this. Few phenomena need a clarifying historical context more than literary theories do; we can identify what past and established theories these words are attacking more easily than we can see, precisely, where they will lead. Thus, Bly's poetics resembles his populist political sentiment: it is rooted in deep feeling, intimately "known" but seldom analyzed, and often more vigorous in its denials than its affirmations.

The positive aspects of Bly's poetics revolve around his concentration on the image. In a series of reviews and essays in *The Sixties,* Bly, in conjunction with James Wright, erected a theory concerning the "subjective image," produced by the workings of the transrational mind, charged with mythical resonances, and bearing the major responsibility for organizing the poem's energies. This image, as the passage above suggests, resulted more from a special gathering of consciousness than from any purely verbal manipulation; it came from a region beyond syntax, and it had powers more than grammatical. To write such poetry, one needed a carefully plotted surrender, and to read it required a discipline less passive than deeply meditative. "But at last, the quiet waters of the night will rise, / And our skin shall see far off, as it does under water." Bly's own images are often liquid and cold, like lake waters soundless and dark, and the poems are often filled with gazes and deep snow. They end with suddenly opened vistas, consoling with something like infinite regress ("Our ears hear tinier sounds, / Reaching far away east in the early darkness.") or vague, indefinable threats ("The doors are open, many are called to silence"). Obviously, the poetry needed the theorizing to clear space for what might otherwise have been a scant, febrile, and barren order.

II

Bly draws up his poetic sensibility out of at least three obvious sources: the heritage of Imagism, with its brevity at once precise and evocative; the argumentative diffidence, especially in metaphysical matters, associated with the haiku; and the body-centered mysticism perfected by such Protestant writers as Jacob Boehme. This relatively wide-ranging literary mix both precedes and results from Bly's interest in translation, for he is quick to appropriate structures of feeling and thought from whatever region or epoch he finds necessary and usable. "We reason with a later reason," as Stevens says, and few writers are more aware that they are drawing on an extensive, multivalent jumble of traditions than is Bly. For all his emphasis on cutting against the grain of too readily accepted poetic modes, and for all his antipathy to questions of technique, Bly demands of himself an unequivocally *centered* sense of his vocation—it is only because his aesthetic geometry seems eccentric to others that his polemics become necessary. What critics might view as the limitations of various modes, he insists on regarding as poetic necessities. For example, I spoke above of the diffidence associated with the haiku; but Bly argues that only when the forces of rationality are stilled, or at least dampened, can the configuration of emotions rightly shape the poem's truth. What some might see as a poetry based on modesty or exclusion, he sees as daring and assertive. Far from reluctant to address ideas in prose argument, Bly makes his own poetic statements turn aside from the ease of identifiable cognitive patterns and plunge instead into dense, pathless areas of experience and darkly associative pools of feeling.

Such a sensibility as Bly has developed could easily lead to a host of predictable enactments and debilitating excesses when the time came to write individual lyrics. A memorable life-style, or even a reassuringly human conscience, as Bly's critics rather smugly repeat, cannot guarantee verbal magic. My sense of Bly's poetry is that it exhibits the skill it does because of its author's high seriousness, but such a sense can only be averred, not demonstrated. However, we can register the characteristic energy of Bly's lyrics by exploring them as resolutions (not solutions, in the sense of problems disposed of, but resolutions, in the sense of a consciousness articulated) through which two apparently opposing compulsions redefine one another. One of these compulsions is most visible as theme, the other as style. Thematically, the concerns of meditative poetry, namely the structures of consciousness and the relation of fact and value, outline the range and subject of these poems. Poetry for Bly offers a criticism of life, but a criticism available only through discipline, by a rectification of thought and feeling. Bly's anti-war poetry doesn't settle for expressing humanistic values; rather, he alleges that the grossest forms of false consciousness are necessary for such inhumanity as a war to occur and that only through a fundamental relearning of the world can it be prevented. This accounts for Bly's aggressive, sometimes intemperate modernism: he sees the poet simultaneously as a solitary craftsman and as a moral scourge.

With regard to style, the language of ecstasy and spiritual autobiography energizes Bly's exploration of his themes. Resembling voices employed by authors as distinct as Thoreau and Mailer, this style employs a dialectical structure as it oscillates between ecphrasis, or heightened description, and a schematizing impulse akin to allegory. Bly insists that the reader surrender to the moment, the intensely peculiar conjunction of sensations stripped of any mediating common circumstances. On the other hand, any satori can be equivalent to any other; the hidden world constantly surrounds us, and any breakthrough, despite and almost by virtue of its arbitrariness, can serve as a template to reassure and instruct readers in the abiding presence of that hidden order. The sacred, masked by the ordinary, escapes our vision, trained as it is to look for the wrong significances. Neither strictly transcendental nor existential, Bly's style owes much to these "methods," especially in their American guises.

This apparent disjunction of theme and style may explain the difficulty many readers have with Bly's poetry. Meditative poetry often conveys a highly developed discursive sense, willing to be patiently self-correcting, never totally sundered from its framework of ideas, though never subsumed by it. To know our own minds or the landscapes that surround, shape, and support us, we must open out deliberately, intent and almost passive, like a snowy field. Autobiographical or ecstatic poetry, on the other hand, proceeds by what Bly calls "leaping," a nondiscursive, elliptical process that stakes everything on the momentary verbal gesture. All accumulative or qualified judgments are untrustworthy; we must be willing to jump from our bodies (or drop, renewed, back into them), as anxious as the silent dark itself to blanket the false lights of the rational mind. Fully responsive readers of Bly's poetry need to undergo long preparation, disciplined and meditative, and yet be willing to undo it all at a moment's notice. This, too, explains why Bly resorts to polemics and chafes at technique: the protective space around his poetry has been laboriously cleared, though he chooses to conceal the evidence of axe and plumb.

Running as an almost silent current beneath this part of Bly's work is a strain of prophetic or chthonic music, a response to very large rhythmic pulses, caught in a vision that can zoom from a nearly microscopic to an archeological measure. This, too, can be confusing, sometimes even toneless, as in "Looking at Some Flowers":

> Light is around the petals, and behind them:
> Some petals are living on the other side of the light.
> Like sunlight drifting onto the carpet
> Where the casket stands, not knowing which world it is in.
> And fuzzy leaves, hair growing from some animal
> Buried in the green trenches of the plant.
> Or the ground this house is on,
> Only free of the sea for five or six thousand years.
>
> (*The Light Around the Body*)

The one word "only" conveys almost all the emotion of the poem, though of course its placement and its context make such emotion available to it. But this is often part of Bly's effect, a sense that we are sharing some secret, glimpsing some long concealed vista that closes shut as soon as the poem ends. In the political poetry this often causes people to complain that Bly is preaching to the converted, but of course such people seldom admit that no poetry built on political vision has much *persuasive* power, whatever its strengths and reassurances. When we call Bly a "nature" poet, we must remember that visions of nature are as various as political opinions and are often the result of an ineffable mixture of temperament, experience, and self-discipline. Also, Bly's political poetry earns some of its most moving successes when he adopts the viewpoint of his political enemies, as in the bizarre "Counting Small-Boned Bodies":

> If we could only make the bodies smaller,
> Maybe we could get
> A whole year's kill in front of us on a desk!

Bly's political poetry plunges past the metaphysical tenuousness of imagism and symbolism into a hidden order. But this hidden order he openly declaims. Like the Marxists with their notions of false consciousness, Bly posits a common awareness of mundane reality as something to be altered, and if necessary smashed, if we are to uncover the true (and truth-revealing) relations that shape the polis and the psyche. Bly's hidden order differs from, say, Mallarmé's because we can trace it from the dailiness of the world—we needn't slip into a world of albums and fauns and cabalism to discover it. On the other hand, it also differs from Stevens's, since we need no patient dialectic, no tone-juggling irony, to coax it from the welter of physical sensations that flood our thirsting eyes. His politics insistently slice along an emotional bias that is essentially populist, though without the xenophobic isolationism of the populists, and tolerate no analysis, no "party structure," no compromised platform.

> The time for exhortation is past. I have heard
> The iron chairs scraping in asylums,
> As the cold bird hunches into the winter
> In the windy night of November.
> The cold miners rise from their pits
> Like a flash flood,
> Like a rice field disintegrating.
> Men cry when they hear stories of someone rising from the dead.
> ("Hurrying Away from the Earth")

Official culture and the State work for the oppression of the spirit, but so pervasive is their success that the evidence of their crimes hides everywhere, and hence is visible only in dreams or trances.

> Ministers who dive headfirst into the earth
> The pale flesh
> Spreading guiltily into new literatures
>
> That is why these poems are so sad
> The long dead running over the fields
>
> The mass sinking down
> The light in children's faces fading at six or seven
>
> The world will soon break up into small colonies of the saved
> ("Those Being Eaten by America")

Bly's political poetry thus arrives repeatedly at a crux: though the language must be hushed or ecstatic, appealing to suprarational truths, the evils must be squarely, almost pictorially, addressed. Part dream-vision, part diatribe, the poems seem laughable to anyone who is unsettled by all-embracing pathos or all-damning bile. Satire and ecstasy make strange bedfellows and often produce a tonelessness, a cancelling out of affect, in the service of an ineffable wisdom.

> The crane handler dies, the taxi driver dies, slumped over
> In his taxi. Meanwhile, high in the air, executives
> Walk on cool floors, and suddenly fall:
> Dying, they dream they are lost in a snowstorm in the mountains,
> On which they crashed, carried at night by great machines.
> As he lies on the wintry slope, cut off and dying,
> A pine stump talks to him of Goethe and Jesus.
> Commuters arrived in Hartford at dusk like moles
> Or hares flying from a fire behind them,
> And the dusk in Hartford is full of their sighs;
> Their trains come through the air like a dark music,
> Like the sound of horns, the sound of thousands of small wings.
>   ("The Executive's Death")

Because Bly mastered the idiom of pastoral ecstasy in *Silence in the Snowy Fields* before the directly political poetry appeared in *The Light Around the Body* (1967), many people will continue to regard his political writings as deviant, as a falling away from a purity of diction and viewpoint that was perhaps too intense for its own good. The voice, however, is a seamless garment, and the "leaping" imaginativeness operates in both field and city, imprinting victim and villain with a distinctive animism.

III

In some instances Bly clearly separates his political poetry from his poetry of pastoral ecstasy, as when he entitles a section of *The Light Around the Body* "The Vietnam War." On the other hand, the two small collections of prose poems, *The Morning Glory* (1975) and *Point Reyes Poems* (1974), are completely without political content, yet they contain some of Bly's most moving and intensely rhetorical writing. His full-length collection, *Sleepers Joining Hands* (1973), though largely ignored by reviewers, contains both sorts of poems (though without being divided into distinct sections). This collection also includes an extended expository prose essay, "I Came Out of the Mother Naked," related directly to the longest poem in the book, "The Teeth Mother Naked at Last," which is the longest poem Bly has written. Concluding this volume is the long poem-sequence that gives the book its title, and it stands as Bly's most challenging and most beautiful poem to date, one that merges perfectly his pastoral and political obsessions and mythologies. "Sleepers Joining Hands," with its five sections and long, loosely cadenced lines, is Bly's celebration of himself, a poem that attempts to reconcile the chanting openness of Whitman with the mythical intensity of Rilke. Before considering it closely, however, we might linger a while on that medium Bly has slowly, unobtrusively, and patiently mastered: the prose poem.

Most readers think of the prose poem in connection with Rimbaud's *Les Illuminations,* in other words, as a series of aggressively scintillating but fragmentary insights spilling from a deranged mind, perhaps the devil's work, perhaps not. Then, too, there is Mallarmé with his imposingly rigorous sophistication, in love with and caused by its own etiolation (Eliot's "Hysteria" obviously belongs to this part of the tradition), while more modern still are the interiorizations of material objects perfected by Francis Ponge speaking "on the side of things." In any case, the prose poem appears decidedly French, a rather bourgeois invention and hardly suited to a Minnesota poet intent on breaking through to mythically resonant images. Yet if his first books showed Bly working with an essentially pastoral poetry, his prose poems illustrate how he has moved closer to a poetry of natural history. The pastoral remains resolutely literary, always conscious of tradition and audience, always at some important level an *exercise,* an attempt to test and redefine the limits of its own saying. Natural history, on the other hand, cultivates a prosaic idiom, it is concerned with observing precisely and labelling tentatively and yields little to its audience by either addressing its emotional needs or reaffirming its metaphysics or even its properties.

In the earlier brief collection, *The Morning Glory,** Bly introduces his prose poems with this short apologia:

> There is an old occult saying: whoever wants to see the invisible must penetrate more deeply into the visible. Everything has a right to exist. If we examine an animal carefully, we see how independent it is of us. Its world is complete without us. We feel separated at first; later, joyful.
>
> Basho says in his wonderful poem:

> The morning glory—
> Another thing
> that will never be my friend.

This becomes the central theme and the recurrent strategy of these poems: the exclusion of the human. Emotion and subjectivity are not totally removed, certainly not denied in these poems, but the phenomena under scrutiny displace ordinary human reactions and relegate them to a subsidiary or marginal role. (This, of course, makes these poems more like Ponge than Rimbaud, but they are quite distinct from either.) We are on the outside, or at the edges, looking in, and our curiosity might exfoliate into any of several emotions. But this perceiving energy dwindles if we lose our curiosity, our reverence, or our patience. Though never directly about "seeing" as both a psychical and physical harmony, these poems presume and demand it as our most human activity. This is the second half of "The Large Starfish," from *Point Reyes Poems:*†

> How slowly and evenly it moves! The starfish is a glacier, going sixty miles a year! It moves over the pink rock, by means I cannot see . . . and into marvellously floating delicate brown weeds. It is about the size of the bottom of a pail. When I reach out to it, it holds on firmly, and then slowly relaxes . . . I suddenly take an arm and lift it. The underside is a pale tan . . . gradually as I watch thousands of tiny tubes

---

*Kayak Books edition, 1969.—ED.

†Mudra press edition, 1974.—ED.

begin rising from all over the underside . . . hundreds in the mouth, hundreds along the nineteen underarms . . . all looking . . . feeling . . . like a man looking for a woman . . . tiny heads blindly feeling for a rock and finding only air. A purple rim runs along the underside of every arm, with paler tubes. Probably its moving-feet. . . .

I put him back in . . . he unfolds—I had forgotten how purple he was—and slides down into his rock groin, the snail-like feelers waving as if nothing had happened, and nothing has.

All the ellipses here are Bly's, and he uses them frequently in the *Point Reyes Poems*. These poems occasionally recall the sensibility of Marianne Moore, or of A. R. Ammons, in their loving care, their careful hovering that sustains itself by shifting from one tack-sharp observation to another. Bly's seeing has seldom been more precise than it is in his prose poems: we are shown gulls "with feet the color of pumpkin" or the orange belly of a salamander that is "the color of airplane gasoline on fire," a seeing that refracts rather than parades the emotional, as in the case of the starfish, "a delicate purple, the color of old carbon paper, or an attic dress."

But the overriding impression of these poems reveals itself as diffidence, almost as if the prose were used to protect the speech act, because formal verse patterns might announce too much of a shaping impulse or initiate a solemnity that could disrupt the ruminative spell. The use of ellipses, along with phrases like "as if" and "a kind of," reinforces the sensation "that we are sailing on skeletal eerie craft over the bouyant ocean," as Bly concludes one of these self-effacing performances. Tentativeness of structure is heightened by similes and metaphors proposed but not pursued, their wayward or incidental charm left to do the work: a wave has the "gentleness of William Carlos Williams after his strokes"; a heron "slowly ascends, each wing as long as Holland"; we see several sea lions "looking neither arrogant nor surprised, but like a billfold found in the rain." In some cases the comparisons are relatively extended, but never to serve as logical support or thematic underpinning: watching the light come through a white bird's nest, "we get the feeling of those cloudy transoms above Victorian doors, or the manless hair of those intense nurses, gray and tangled after long nights in the Crimean wards." Human emotions and human weaknesses, though submerged, are omnipresent. Humility of format has its purposes, for it tends to reveal its own vulnerability, to get close to those moments of connectivity and insight that ordinarily we quickly dismiss with an antisentimental jab at our reverie.

Closely related to this tentative sense of structure, a thematic concern with various kinds of movement and growth makes itself felt throughout these poems. The variety extends from motility to glaciation, and the "leaping," associative energies of Bly's poetic attentions test themselves against a world where surprise, spontaneity, immeasurably slow drifts, or immense geological transformations are the order of the moment. These various modes of motion become evident to the human senses only at moments of great stress or utter freedom; they are available only to a haptic or body-centered consciousness, an awareness that cuts across perspectives and breaks down discursive categories. You can well read these poems with a sense of Bly's pragmatism in regard to form, as though a primer course is developmental biology were a prerequisite. The scale can be either macro- or microscopic, focusing on life at either end of the spectrum, exploring the growth of cells or of galaxies. Our vision must learn a different pace and a new frame of reference, until, like the moon, it "moves slowly southward as the clouds flow past. It is an eye, an eye-traveller, going so alone . . . sturdy as an orphan. Bold and alone and formed long ago."

Here is "Walking among Limantour Dunes" (the *Point Reyes Poems* are topographical, even incipiently chthonic in their pursuit of the genius loci):

Thinking of a child soon to be born, I hunch down among friendly sand-grains . . . And the sand grains love us, for they love whatever lives with force not its own, a young girl looking out over her life, alone, without horses, with no map, a white dress on . . . whatever is not rushing blindly forward, the mole blinking at the door of his crumbly mole Vatican, the salmon sensing in his gills the Oregon waters crash down, or this planet abandoned here at the edge of the universe, the life floating inside the Pacific of the womb, near the walls, feeling the breakers roaring.

Bly's objective here clearly is to create something resembling those evanescent moments of sudden expanded consciousness he rendered so often in the early books, as in the following example:

DRIVING TO TOWN LATE TO MAIL A LETTER

It is a cold and snowy night. The main street is deserted.
The only things moving are swirls of snow.
As I lift the mailbox door, I feel its cold iron.
There is a privacy I love in this snowy night.
Driving around, I will waste more time.

(*Silence in the Snowy Fields*)

However humble these early poems may be, however concerned to defeat their own ambitions and lose the ego in the momentary sensations and prevailing drift of the scene, they remain vaguely "confessional," lyric celebrations of an exacerbated, private sensibility. But the later prose poems develop a different consciousness, one no less emotional but much more impersonal (if that distinction will stand), in which the ego is always measured against contexts capable of rectifying our obsession with it. Here is the end of "A Turtle," from *The Morning Glory* sequence, where Bly inverts the animal and sees:

The bottom is a pale, washed-out, rose from being dragged over the world—the imagination is simplified there, without too much passion, business-like, like the underside of some alien spaceship.

This clearly sounds a note not heard in *Snowy Fields*. The prose poems speak more self-sufficiently, with less protection from the sometimes hectoring theory of the deep image; they clear their own ground as they go, or rather float like fog "over soaked and lonely hills." Bly continues to use many of the strategies of the earlier poems, such as those deep images, sprung loose from Jungian depths; the barebones narratives, exemplumlike in their simplicity; and the heightened descriptions. But Bly has realized that the image alone can't do the work of the poem, that the ego and pseudorationality will make themselves felt in any surrealist attempt (especially a programmatic one) to escape them. If we trust too much in the theory, "mind" will be there anyway, not necessarily supplying significant form, but more likely having designs on *us;* and the only way to keep the possibilities of discovery open is to acknowledge the presence of the intellect but relegate it carefully from the seat of control. Much of the putatively surrealist poetry spawned by Bly's theories comes out clichéd and conceited, in both senses of the term, as the farfetched and the self-advancing merge histrionically. But Bly, especially in his prose poems, manages to skirt the foolishness of his students. Here, as coda to these points, is the conclusion of "The Dead Seal near McClure's Beach":

> He raises himself up, and tucks his flippers under, as if to keep them warm. A wave comes in, touches his nose. He turns and looks at me—the eyes slanted, the crown of the head like a leather jacket. He is taking a long time to die. The whiskers white as porcupine quills, the forehead slopes, goodbye brother, die in the sound of waves, forgive us if we have killed you, long live your race, your inner-tube race, so uncomfortable on land, so comfortable in the sea. Be comfortable in death then, where the sand will be out of your nostrils, and you can swim in the long loops through the pure death, ducking under as assassinations break above you. You don't want to be touched by me. I climb the cliff and go home the other way.

IV

If somewhere behind his prose poems stand Francis Ponge or even Robinson Jeffers, the tutelary spirit of *Sleepers Joining Hands* is surely Pablo Neruda. It is odd, but beneficially so, that a Norwegian immigrant meditating in the snowbound isolation of Minnesota should, in part, extend his resonance by way of the tropically surreal imagination of a Latin diplomat. Though there are only ten short poems included in *Sleepers Joining Hands,* the language is whittled out of a sense of distance and anguish, and the poems tell of a natural world almost preternaturally capable of storing and releasing great depths of human emotions. Some of these poems are like Neruda's early work, such as *Twenty Love Poems and a Song of Desperation* (1924), and they make us realize the poetic value of constant separation working in consort with the hope of ultimate possession. This passage is from "Water under the Earth," and the lines in which the poem describes itself recall Neruda's self-conscious modesty, born of a desire to create an organic language at home in the world of growth and decay:

Everything we need now is buried,
it's far back into the mountain,
it's under the water guarded by women.
These lines themselves are sunk to the waist in the dusk under the
    odorous cedars,
each rain will only drive them deeper,
they will leave a faint glow on the dead leaves.
You too are weeping in the low shade of the pine branches,
you feel yourself about to be buried too,
you are a ghost stag shaking his antlers in the herony light—
what is beneath us will be triumphant
in the cool air made fragrant by owl feathers.

In the surrealism of the long antiwar poem "The Teeth Mother Naked at Last" we can again hear the influence of Neruda, as here, where the central image might have come from a carnival fairgrounds, but its new context renders it anything but entertaining:

There is a black silo inside our bodies, revolving fast.
Bits of black paint are flaking off,
where the motorcycles roar, around and around,
rising higher on the silo walls,
the bodies bent toward the horizon,
driven by angry women dressed in black.

160

This dissociating juxtaposition of images with associative complexities alternates with straightforward connections between mundane surfaces and horrifying realities:

It's because the aluminum window shade business is doing so well in
     the United States that we roll fire over entire villages
It's because a hospital room in the average American city now costs
     $90 a day that we bomb hospitals in the North
. . . .
It's because we have new packaging for smoked oysters that bomb
     holes appear in the rice paddies

It is because we have so few women sobbing in back rooms,
because we have so few children's heads torn apart by high-velocity
     bullets,
because we have so few tears falling on our own hands
that the Super Sabre turns and screams down toward the earth.

Some will mutter in disbelief at these lines; others will think of Sidney's "The poet, he nothing affirms, and therefore never lyeth" and wish that Bly had heeded the advice. But like Neruda's anti-imperialist poems in *Canto general* (1950), I think Bly's antiwar poems will become even clearer and more striking in time, and their "excess" will be recognized as Blakean.

"The Teeth Mother Naked at Last" is followed, and its title image explained, by an essay Bly wrote and included in the midst of *Sleepers Joining Hands* to outline his theories and his method of "psychic archeology." The tone of his argument is, by turns, allusive, hectoring, suggestive, definitive, and exploratory. The essay shows Bly at his rhetorical best and at the same time shows how far beyond even Neruda his search has carried him.

Whenever a man enters the force field of a Mother, he feels himself being pulled toward mothers and childhood, back toward the womb, but this time he feels himself being pulled *through* the womb, into the black nothing before life, into a countryside of black plants where he will lose all consciousness, both mother and father. The teeth in the vagina will strip him as he goes through. He is dismembered while still alive. The job of this Mother is to end the intensification of mental life that the Ecstatic Mother began, to end ecstasy and spiritual growth. The alcoholic has seen the Stone Mother, and he drinks to dull the fear that his inner rivers will turn to stone. He avoids looking at the Mother and the alcohol turns him to stone. The Stone Mother stands for numbness, paralysis, catatonia, being totally spaced out, the psyche torn to bits, arms and legs thrown all over. America's fate is to face this Mother before other industrial nations; Poe's "Descent into the Maelstrom" suggests the horror of the descent. My Lai is partway down; hard drugs that leave the boy-man permanently "stoned" are among the weapons of this Mother.

Though virtually every aspect of this argument can be traced to some previous writer—the dichotomy between "mother consciousness" and "father consciousness" echoes and parallels Lawrence's "blood consciousness" and "mind consciousness"; Bachofen's *Mother Right* is openly acknowledged as a source; the interest in force fields and the archaic consciousness as energizing templates for contemporary poets recalls Charles Olson—the essay is distinctive and revealing for Bly's poetry. Bly continues to favor images and associative structures over ideas and logical distinctions, and he continues to see good poetry as being a result of disciplined consciousness, not so much a criticism of life (though it is that, too) as a search for almost lost origins, a patient surrender almost Christian:

> I see in my own poems and the poems of so many other poets alive now fundamental attempts to right our own spiritual balance, by encouraging those parts in us that are linked with music, with solitude, water, and trees, the parts that grow when we are far from the centers of ambition.

But the most praiseworthy achievement in *Sleepers Joining Hands* is the title sequence, a five-part dream-vision deserving comparison with the best of contemporary poetry. As I suggested above, this sequence has affinities with Whitman, especially as it announces a new consciousness founded on a new sense of the ego, and also with Rilke, for it develops a complex symbolism in its search for a transcendent vision, a desire "to see things from the other side." Bly attempts to formulate a special sense of space and time in this poem; although his predecessors are apparent and many, he succeeds, and succeeds largely in his own terms. Simply put, Bly's temporal sense places the perspectives of a floating present, such as we experience in dreams, within an archeological, even a geological framework. At the same time, this temporal sense accompanies and is supported by a spatial sense, really an awareness of "inwardness" in which, again, a dreamlike space is modified by a consciousness directed toward the inner reaches of the body.

Thematically, discussions of the poem are apt to be clumsy, for reasons that should now be obvious. Yet the sequence does offer vague outlines for its "argument," and careful readers can sense a "plot" rising and falling with the speaker's energies, with his trust and doubt concerning his own visionary powers. The point of simplest and most intense affirmation comes in the third section, "The Night Journey in the Cooking Pot":

> Leaves slip down, falling through their own branches.
> The tree becomes naked and joyful.
> Leaves fall in the tomby wood.
> Some men need so little, and even that I need very little.
> Suddenly I love the dancers, leaping
> in the dark, jumping
> into the air, and the singers and dancers and leapers!
> I start to sing and rove around the floor,
> singing like "a young Lioun"
>
> I want to rise far into the piney tops
>
> I am not going farther from you,
> I am coming nearer,
> green rain carries me nearer you,
> I weave drunkenly about the page,
> I love you,
> I never know that I loved you
> until I was swallowed by the invisible

This acceptance, however, is much more problematic than it appears in this passage, and the poem goes on to record self-hatred and despair. Slowly the necessity becomes clear: we must accept our mortal bodies. But the necessity can be cruel long before it is kind:

> I fall into my own hands,
>   fences break down under horses,
> cities starve, whole towns of singing women carrying to the burial
>   fields the look I saw on my father's face,
> I sit down again, I hit my own body,
> I shout at myself, I see what I have betrayed.
> What I have written is not good enough.
> Who does it help?
> I am ashamed sitting on the edge of my bed.

Like many dream-visions, "Sleepers Joining Hands" unravels the speaker's vocation, his being called to the knowledge of a higher, hidden order. Though his guides announce their other-worldly origins, the speaker must finally conduct his own initiation:

> I have been alone two days, and still everything is cloudy.
> The body surrounds me on all sides.
> I walk out and return.
> Rain dripping from pine boughs, boards soaked on porches,
> gray water awakens, fish slide away underneath.
> I fall asleep. I meet a man from a milder planet.
> I say to him "I know Christ is from your planet!"
> He lifts his eyes to me with a fierce light.
> He reaches out and touches me on the tip of my cock,
>   and I fall asleep.
>
> ("Meeting the Man Who Warns Me")

The sleep within sleep, the savior who rejects our recognition, and the symbol of assertive power rendered weak by gentleness: we are clearly closer to Jung than to Freud, to hermetic rather than rational knowledge.

Some savior appears to have come, but the arrival is on a different scale, in a different world, than we expected:

The barn doors are open. His first breath touches the manger hay
and the King a hundred miles away
stands up. He calls his ministers.
"Find him.
There cannot be two rulers in one body."
He sends his wise men out along the arteries,
along the winding tunnels, into the mountains,
to kill the child in the old moonlit villages of the brain.
                              ("The Night Journey in the Cooking Pot")

The body politic merges with the transfigured body, for this poem wants a new consciousness and a new world, and it will settle for nothing else, even if it must live in dreams and fantasies:

Sometimes when I read my own poems late at night,
I sense myself on a long road,
I feel the naked thing alone in the universe,
the hairy body padding in the fields at dusk. . . .

I have floated in the eternity of the cod heaven,
I have felt the silver of infinite numbers brush my side—
I am the crocodile unrolling and slashing through the mudded water,
I am the baboon crying out as her baby falls from the tree,
I am the light that makes the flax blossom at midnight!
I am an angel breaking into three parts over the Ural Mountains!
I am no one at all.
     ("An Extra Joyful Chorus for Those Who Have Read This Far")

Whether passing "under the earth through the night-water" or "all alone, floating in the cooking pot on the sea," the speaker remains isolate, selfless, lost through his own irresolution or defeated by false energy. But if he is "the last inheritor crying out in deserted houses," he also sees himself as "an eternal happiness fighting in the long reeds."

The poem spills out images, it gathers toward clarity, it

moves through thickets of association, and through it all develops an emotional force field, a sense of temporal simultaneity and spatial diffusion. Quotations, even frequent and lengthy, will not convey this force, and with associative poetry this critical axiom becomes freshly true. We must become patient readers, for the lyric bursts of the shorter poems are here protracted, though with no dampening of the lyric intensity. The poem *is* lyrical, its audience is a better, secret part of the speaker, or of someone willing to assume that role. The speaker imagines himself joining an Indian tribe; and, as "the suppressed race returns," Bly resembles Thoreau, another spokesman for solitude who desperately wanted to be inside the body of the redskin. Echoing the poet-naturalist, the transcendentalist, Bly waits to give birth to the new man:

> There is another being living inside me.
> He is looking out of my eyes.
> I hear him
> in the wind through the bare trees.
> . . . .
> That is why I am so glad in fall.
> I walk out, throw my arms up, and am glad.
> The thick leaves fall,
> falling past their own trunk,
> and the tree goes naked,
> leaving only the other one.
>
> ("Water Drawn Up into the Head")

One can hear some Thoreauvian puns here as the tree and the man uncover their common state. The poem ends with the following lines, and their utter difference from the rest of the poem recalls the end of Eliot's "Prufrock" with its two three-line stanzas, but the mermaids and the solitude and the destroying waves are replaced by something shared, a joy, and by the waters of release:

Our faces shine with the darkness reflected from the Tigris,
cells made by the honeybees that go on growing after death,
a room darkened with curtains made of human hair.

The panther rejoices in the gathering dark.
Hands rush toward each other through miles of space.
All the sleepers in the world join hands.

V

The publication of *This Body Is Made of Camphor and Gopherwood*
(1977) signaled a decisive change in Bly's poetry. Though continuing to use the prose poem as he had in *The Morning Glory*
(1975), in the later work Bly concentrates his vision more directly on ecstatic moments and writes what must be described as
religious poetry. These moments, or nodes of psychic energy,
have only a fleeting relation with the subjects of natural history
over which Bly lingered so lovingly in *The Morning Glory*. That
earlier collection was dominated by a sense of animal delight and
keen observation. Its middle section, "The Point Reyes Poems"
(earlier printed as a separate volume), struck me as Bly's finest
work: a celebration of presence and vision, a peripatetic delight
in the evidences of process and system that avoided both the
disappointments of self-conscious closure and the overreaching
of the glib sublime. But Bly, ever aggressive, was obviously not
content to rest there. The publication of *This Body Is Made of
Camphor and Gopherwood* moves Bly beyond *The Morning Glory*,
just as *The Light Around the Body* (1967) moved him beyond
Silence in the Snowy Fields (1962). In both instances, a continuity
of idiom and style contrasts with a shift in the central subject
matter. To simplify the matter grossly, Bly first went from
midwestern pastoral to antiwar polemic, and now he has gone
from natural history to religious vision. However, what looks
ostensibly like a change in subject can be read as an intensification in style (taking *style* in the largest sense, as the intersection
of temperament and vocation), since the pastoral can readily
turn into polemic, as with Vergil's first eclogue and Milton's
"Lycidas." Likewise, celebrations of natural history are often
possible only through a sublimated religious yearning, as is apparent in Lucretius, Erasmus Darwin, and, in some senses, even
in Whitman.

Of course this schematizing of Bly's work ignores much detail and overlapping. To take the most obvious point, *The Light Around the Body* has both pastoral and political polemics as its subject matter. Also, there are in *Camphor and Gopherwood* moments of sheer pastoral delight, and even domestic relaxation, that are not directly religious. And my scheme ignores *Sleepers Joining Hands* (1973), which is best assimilated as a "transitional" volume (what would any scheme do without its transitionals!), part way between the antiwar polemics of the late sixties and the religious-ecstatic poetry of the seventies. In fact, *Sleepers Joining Hands* gathers together Bly's highest utterances in both the polemical and the religious modes: "The Teeth Mother" and the title poem, respectively. But the general shape of Bly's growth exhibits at least the outline I have sketched. I would argue further that the continuity of idiom, contrasted with the shift in subject matter, makes Bly's development both dramatic and instructive; moreover, such change with continuity is in fact a working out of poetic problems that remain central to contemporary poetry.

What is distinctive about *Camphor and Gopherwood* is the persistence and dominance in it of the religious impulse. Or, to put it in broader terms, Bly exemplifies the curious persistence of theological modes of experience and feeling in our present-day, secularized culture. This persistence often poses a scandal for criticism. For many readers, especially those with secularized imaginations, Bly's work strikes a thoroughly false, and what is worse, an utterly outmoded, note. For others, the religious is simply assimilated to that other category, the supercharged "poetics," a post-Arnoldian preserve of the literary, where we safely store away all that is not marketable, all that is not "operative" in today's society. These readers are likely to overpraise Bly, to read him with little critical or historical awareness, and to accept his religious yearnings simply as a sort of Jungian compensation and corrective to technocratic thought. It is difficult to know a way other than these two alternatives, the dismissive and the obsequious. The former often degenerates into ad hominem attacks, while the latter becomes a twisted form of condescension.

But some middle ground might be claimed. Bly, like some of his contemporaries, can be seen as fighting (a rearguard action? a border skirmish? or the start of a pitched battle?) against the too-pat assumptions of late modernism. In this view, Bly wants to move beyond irony, past the fourth stage of Vico's historical cycle, past the low-mimetic irony of Frye's system, into some challenging affirmation. If we put Bly's work in this sort of context, we can treat its religious impulses seriously and still see how the poems remain essentially poetry and not sacred texts. In other words, Bly writes in such a way as to reaffirm the value of spontaneity, the emphasis on process and sudden illumination often associated with certain trends in modernism (from surrealism to John Cage). But he also wants out of the modernist trap of autotelism, the sense of poetry as "just another" language game. His poetry registers a desire to move beyond what we can call the problem of the symbolic, the modern notion that since reality is constituted by language, everything is (or can be read as) a text. To borrow terms from linguistic theory, in modern consciousness generally there is no signified, and hence there can only be an excess of signifiers; in which case, each code must do what it can to claim autonomy, or else poetry must surrender any claim to a special linguistic status (hence, we have "found poetry," the lingua franca campiness of the epigones of the New York school, and so forth). But one way out of the traps of autotelism and excessive self-consciousness is the insistent affirmation of some indisputable "signified," a "beyond," a realm where value is generated and confirmed. This realm becomes the ground of ultimate concern, a place where irony must fall silent or else change into celebration. But how can Bly hope to find a language that will take him beyond the ironic, especially when irony often seems the only language?

One key to Bly's latest volume lies in his fascination with the medium of the prose poem. Baudelaire described the "miracle of a poetic prose, musical, without rhymes and without rhythm, supple enough and rugged enough to adapt itself to the lyrical impulses of the soul, the undulations of the psyche, the prickings of consciousness." Impulses, undulations, prickings: with this category of gestures, each bordering suggestively on half-liberated, half-choked releases of the unspoken, we begin to sense why Bly has turned to the prose poem. His needs and vision have led him to the point where spontaneous revelations must be somehow both respected for their contact with the marvelous and incorporated into an everyday idiom, a language both supple and rugged. Bly, in other words, wants to domesticate the sublime.

> We love this body as we love the day we first met the person who led us away from this world, as we love the gift we gave one morning on impulse, in a fraction of a second, that we can still see every day, as we love the human face, fresh after love-making, more full of joy than a wagonload of hay.
>
> ("We Love This Body")

The spontaneous ("fraction of a second") becomes the quotidian ("every day"), as the palpable flesh ("this body") is equated with transcendence ("away from this world"). For such eruptions of the marvelous and such blessed sinkings-back into the everyday no strict verse form will suffice. Verse, even intense lyric poetry, has traditionally had a public dimension; it cannot be whispered. It can pretend to be overheard, as "Prufrock," but it almost always has its eye on the larger audience. (Think of Donne, even Catullus, winking at *us* over the shoulder of his mistress.) But prose poetry sets up a different writer-reader contract by asking the reader to surrender his or her sense of regular measure. Verse promises a return to some unit of measure that implies, however weakly, a mediation between the cry of a revealing truth and the closure of a presentable argument. By their very irregularity, prose poems *suggest;* the best of them almost always are masterpieces of insinuation. They are less achieved mediations than a sort of self-erasing indicator of something beyond themselves, hushed pointers to the ineffable.

Many of the prose poems in *Camphor* include passages that announce themselves as dreams; still others suggest a dreamlike structure, as does "Galloping Horses." Even "Walking Swiftly," which begins "When I wake . . . ," has the characteristics of a dream-vision, where impulses, undulations, and prickings are the dominant kind of occurrence. Such concern with the texture and the ultimate moral meaning of dreams has been crucial to Bly's poetry from the beginning. Articulating such concern in prose poems seems natural; besides, Bly has never had an ear that was musical at the level of the poetic line. One sensed from the first that he composed by phrases and clauses, that he wanted more a suggestive cadence than a measured rhythm. So the spontaneous "gesture" of the prose poem has been suited to the "word" of the dream-vision. Falling into holes, leaping through and by images: both types of motion are made possible by the spontaneous, insinuating discursiveness of prose poetry. We can summarize this sort of movement as "motile," defined as having the power to move spontaneously, like certain spores and microorganisms. (A secondary meaning of motile is drawn from psychology, where the word describes a person whose mental imagery consists of his own bodily motion. This word thus relates the movement of Bly's sentences to his "body-centered" mysticism.)

For Bly, motility represents more than a stylistic tic. It stands for the particular form of heuristic discovery that alone can do justice to his religious imagination. Central to this imagination is the belief, itself a vital part of the Portestant mystical tradition from which Bly borrows much of his imagery, that conversion is most strong when it is most sudden. In *The Varieties of Religious Experience* (1902) William James discusses this phenomenon of sudden conversion. By using the then new notion of a "field of consciousness," James analyzes sudden religious conversions as resulting from a change in relative importance between what had been centered in the "field" and what had been only marginal to consciousness. To illustrate such repolarized fields, or " 'uprushes' into ordinary consciousness of energies originating in the subliminal parts of the mind," James refers to cases of posthypnotic suggestion. This persistence of mental energies and their eventual irruption into a waking state of mind, though originally discovered in a sleeplike state, is, of course, at the center of Bly's poetic project.

James then goes on to discuss (in the same lecture) the difficulty of ascertaining the "class-mark distinctive of all true converts." James concludes that such identification is difficult, if not impossible. Spontaneous conversion leaves no specific evidence; as such, it is indistinguishable from conversion occurring over a protracted period. Likewise with Bly's poetry. Its religious intensity leaves no mark except its own spontaneous, motile discoveries. Bly's political poems, for example, strike many as unsuccessful because they are based on no apparent understanding of social cohesiveness. For Bly, the only important ingredient in the *social* is the ecstatic; the ordinary demands of social mediation and historical necessity go largely unregistered in his poetry. This raises a problem that many readers face with Bly, both in his political and in his religious visions: they feel that his salvation is less suffered than willed. Since there is little social experience in his poems, little evidence of how his conversion affects his daily intercourse with others, the reader must react from inner, subjective criteria. Bly's is essentially a utopian vision. Furthermore, the negative element of his vision, his sense of satiric correction, can hardly extend beyond labelling the unawakened as unawakened. On the positive side, he preaches not simply to the converted, but to the transformed. The social does not necessarily obliterate the spontaneous, but it remains a fact that when American poets glorify the spontaneous and inner life, then the programmed and exterior life—and hence inevitably society itself—becomes the undesirable.[2]

Now, generally, religion (as the root of the word tells us) has a social, communal element: one is "bound" not only to a higher force, but also with others. (Wittgenstein's argument against a private language would apply equally strongly against a private religion.) But Bly's religious intensity has no immediate social content; it is a religion of one. Throughout *Camphor* Bly addresses a "friend." This "friend" can be viewed as the polar opposite of Baudelaire's "hypocrite lecteur," but as with some polar opposites, there are strange resemblances. Bly's friend is an interlocutor, a psychological necessity that permits communication to continue; such interlocutors are necessary when the very status of the lyric voice has been called into question. As Walter Benjamin says of Baudelaire, he conceived of his poems as being written for an audience that no longer read lyric poetry. So Bly writes his religious meditations for a public that is no longer ostensibly religious. But a more positive perspective on this "friend" would relate him to the friend addressed by George Herbert in *The Temple*. In this sense the friend is not merely a rhetorical crutch, or a way to domesticate the sublime, but the very divinity made companionable. In other words, the friend is the savior, or us, or the savior-in-us, less a social force than a private, inner healer.

> My friend, this body is made of camphor and gopherwood. Where it goes, we follow, even into the Ark. As the light comes in sideways from the west over damp spring buds and winter trash, the body comes out hesitatingly, and we are shaken, we weep, how is it that we feel no one has ever loved us?
>
> ("The Left Hand")

The Ark is the vessel of love, both the covenant that demonstrates we will be saved and the body scented with eros. (Gopher wood is traditionally the wood Noah used to construct the Ark. The camphor tree is aromatic, and its gum has legendary ritual uses. Although the Song of Songs clearly uses camphor in an erotic metaphor, it developed a certain reputation as an anaphrodisiac. But whether used erotically or ascetically, its odor is sensuous.)

Such religious feeling exists, however, only in a "sideways" light, in the subliminal or marginal consciousness. (This is perhaps why Bly often uses olfactory imagery.) As soon as the feeling is called into the light it may begin to petrify and die:

> Then what is asked of us? To stop sacrificing one energy for another. They are not different energies anyway, not "male" or "female," but whirls of different speeds as they revolve. We must learn to worship both, and give up the idea of one god. . . .
>
> ("Walking to the Next Farm")

Does Platonism lead inevitably to pantheism? Even without tackling that question, we can see how Bly's trust in a realm beyond matter leads him to "recontain" things material as suffused with divinity. Because faith, the "evidence of things that do not appear," is so strong, it can only be located in *every-thing;* and because every thing is thus (at least potentially) sacred, no institutionalization of religious feeling is permissible. The temple always leaves something outside, something "pro-fane," but Bly cannot accept this. Before any temple he prefers the upright heart, but the upright heart must be prepared to cast down its glance—and its attachments—to the lowliest things. Like many American poets before him, from Whitman to Roethke, Bly believes that what Stevens called "the malady of the quotidian" must be rescued by and for the poetic consciousness. As Emerson argued, "The poet, by an ulterior intellectual perception, . . . puts eyes, and a tongue into every dumb and inanimate object." So a wagonload of hay can be full of joy.

But in this religion without priest or hierarchies, what and how should the poet celebrate? If, as Emerson says, "Small and mean things serve as well as great symbols," isn't the worshipful act indistinguishable from the casual, unthinking acts of everyday consciousness? An answer is offered by Emerson:

Here is the difference betwixt the poet and the mystic, that the last nails a symbol to one sense, which was a true sense for a moment, but soon becomes old and false. For all symbols are fluxional; all language is vehicular and transitive, and is good, as ferries and horses are, for conveyance, not as farms and houses are, for homestead. Mysticism consists in the mistake of an accidental and individual symbol for an universal one. . . . The history of hierarchies seems to show, that all religious error consisted in making the symbol too stark and solid, and, at last, nothing but an excess of the organ of language.

The poet then becomes a priest of process; he must constantly throw off his own symbols and perceive "the independence of the thought on the symbol, the stability of the thought, the accidency and fugacity of the symbol," as Emerson goes on to say. What better instrument to use for such throwing away than the motility of the prose poem, that most protean of forms? What better divinity than the yet to be disguised as the castoff, the fugitive cloaked in the forgotten? Bly says:

The dream said that The One Who Sees The Whole does not have the senses, but the longing for the senses. That longing is terrible, and terrifying—the herd of gazelles running over the savannah—and intense and divine, and I saw it lying over the dark floor . . . in layers there.

("A Dream of What Is Missing")

It is also possible to see here how Bly escapes the problem of the symbolic. As for a true Emersonian, language is for him transparent, even fugacious. The opacity of language, which has long provided one basis for the autotelic theories of modern poetry—"a poem should not mean, but be"—is simply willed away. Language, for Bly, always offers a way of encapsulating the longing for the senses and is therefore a way of going beyond the senses.

All this might be taken as another way of saying that Bly is a typical post-Romantic poet, that he faces the same problem the symbolists faced, namely, how to discover an entrancing language without a binding social myth, or how to write a liturgy without a theology. In part, Bly's response has been to join that sector of the modernist movement that sacralizes the unconscious. (His closest *poetic* forerunner may be D. H. Lawrence, especially in the "Preface" to the 1923 volume of his poems.) But the most important aspect of the unconscious is that it is a process. *Camphor* is filled with revealing processes, appearances, the comings-on of a guide or the discoveries of a traveler, a catalogue of Poundian *periploi*. But it records slower processes as well, like falling snow and rising smoke, pilgrimages in a slow, protozoic time frame, "the sweetest pools of slowly circling energies." To anchor his sense of a nonbinding religion of process, Bly rewrites the Freudian "return of the repressed" as an activity best registered by the body, not sublimated into the "beautiful" or the therapeutic. This is, among other things, Bly's way of avoiding the "religion of art," that other tendency in modernism that would aestheticize all experience and thus render religion superfluous.

We take our first step in words each day, and instantly fall into a hole in the sounds we make. Overly sane afternoons in a room during our twenties come back to us in the form of a son who is mad, every longing another person had that we failed to see the body

returns to us as a squinting of the eyes when we talk, and no sentimentality, only the ruthless body performing its magic . . .

("Falling into Holes in Our Sentences")

It is the body, the individual human body, that best incorporates
both the spontaneous discoveries and the longer, slower processes. If the body becomes "the field of consciousness," then
bodily ecstasy becomes a sort of sacred unconsciousness, that is,
a something beyond that can suddenly become central and in
turn redefine all value.

I would offer a formulation at this point. What Bly's religion
does is substitute the body for the soul as the privileged term in
the traditional body-soul dichotomy. (The negative term then is
not soul, but conscious rationality.) This dichotomy has been
traced by Paul Ricoeur, in *The Symbolism of Evil*, back to orphic
religion. It was in Orphism that the "body" was first named,
and it was there regarded as "an instrument of reiterated punishment." Once the body was termed evil, the next step was inevitable: the soul is not a part of the body, it "is not from here; it
comes from elsewhere; it is divine." At this crucial point in
Western culture, myth is not yet separated into religion and
philosophy, but a lasting assumption is made about experience:

> Other cults taught enthusiasm, the possession of the soul by a
> god. What seems to be original in Orphism is that it in-
> terpreted this sudden alteration, this rapture, as an excursion
> from the body, as a voyage in the other world, rather than as
> a visitation or a possession. Ecstasy is now seen as manifest-
> ing the true nature of the soul, which daily existence hides.

Ricoeur goes on to argue that Greek philosophy was to take this
body-soul dichotomy as the basis of its definition of the soul, as
that essence that remains identical, the same as itself. Thus, the
body is seen as change, as the subject and locus of decay, while
the soul is eternal and immutable. But for Bly ecstasy is not an
excursion from the body; it is an excursion *with* and *into* the
body. Ecstasy manifests the true nature of the body, which is to
be the evidence of the divine.

Bly's poetry, in *Camphor* especially, is best understood as an attempt to get back to a preorphic sense of the body. The body is sacred for Bly because, as the subject and locus of change and process, it becomes the perfect universal symbol. The body, in *Camphor,* provides the stability, while it is thought that bears the burden of "accidency and fugacity." Paradoxically, it is the body-as-process that by its very nature provides this stability. This "curiously alive and lonely body" is what loves; it "offers to carry us for nothing"; it "is made of energy compacted and whirling." In a passage that would read more traditionally if we could reverse the poet's usage and put "soul" where he puts "body," Bly says:

> This body longs for itself far out at sea, it floats in the black heavens, it is a brilliant being, locked in the prison of human dullness. . . .
>
> ("Going Out to Check the Ewes")

Here we see what is distinctive about Bly's religion: he has made the body equivalent to the Western-Christian-Protestant "soul," an entity of nearly unspeakable longings that has its true abode in the vast beyond and that can realize its essence only in the momentary gestures of escape and ecstasy.

> Friend, this body is made of camphor and gopherwood. So for two days I gathered ecstasies from my own body, I rose up and down, surrounded only by bare wood and bare air and some gray cloud, and what was inside me came so close to me, and I lived and died!
>
> ("The Pail")

Ecstasy now manifests what daily existence hides: the true nature of the body. The body is both a passage to the bare elements and itself a congeries of religious and erotic scents; it is its own ark and covenant.

It is difficult to transform—or translate, or convert, or institutionalize: whatever the metaphor, the difficulty remains—the ecstasies of one's body into a shareable, communal vision. What I think Bly's poetry enacts, especially in the strengths and weaknesses of *Camphor,* is the persistent desire of American poets simultaneously to celebrate the body and to incorporate the universal energies, thus making them available to all. How to domesticate the sublime? Bly's answer seems to be to deify the *truly* immediate, that is, the data of consciousness understood not as thought, but as bodily sensation. Bodily presence and process—the purview of natural history, with its emphasis on seeing, on turning the given into a specimen by an act of loving attentiveness to detail and change—thus become equated with bodily ecstasy—the evidence of religion, with its proffered hope that the bodies of men and women can become one body, which will manifest, in a Blakean way, the transforming and divine energies of the universe.

NOTES

1. In *Tennessee Poetry Journal 2,* no. 2 (Winter 1969):14. This issue contains several assessments of Bly's work, some sharply negative.

2. In an excellent essay on James Wright in *Ironwood* 10 (1977):74–76, Robert Hass discusses Bly's attack on American society, with its prizing of outer as opposed to inner reality. Hass is perceptive and eloquent in formulating the limits of this polemic, and the anti-intellectual, eventually antihuman, positions it can lead to.

RALPH J. MILLS, JR.

"Of Energy Compacted and Whirling"

Robert Bly's Recent Prose Poems

I

Readers of Robert Bly are well aware of the deep, substantial connections existing between his poems and the ideas he explores, the critical opinions he expresses in his essays and reviews—to say nothing of the relationships between the various larger forms of his literary enterprise: writing, translating, editing, lecturing, and reading his work. The elaborate, detailed scrutiny of Bly's intellectual interests, his reading and the development of his thought I leave to those who are engaged in a comprehensive study. I want to examine here some of his new prose poems, to note some of their striking features, and to point to correspondences of imagery and thought between these poems and several of the author's recent essays, such as "I Came Out of the Mother Naked" from *Sleepers Joining Hands,* "The Three Brains" from *Leaping Poetry,* and "Wallace Stevens and Dr. Jekyl" from *American Poets in 1976* (edited by William Heyen). These preoccupations of Bly's, not surprisingly, appear in the versions and commentary of *The Kabir Book,* and so this latter volume is also closely involved in my remarks as well.

The concerns fundamental to these poems and essays are surely no novelty to Robert Bly. His work is organic, much as a tree or plant in the natural world he contemplates and loves so well: he strives in it for a healing, an integration of the extreme polar-

New Mexico Humanities Review 4, no. 2 (1981):29–49. Reprinted with permission.

ities humans experience (as did such modern masters, say, as Yeats or Lawrence) between the masculine and feminine, the "light" and "dark" or "shadow" sides of personality, between the "reptile," "mammal," and "new" brains; or again, between body and spirit, individual and nature. Always, Bly takes considerable pains to avoid anything resembling a false or imposed unity, a generalization which excludes; we must, he says in one of his prose poems, "give up the idea of one god." This is less a call to abandon monotheism, I think, than it is an effort to arrive at a more expansive, inclusive sense of deity. Indissolubly bound up with this devotion to balance, to an absorption in all of the differing, contradictory aspects of man's makeup and experience (which we might say in passing parallels his belief that a truly vigorous associational poetry of the sort he admires has the capacity to "leap" in its energies from one brain to another, making use of each of them) is Bly's romanticist, visionary commitment to the singularity, the particularity of each thing, creature, incident; and he often firmly and angrily rebukes the contemporary abstracting, classifying mentality or "mind-set" he notices in politicians, city-planners, literary critics, and doubtless in many other occupations. In *The Kabir Book,* to which we can assume the poet gives rather strong assent, the deity is indwelling, a divine being discoverable within man as he lives in the physical world—and lost by denying that corporeal nature:

Fire, air, earth, water and space—if you don't want the secret one, you can't have these either.

(poem 4)

If you want the truth, I will tell you the truth:
Friend, listen: the God whom I love is inside.

(poem 5)

But the polarities of existence are not easily resolved, though they can be experienced and named. Bly's writings, whether in poetry or prose, participate in a continuing process on his part, an imaginative and intellectual pursuit of a very elusive harmony for these age-old conflicts and divisions.

An increased attachment to and practice of the prose poem

seems appropriate to the endeavors I've mentioned. Bly's *This Body Is Made of Camphor and Gopherwood* consists of twenty such poems; it was preceded by *The Morning Glory* (1975), a larger gathering which included pieces from earlier chapbooks published by Kayak and Mudra. A very few prose poems were printed in Bly's initial books, but all the external signs indicate a considerable recent concentration on this form. His books coincide as well with a widespread growth of interest by Americans in the possibilities of the prose poem genre, and with the appearance of Michael Benedikt's big, authoritative "international" anthology. Both established and new poets have started to test the form—and themselves in it—while still, of course, there is some evident resistance to its introduction. In these pages we can only glance at some of the qualities which Bly conceives of special value and attractiveness in the prose poem, and how his own pieces reflect these conceptions, in addition to themes and predilections already cited.

In a brief but compelling article, "What the Prose Poem Carries With It" (*American Poetry Review,* May/June 1977), Bly sets forth notions about the prose poem important for a reader of his or anyone else's work of this kind. Contrasting the "quiet and low voice" with the "elevated or 'raised' voice," he indicates that, in his view, "the more original thoughts" have been articulated usually in the former. The prose poem he links with that voice, where "we often feel a man or woman talking not before a crowd but in a low voice to someone he is sure is listening." (This quiet speaking bears some resemblance to the "first" of Eliot's "Three Voices of Poetry," a lyric or meditative voice; but for Eliot the poet in this voice talks to himself, wishes to relieve himself of an inner burden or pressure: the reader merely, as it were, overhears him.) Behind the prose poem also there frequently lies calm or meditativeness, familiar enough to those acquainted with Bly's writings; but then "buried impulses toward joy" rise up through this mood in the prose poem's form as if from an "artesian well." So for our poet the quietly speaking voice, which doesn't seek large pronouncements or effects— though it must necessarily gravitate toward them in dramatic moments—moving within the relative freedom of prose, is capable of releasing "some feelings or half-buried thoughts in us [which] would remain beneath the consciousness, unsure of themselves, unable to break through." He warns of the statues of esteemed dead poets who stand behind an author as he writes, requiring of him sympathy and cooperation in the maintenance of poetic forms stiffened with age and almost incapable of animation or resilience. "The man or woman writing a poem in this century has to deal with these white shapes, either outdoing them by tripling the energy in the poem—Yeats does that—or by doing something they don't notice"—that is, composing the poem in prose.

In the second part of this article Bly discusses the prose poem's content, but he approaches it from a new angle, not in terms of voice or the unconscious or past poetic conventions. Instead, he stresses perception, whatever engages the poet's senses, the immediacy of perceiving something and its accurate transfer into the poem. With characteristic sensitivity he remarks: "I have a feeling that the contemporary poem longs for what takes place only once." The prose poem with its loose formal requirements can at least try to accommodate the unique attributes of a momentary perception, which ordinarily we fail to regard, forget, or absorb into abstract summary or information. "I like the way the prose poem so easily allows the original perception to live," Bly writes, "so that in a good prose poem— just as in a good lined poem—it's possible that every noun would be a singular noun! No one plural noun in the whole poem!" An impossible ideal, no doubt, but perhaps worth working toward. Such a poem would truly be, as Wallace Stevens said, "the cry of its occasion," utterly faithful to the particulars of an experience. Likewise, for Bly it should aid in rejecting the "generalization" into which "we have been pushed too early" in school and elsewhere, our "original perception" forced to disappear in some larger categorical scheme.

Of course, the prose poem is not alone in permitting this desirable truth to individual detail or sensory experience; among other things, that is the province of all literature. And after all, isn't exactly this kind of seeing one of the most impressive elements of this first *lined* stanza of the first poem in Robert Bly's first book?

Sometimes, riding in a car, in Wisconsin
Or Illinois, you notice those dark telephone poles
One by one lift themselves out of the fence line
And slowly leap on the gray sky—
And past them, the snowy fields.

("Three Kinds of Pleasures")

All the same, while the prose poem allows for the sort of creative observation of particulars we see registered in these lines, it further encourages the writer to float about freely in his perceptions by affording him space—blocks of prose paragraphs—where his consciousness can exercise a flexibility not constrained by problems of the line. In such paragraphs, as Michael Benedikt says in his significant introductory essay to *The Prose Poem,* any or all of the other devices of poetry may be called into use—and Bly employs them too. Benedikt also points out that this "genre" of poetry aids our "need to attend to the priorities of the unconscious. This attention to the unconscious, and to its particular logic, unfettered by the relatively formalistic interruptions of the line break, remains the most immediately apparent property of the prose poem." It becomes obvious then that the form makes "association" or "leaping" in which the unconscious plays a leading part, and which Bly defines as "a form of content" in itself, not merely a poetic technician's method but an essential directing of imagination currents in the composition of a poem. Bly's musings in *Leaping Poetry* about Wallace Stevens's early poems have, I think, a value as indirect illumination of the procedures in many of his own prose poems. He notes, "Often in *Harmonium* . . . the *content* of the poem lies in the *distance* between what Stevens was given as fact, and what he then imagined. The farther a poem gets from its initial worldly circumstance without breaking the thread, the more content it has." The key phrase here is "without breaking the thread," for the poem begins with its "original perception," a "fact" of observation or circumstance, which the imagination, the forces and dream logic of the unconscious subsequently transform, transfigure, attenuate to the limit, or compress to an opposite extreme—in short, whatever associational "leaping" and imagery will do—remaining all the while tied, however lightly, to the object or complex of elements with which it originated. Within its framework of the paragraph, the prose poem has ample opportunity for such give and take, expansion from and tension with a certain beginning point. "Rapid association," as Bly calls it, exhibits itself at once in the prose poems of his earlier collection, *The Morning Glory*. In "A Bird's Nest Made of White Reed Fiber" there is swift movement from the title object toward things associated with it by imaginative jumps. The poem proceeds in a breathtaking way from simile to metaphor, likeness to identity; the concluding third sentence is climactic and visionary:

> The nest is white as the foam thrown up when the sea hits rocks! It is translucent as those cloudy transoms above Victorian doors, and swirled as the hair of those intense nurses, gray and tangled after long nights in Crimean wards. It is something made and then forgotten, like our own lives that we will entirely forget in the grave, when we are floating, nearing the shore where we will be reborn, ecstatic and black.

How long a poem stays close to its "initial worldly circumstance" varies with each one. Often, a poem returns to that circumstance in some fashion in the course of its movements, and may then depart from it again; or it may return there at the end; but in any case for the reader the first circumstance or object will have been changed by the imaginative operations occurring in between. To Bly's thinking—as the term "leaping" implies—the author's mind during composition should dance among images derived from different areas of the brain, from both the conscious and unconscious levels. When this activity is accomplished with a great flow of imaginative and emotional power—Bly selects Lorca's poetry as a primary example—"we have," he says, "something different from Homer or Machado; a new kind of poem (apparently very rare in the nineteenth century) which we could call the poem of 'passionate association,' or 'poetry of flying.'"

II

The prose poems of *This Body Is Made of Camphor and Gopherwood* comprise a smaller, more closely knit group than those of *The Morning Glory;* there is less variety, greater intensity of purpose—it can, and in some ways should be read as a sequence. Bly's theme, as the title makes plain, is the body. In poem after poem he explores with precision and strength of imagination the body's relationships of earth, death, selfhood, joyousness, dream, consciousness, and mystical apprehension. This last phrase I use to suggest how the poems progress toward—and not seldom either—one or another state of visionary awareness: for instance, when the poet envisages powerfully the life of protozoa within man's physical structure, in the amazing "The Origin of the Praise of God." At this stage in his career it is no more than commonplace to remind ourselves that Bly's literary impulses contain a sizeable mixture of moral and religious, as well as aesthetic, ingredients, and that his religiousness is involved with psychology and is in no sense conventional. But heterodox visionary qualities are familiar components of American writing and are inseparable from its appeal. "Sometimes the spirit even begins to flow upward a little in the language of the prose poem," Bly admits in the article quoted before. "So prose poems perhaps resemble home or private religion, lined poems are like public churches. The ancient world had both, and, strangely, different gods for the public religion than for the private, which were appropriately called 'Mysteries.'"

In keeping with Bly's comments and speculations on the prose poem, "Walking Swiftly," the opening piece in the book, begins descriptively with "separate events" early in the morning on the farm just beyond his house. The poet wakes to a reality which is clearly familiar, immersed heavily in its own physical properties. But contrast and change set in; and uneasiness on Bly's part leads without transition to sentences about an unspecified "Emperor" and his demands for exotic objects, all of which violate the natural order. The poem continues to a passage about the "heat inside the human body," forces generated in and through man, and seeking proper realization. A final sentence tells us, as in a proverb or the fragment of some parable, how "the artist" expends his energy. My quick summary here breaks up what is in Bly's poem a distinct progression, though not a rational one, from sentence to sentence. It is for the reader to recognize, perhaps after several trips through the text, the way along which these sentences take him, building up a cluster of imagery or thought through one or two, let us say, and then stepping off without warning across a considerable gap to a new one, which presents in turn a quite different, but not unrelated perception or grouping of details. Variations on a pattern of this sort appear constantly throughout these prose poems. Here now is the text of "Walking Swiftly":

> When I wake, I hear sheep eating apple peels just outside the screen. The trees are heavy, soaked, cold and hushed, the sun just rising. All seems calm, and yet somewhere inside I am not calm. We live in wooden buildings made of two-by-fours, making the landscape nervous for a hundred miles. And the Emperor when he was sixty called for rhinoceros horn, for sky-blue phoenix eggs shaped from veined rock, dipped in rooster blood. Around him the wasps kept guard, the hens continued their patrol, the oysters open and close all questions. The heat inside the human body grows, it does not know where to throw itself—for a while it knots into will, heavy, burning, sweet, then into generosity, that longs to take on the burdens of others, then into mad love that lasts forever. The artist walks swiftly to his studio, and carves oceanic waves into the dragon's mane.

The "calm" of the poem's setting at first and the contrasting disturbance within the poet betray a fundamental absence of harmony or reconciliation which, as we said, troubles Bly elsewhere and gives impetus to his writing. In this poem, man's dwellings, farmhouses, "buildings made of two-by-fours," are inimical to their environment, sending out tremors that bother a world otherwise balanced within itself. A passage from the essay, "I Came Out of the Mother Naked," helps to explain this negative vibrancy. There Bly reminds us that matriarchal consciousness favors curves and circles, while the patriarchal plans "the ground in huge squares" and "creates straight roads." A little further on he refers to Drinks Water, "an old Dakota [Indian] holy man" who admonished his people of defeat by the whites, "and warned that when that happened, they would have to live in square houses." Bly goes on to quote Black Elk on living in square buildings: "'It is a bad way to live, for there can be no power in a square. You have noticed that everything an Indian does is in a circle, and that is because the Power of the World always works in circles, and everything tries to be round. . . . Everything the Power of the World does is done in a circle. . . .'" We see as we read these prose poems how essential circular imagery is for the poet; here it is sufficient to note how it clarifies by antithesis the disruptive character of the "wooden buildings" with their square or rectangular design, which is not in conformity with the rounded patterns of the "landscape."

Bly's sudden "leap" to the apparently remote figure of the Emperor adds a sharp new perspective to the poem's theme, for he represents power and domination, and yet he too is a man, driven by human compulsions. He wishes for objects manufactured from other creatures. Readers may want to determine for themselves the significance of eggs and horn: the objects leave room for a variety of interpretations. Does the aging Emperor in fact hope to win renewal from these concocted symbols of life and fertility, constructed at his command? We aren't told; instead, the next sentence reaches out to the surrounding realm of nature to garner images: there wasps and hens behave protectively and oysters, strangely, appear to pronounce judgments, render decisions by moving their shells. The last is, I suppose, a surrealist detail: but we know from Bly's essay on the Mother that "four favorite creatures [of hers] were the turtle, the owl, the dove, and the oyster." The natural activities of these creatures in the poem contradict the Emperor's will. The subsequent passage on the body's "heat" and the forms it takes, while comprehensible in itself, gains in meaning when connected with Bly's article, "The Three Brains." A correspondence seems to me to exist between the different outlets this heat finds in the poem and the identifying characteristics of the reptilian, mammalian, and new brains described in the article, but I won't attempt any investigation here. Indecision about the heat or energy's disposal appears central to the poem's implications.

Sheep, trees, wasps, oysters, hens, and so on, do not have such questions raised with regard to them; only man does. The poem ends with the emergence of an artist figure who releases his force (or the heat inside himself) in appropriately harmonic, imaginative fashion. The curved "oceanic waves" of his carving relate him to the "feminine consciousness" Bly believes necessary to human balance and wholeness, for one of the Mother's images is also "the sea," and to the rounded forms of nature in general. He says of the dragon that "in inner life [it] is man's fear of women, and in public life, it is the matriarchy's conservative energy." Surely, the second meaning is the one most applicable to the artist's activity in the poem; but any such interpretation must be tentative. Bly has advised his readers not to attempt to use "I Came Out of the Mother Naked" as an index to his poems. That seems fair enough; the author should know best, we say. On the other hand, I have obviously not obeyed him in this essay, at least not to the extent of bypassing connections which are too evident to ignore. "Walking Swiftly" reveals itself as a poem divided between conflicting modes of consciousness (masculine and feminine, or light and dark, in the poet's terms) and the manner in which human energy or heat is utilized by each of them. The Emperor remains stolidly patriarchal, demanding the phallic, and also weaponlike, rhinoceros horn, the Apollonian "sky-blue" eggs, and he is, of course, a figure of will and domination. The artist stands perhaps in the antithetical position, or nearly so. In his figure we presumably find a balance of conflicting elements; for the artist belongs to the side of "mother consciousness" and puts will and energy to the service of imagination or art, carving forms harmonious with nature's. But we are talking of a poem, and it does not deliver its secrets to dissection. I believe, however, that Bly conveys some of the implications I've discussed in a fluid, elliptical prose, its language, phrasing, and imagery as full and rich as we would expect to discover in his lined poems.

Each poem in the book emerges from one or another kind of meditation on man's body, I have said, but that is simply the beginning. A poem may lead in any number of directions, become enmeshed in the most intricate webs of experience; and it will usually shift abruptly, yet with apparent ease, from one perception to the next. Quite often Bly starts a poem with an invocation both to his reader and to some of the body's metaphorical components, thus directly or obliquely, as the case may be, echoing his book's title. Here are some examples: "My friend, this body is made of camphor and gopherwood"; "My friend, this body is food for the thousand dragons of the air, each dragon light as a needle"; "This body holds its protective walls around us, it watches us whenever we walk out"; "My friend, this body is made of bone and excited protozoa . . . and it is with my body that I love." In the final poem he begins with a direct address to a loved one which becomes also, in its way, an appeal for human community, reconciliation and kinship with the world: "I love you so much with this curiously alive and lonely body." Other poems may originate, as "Walking Swiftly" does, in an ordinary or familiar situation, with weather, landscape, objects: "It has been snowing all day. Three of us start out across the fields"; or "The cucumbers are thirsty, their big leaves turn away from the wind." Only a few of them open having already taken a stride into dream or vision: "The horses gallop east, over the steppes, each with its rider, hard. Each rider carries a strip of red cloth raised above his head"; or "Smoke rises from the mountain depths, a girl walks by the water. This is the body of water near where we sleep."

From beginnings such as these Bly gets under way rapidly. Prose paragraphs, as we've noted, supply a medium in which he can attend to particular detail if he desires, or alternate quickly from one dimension of reality to another with no hesitation or explanation, slipping in and out of the factual and the visionary while avoiding some of the conventional problems of technique that might interfere with those motions: he need only decide when and if to use more than one paragraph. In "The Sleeper," for instance, a poem which appears to record an extreme of withdrawal or self-enclosure, Bly can simultaneously adopt the roles of the dreamer and of an anonymous, transparent speaker who watches from outside, describing what takes place while the first figure sleeps:

He came in and sat by my side, and I did not wake up. I went on dreaming of vast houses with rooms I had not seen, of men suddenly appearing whom I did not know, but who knew me, of thistles whose points shone as if a light were inside.

A man came to me and began to play music. One arm lay outside the covers. He put the dulcimer in my hand but I did not play it. I went on, hearing.

Why didn't I wake up? And why didn't I play? Because I am asleep, and the sleeping man is all withdrawn into himself. He thinks the sound of a shutting door is a tooth falling from his head, or his head rolling on the ground.

Flexibilities of this sort make the prose poem a very suitable form for various poetic or imaginative intentions. Bly can introduce, as he does in "Going Out to Check the Ewes," what one might call different or contrasting manners, place them side by side without advance notice and with no transition between them, and then let them work with, around, and upon each other as the developing poem requires:

My friend, this body is food for the thousand dragons of the air, each dragon light as a needle. This body loves us, and carries us home from our hoeing.

It is ancient, and full of the bales of sleep. In its vibrations the sun rolls along under the earth, the spouts over the ocean curl into our stomach . . . water revolves, spouts seen by skull eyes at mid-ocean, this body of herbs and gopherwood, this blessing, this lone ridge patrolled by water. . . . I get up, morning is here. The stars still out; the black winter sky looms over the unborn lambs. The barn is cold before dawn, the gates slow. . . .

The body longs for itself far out at sea, it floats in the black heavens, it is a brilliant being, locked in the prison of human dullness. . . .

In the first paragraph two sentences are juxtaposed which, so to speak, call up for the reader separate planes of awareness without any jarring incongruity and in such a fashion that they seem to belong with one another, or indeed participate mysteriously each in the other. The poem takes for its point of departure a near-mystical kind of declaration, set in that form of address we've specified previously. But the body is lowered to the ground from this metaphoric, visionary height by the second sentence; yet the two statements don't struggle against one another; they operate as a pair, complementary, necessary companions reflecting the antitheses Bly encounters everywhere. Moreover, the repetition of "this body" fixes ties between the sentences, so the ecstatic definition of the first combines readily with the more earthly harmony of the second. Thinking about these two sentences and their relationship can help us to grasp the type of subtlety and suppleness Bly manages in these poems.

The next of the poem's three paragraphs maintains that subtlety from the outset. The opening pronoun refers to the body, which is "ancient," recalling the dragon image; "bales of sleep" beautifully serves as a reminder of daily labor, keeping us in mind of the "hoeing" of paragraph one. At the same time this phrase designates the hidden, unconscious self waiting to be revealed with coming night, for the workday world is left behind at the initial paragraph's close. Now night overtakes the poem completely: "the sun rolls along under the earth," and the reader finds himself confronted with a sudden abundance of imagery associated both with the feminine consciousness, or Mother, and with the propulsive force of life and creation. "This body is made of energy compacted and whirling," Bly states at the beginning of "We Love This Body," and it is quite clear from that poem, as well as from innumerable instances in others, he means not simply the human body—though certainly it too—but the entire body of creation, the physical cosmos and the life or vitality of spirit, soul, psyche, call it what you will, which infuses, sustains, and orders it. In the poem under discussion those images of energy are plentiful and undisguised, ranging from the sun which "rolls," through "spouts" that "curl" into us (drawing together images of large or universal energies with those implying their functioning in individuals), the "water" that "revolves," back again to the "spouts," which seemingly even the dead know, finally arriving at a calm and an echo of the title with an evocation of the body in terms of natural things ("herbs and gopherwood"). Before the paragraph swings upward again on the diurnal cycle, the body is praised as a "blessing" and, immediately after, viewed as solitary, a rocky "ridge" surrounded by, protruding from "water." It is then the poet awakens, as if all that has just occurred were part of his dreaming or else the imagery of forces at work beyond dreams, far off in the inner reaches of being in person and cosmos. Bly goes now to perform the early chores of the farm before daybreak; but even here, in the morning routine, the drawing of detail turns teasingly allusive—sky, unborn lambs, stiff gates seem disturbingly mixed with memories of the night.

In this paragraph's nocturnal journeying we have happened once more on that imagery of the circular mentioned earlier in correspondence with Bly's ideas about "Mother consciousness" and with the Indian sense of "the Power of the World" to which he refers. Bly lists additional images allied to the feminine in his essay: "the night, the sea, animals with curving horns and cleft hooves, the moon, bundles of grain." Furthermore, he argues that "matriarchy thinking is intuitive and moves by associative leaps," to which we can see the poet's should be kindred. "Masculine consciousness," he asserts, following a number of scholars, comes chronologically or historically after the feminine, has for "its main image the bright blue sky surrounding the sun—its metal, gold." It plots straight lines, as implied before, thinks with straight logic, distrusts myth and imagination, proliferates regulations, moral dicta, "and tries to reach the spirit through asceticism." To Bly's way of thinking (as to many another poet's) these masculine values have wrongly created our modern technological civilization and prevailed over it; only now, he tells us, there are indications of change, of righting the balance: "Intuitive gifts are being given." Anyone who has looked at Bly's essay also knows that he names, speculatively, four Mother figures, representative of different energies and impulses. The Death Mother and the Stone or Teeth Mother are icons of danger and destructive forces as real as their positive, creative counterparts, the Good Mother and the Ecstatic Mother. For our purposes, however, in talking of this sequence of prose poems and some of its themes and images, I will be occupied largely with the affirmative aspects of feminine or dark consciousness. And as Bly has remarked: "All men's poems are written by men already flying toward the Ecstatic Mother. It's possible for a poem to talk about the Death Mother, but I think the energy that brings the words alive belongs to the Ecstatic Mother."

The single sentence paragraph which finishes "Going Out to Check the Ewes" guides us again into regions of metaphor and vision, away from the mundane reference of the poem's title and the descriptive particulars of the barnyard. Yet, as before, connections are present between the rest of the text and what is said at its ending. From the start I have indicated the feeling of dividedness Bly finds prevalent in experience, and it is surely visible in these poems. Of course, some sense of harmony and security makes itself felt in the first paragraph of "Going Out . . ." A self-unity, the body's supportiveness appear to harmonize existence there. But the imagery of night with its wealth of creative potentiality and energetic expenditure also seems partially imprisoned within sleep or the unconscious. So as morning inevitably recurs at the poem's conclusion the force of those night or feminine energies becomes diminished: division takes hold of the poet's sensibilities—the true or wholly unified body, the human-as-he-should-be, is projected distantly, "far out at sea . . . in the black heavens," with the water and darkness which are among its elemental symbols. Still, it is termed "a brilliant being" too, implying possibly a new kind of radiance or light that reconciles the opposing consciousness, "the Secret One" or inward divinity of *The Kabir Book,* an unrealized God longed-for but secreted behind "human dullness."

The condition enacted in "The Sleeper" is basically the same, especially if we use poem 35 from Bly's Kabir versions as a source of illumination for it. The Kabir poem goes:

> Listen friend, this body is his dulcimer.
> He draws the strings tight, and out of it comes
>   the music of the inner universe.
> If the strings break and the bridge falls,
> then this dulcimer of dust goes back to dust.
>
> Kabir says: the Holy One is the only one who can
>   draw music from it.

In Bly's poem we recall how the speaker (or one aspect of him— he plays a dual role), asleep, is visited by an unnamed man who plays music to him, then places a dulcimer in his hand, but the sleeper refuses to play it and only listens. Questioning himself about this rejection, Bly answers that it has occurred because he hasn't wakened, remains "asleep," not certainly in the limited everyday meaning but in a spiritual sense, which the Kabir poem touches on quite clearly. Earlier I said "The Sleeper" treated a withdrawn state. The dulcimer suggests a music of wholeness vibrating with one's entire being, that "inner universe" of the Kabir version which will be compelled outward if the "Holy One" plays upon it. Bly's sleeper stays exiled in himself, hence he misunderstands even ordinary external sounds as events happening within his own body, or to it, events that are, as the poem shows, destructive or fatal in their significance. Reading his situation in the light of Kabir, we may think the sleeper resembles an unused instrument, falling back to dust, having failed to discover or accept the deity waiting inside him. Obviously, a close affinity exists between this unhappy resolution and the frustration of unfulfillment in the body's "brilliant being, locked in the prison of human dullness."

"How do I know what I feel but what the body tells me?" Bly queries in one of the poems; but the restriction his words could seem to denote must not be taken literally. In "Looking from Inside My Body," the title of which shares the viewpoint of this rhetorical question, recurrent images, objects, details we should by now easily recognize are on display. But the substance of this poem, once we have passed its beginning sentences, is unmistakably visionary: after all, Bly never confines bodily knowledge, here or elsewhere, to basic sensory impressions. Doesn't he tell us in *Silence in the Snowy Fields* that "the quiet waters of the night will rise, / And our skin shall see far off, as it does under water"? Description always gives place to intuition, embodied imagination.

"Looking from Inside My Body" can be called a quest poem, in which the author discovers himself pulled toward two contrary bodies, earth and moon, while confusion, irresolution, and inner division rule. His meditations originate with sunset, the encroaching darkness: "night thickens near the ground, pulls the earth down to it." Bly in his own physical body must remain where he is, a figure composed of earth and so part of it—"down here, thickening as night comes on." This is, all the same, the night of objects, of nature, of other creatures than man too; but in him another element—of spirit—cannot be satisfied with earth alone and yearns toward the moon, locating this second aspect of his being in that lunar image with the feminine associations it bears. Around him he witnesses in the natural world a unity he doesn't possess but must envy:

> There are earth things, earthly, joined, they are snuggled down in one manger, one sweep of arms holds them, one clump of pine, the owlets sit together in one hollow tree. . . .

Again he questions what will happen with night's advent. He faces now the fact that consciousness, reason, intention—all the powers by which he has navigated existence throughout the day—must necessarily be lost, forsaken at this hour: they are all concentrated in the single image of the sun pursuing its routine course—but he has this solar correspondence within that will likewise lose strength. (We remember the sun is for Bly a central symbol of the masculine or patriarchal disposition.) Yet as such thoughts occur to the poet, the loss of solar energy is suddenly combined with a mystical or religious realization on which the paragraph then trails off inconclusively but not negatively:

> What has been sun in me all day will drop underneath the earth, and travel sizzling along the underneath-ocean-darkness path. . . . There a hundred developed saints lie stretched out, throwing bits of darkness onto the road. . . .

In this rather unexpected turning the poem takes we come near some of Bly's Kabir versions again. Plainly, the actions of the saints in the above passage appear in contrast with what the poet has done so far in the poem. In curious fashion they toss "bits of darkness" on a road which is in one sense the sun's "path" along the underside of the globe at night but is likewise, I think, the path of individual destiny, the Way, or the "bhakti path" of which Bly speaks in his comments on Kabir. Their gesture is one of reconciliation, harmonizing the polar extremities of light and dark, masculine and feminine which the poet has viewed anxiously in separation.

The end has yet to come; two more paragraphs complete the poem. In the first of them Bly sees himself in the literal situation sketched at the beginning. Nightfall: soon he must retire from the darkened external scene before him, the moon still risen overhead, and enter his room to submit to sleep. Losing this external actuality, he fears that he will surrender all it symbolizes for him. Considerable agitation seems to underlie his anticipated descent into sleep, solitude, incarceration, blackness, and the riddling encounter with "another prisoner" there.

> . . . suddenly my moon will vanish. The sleeper will go down toward utter darkness. . . . Who will be with him? He will meet another prisoner in the dungeon, alone with the baker.*

Concluding sentences depict the "moon outside the bedroom," moving through the night sky by itself, "slipping through the arms reached up to it. . . . It will go on, looking. . . ." Several implications at least can be found in this ending, though I cannot cover all of them here. It can be said, referring once again to the Kabir poems, that both external and internal suns and moons exist: the physical bodies in space and the polar opposites in humans, as we say Bly's connotations suggest. Kabir version 13 begins like this:

> There's a moon in my body, but I can't see it!
> A moon and a sun.
> A drum never touched by hands, beating, and I can't
>   hear it!
>
> As long as a human being worries about when he will
>   die, and what he has that is his,
> all of his works are zero.
> When affection for the I-creature and what it owns
>   is dead,
> then the work of the Teacher is over.

---

*Bly has recently mentioned in a letter to the author that the other prisoner and "the baker" refer to the story of Joseph's imprisonment and dream interpretation, Genesis 40.

Ownership of this sun and moon then is not possible in the usual sense of property or an object. In Bly's poem the quest will be fruitless if that impossible possession constitutes its goal: the sun sinks past the earth's rim; the moon eludes those grasping arms extended toward it. Besides, of course, the correspondences and the basic significance of these celestial entities are inward, reaching to those opposing extremes which need to be merged in order to achieve human wholeness or balance. The saints, being wiser, further along the path, keep repose, "lie stretched out"; the "bits of darkness" they toss on the sun's route imply a spiritual corrective by means of which these sages work for, or attain, a blending of the antitheses—that very harmony the poet desires. In addition to which Kabir says in another poem not to gaze beyond but to "stand firm" in one's body.

III

Much of my attention till now has been devoted to some poems about "What Is Missing"—the lack of self-unity and of the congruent flow of energies—if I may borrow that half of the poem title "A Dream of What Is Missing." My remarks naturally neither exhaust the subject in those pieces, nor in Bly's collection as a whole. I should like, however, to focus at this point on several poems from the middle and later pages of the book, poems which do realize moments of elation, ecstasy, or fulfillment—a level of intense, heightened perception. This sort of mood predominates in the second half of the sequence and brings the work to a moving, joyous climax.

At the heart of the book the tenth poem, "Walking to the Next Farm," acts as a transitional piece, a bridge to affirmative vision, as well as a companion to the poem that follows, "The Origin of the Praise of God," the most unusual, difficult, and strangely mystical of all. The setting should be well-known to Bly's readers: Minnesota farmlands at midwinter, earth and air heavy with snow. The poet and two others are walking over the fields. Gradually, as is so often the case with these poems, Bly's awareness is brought to bear on a specific quality of the phenomena about him. He abandons other description as extraneous, drawn by his senses, then by intuition, insight, imagination—whatever you wish—to the center of the experience, which amounts to nothing less than some kind of revelation for him. Such is the structure and progression of this starting paragraph:

It has been snowing all day. Three of us start out across the fields. The boots sink in to the ankles, but go on; our feet move through the most powerful snow energy. There is falling snow above us, and below us, and on all sides. My eyes feel wild, as if a new body were rising, with tremendous swirls in its flow; its whirlpools move with their face upward, as those whirls in the Missouri that draw in green cottonwoods from collapsed earth banks, pull them down with all their branches. And our feet carry the male energy that disappears, as my brother's energy did, in its powerful force field his whole life disappeared, and all the trees on his farm went with it. . . .

In the dreamlike qualities the poem assumes, which are perfectly in keeping too with the weather's behavior, Bly becomes cognizant of what amounts to a full-scale combat between male and female energies in which the stakes can be mortality. The men with their physical strength, will, endurance (even the male sexual attributes of their feet and boots) push through lifting "whirlpools" of snow and the rounded swirls of energy we have come to identify as inherently figurative of feminine power. Yet if the two sides are locked in struggle, Bly also glimpses—though the verb is perhaps not adequate to the instantaneous perceiving he experiences—a moment of their union in his reference to "a new body . . . rising." Ostensibly, this alludes to the invasion of feminine energy in the whirling columns of snow, but in view of what the remainder of the poem calls for, it appears rich with prophecy as well. The paragraph proceeds by tracing analogies, instances of the collapse of masculine objects and individuals into the fierce, revolving "force field," where they are destroyed. Bly's brother, whose death is included in a poem close to the end of *The Morning Glory,* is swallowed up here too. Throughout the paragraph, the fatal, ruinous aggression of matriarchal consciousness perseveres: an engagement with its negative dimensions, I should guess, the Death Mother or the Teeth Mother.

The following section doesn't offer much respite. There are multiple references to a Tibetan, Huns, Vienna, "the doctor," and Lenin, prefaced by a depiction of "energy that comes off the fierce man's hair . . . not a halo, but a background of flames." Bly seems to be concerned to represent here the involvement of these various persons with the release or frustration of male forces or concepts. The doctor is most likely Freud, who, Bly notes elsewhere, "could only imagine a great father running the primal horde." This collocation of figures, activities, and images is for me highly reminiscent of portions of the poems in *Sleepers Joining Hands*.

But the final paragraph steps back from this turbulence and conflict. The poet opens with a question, and promptly answers it, giving a reply he believes will lead toward the balance he searches for. Like Yeats, he approves the embrace of contrarities, rather than a fixed selection between alternatives. The passage returns to imagery, to the poet still walking through the snow, to the vortices of energy in their costly battle. A three line lyric coda is appended to this paragraph, a tiny poem of balance or reconciliation in its own right; and, as we'll see, a similar piece is used as an interlude in "The Origin of the Praise of God":

> Then what is asked of us? To stop sacrificing one energy for another. They are not different anyway, not "male" or "female," but whirls of different speeds as they revolve. We must learn to worship both, and give up the idea of one god. . . . I taste the snow, lying on a branch. It tastes slow. It is as slow as the whirl in the boulder lying beneath the riverbed. . . . Its swirls take nine thousand years to complete, but they too pull down the buffalo skin boats into their abysses, many souls with hair go down.
>
> > The light settles down in front of each snowflake,
> > and the dark rises up behind it,
> > and inside its own center it lives!

What startles the reader is Bly's unexpected denial of the masculine and feminine identities of these "whirls" of force; now he has translated their differences into "speeds" of revolution, envisaging them as operating at fast or slow tempos as the means for explaining their conflict. One shouldn't balk at the change. Bly doesn't write as a philosopher who has restricted himself to the limitations of a special terminology but as a poet free to lend himself to imaginative impulses. The reader will notice that the male/female polarity hasn't vanished anyway from the poems at this point; we shall meet up with it again. In fact, the details of the explorers dragged into watery "abysses" obviously retains associations with the two extremes. Of greater importance is Bly's requirement that we "worship both" energies, abandon the habit of refusing one for its opposite. The small lyric renders this notion quite beautifully—revolutions of light and dark, as with earth's day and night, and the snowflake poised between, secure in its own being.

"The Origin of the Praise of God" is a visionary hymn to the body, its architecture and existence, but most astonishingly this poem travels far beyond the outward, ordinarily visible lineaments and forms to evoke the myriad lives of the cells of which it consists. Bly brings together unforgettable images here to provide a marvelous enactment of the motions and responses of protozoa, the simplest single-celled creatures. In such finiteness and simplicity, and yet with internal complexity, it is not difficult to see an analogy with the previous poem's snowflake. The present poem Bly has dedicated to Lewis Thomas and his book *The Lives of a Cell.*

Starting once more with a simultaneous address to his reader and declaration of the body's composition—in this instance "made of bone and excited protozoa"—the poet claims that only through his corporeal being can he "love" external creation or know his own feelings. He completes the first paragraph with allusions to bodily formation, differentiating the inside ("so beautifully carved . . . with the curves of the inner ear") from the outside ("the husk so rough, knuckle-brown"). With the shift to the next paragraph Bly advances boldly into "the magnetic fields of other bodies"—thus announcing a theme of attraction and union occupying him from his poem to the last—and then further, into the responsiveness to such stimuli of countless cellular lives within us:

. . . every smell we take in the communities of protozoa see, and a being inside leaps up toward it, as a horse rears at the starting gate. When we come near each other, we are drawn down into the sweetest pools of slowly circling energies, slowly circling smells. And the protozoa know there are odors the shape of oranges, of tornadoes, of octopuses. . . .

> The sunlight lays itself down before the protozoa,
> the night opens itself out behind it,
> and inside its own energy it lives!

The lyric triplet, appearing at the middle of this poem rather than at its finish, restates the harmony, the integration or balance observed in the snowflake image. Bly constructs too with scientific accuracy, in that the one-celled creature does indeed live its own life—is born of fission, feeds and reproduces by dividing, and finally dies. In the poem the poles of light and dark lie before and behind it, while the protozoa exists within "its own energy," just as the snowflake sustains itself at its own central point. Both become emblems of equilibrium, which Bly has purposely set off by themselves to draw our notice.

It is necessary to recall as well the magnetism of bodies coming into proximity to one another in the quoted passage, with the extraordinary, complicated reactions caused inside of us, of which we can be scarcely conscious except in terms of general effect. The poet looks outward momentarily to introduce a couple approaching each other—to put us in touch again with a familiar circumstance—then turns once more to the swarming cellular reality within, seeing the compulsions, the synesthetic impressions, the huge movements of microscopic bodies in light of a religious "pilgrimage." Details of Christ's tomb, the stone blocking its entrance, and a reference to the Resurrection are worked into a scheme of rebirth or renewal for the persons of whom these cells are a part. As the individuals unite, so the "clouds of cells" in each of them, mutually attracted or magnetically compelled, journey toward their bodies' boundaries. In the union of persons opposites fuse, contrarities and antitheses are overcome, they find completion. Inside them the cells perform a dance of ecstasy, of mystical achievement. Here we must

not forget that the God for whom both Bly and Kabir are looking lives in them and has to be discovered initially in mortal,
physical existence, not afterwards. This lengthy concluding portion of the poem dramatizes an experience of the inner deity; it is
sanctioned at the close by a sage figure whose final question
clarifies for the reader the route Bly's visionary pursuit in this
prose poem sequence has traced:

> So the space between two people diminishes, it grows less and less,
> no one to weep, they merge at last. The sound that pours from the
> fingertips awakens clouds of cells far inside the body, and beings
> unknown to us start out in a pilgrimage to their Saviour, to their
> holy place. Their holy place is a small black stone, that they re-
> member from Protozoic times, when it was rolled away from a
> door . . . and it was after that they found their friends, who helped
> them to digest the hard grains of this world. . . . The cloud of cells
> awakens, intensifies, swarms . . . the cells dance inside beams of
> sunlight so thin we cannot see them. . . . To them each ray is a vast
> palace, with thousands of rooms. From the dance of the cells praise
> sentences rise to the throat of the man praying and singing alone in
> his room. He lets his arms climb above his head, and says, "Now do
> you still say you cannot choose the Road?"

Evidently, much more could be contributed to any thorough
reading of this poem. I can't pretend to have dealt with its scientific sources, but my remarks have, I hope, touched some of its
essential intentions. The theme of union in "The Origin of the
Praise of God" prepares for consideration of some of the later
poems in the book. For obvious reasons I must skip over pieces
which are excellent and worthy of close, appreciative study in
order to give attention to a few of the last. I will, however, pause
to quote one of them, "The Pail," because in its opening paragraph Bly reflects in a personal way, and even retrospectively,
on the quest for and accomplishment of revelatory experience.
These ecstasies are hard won, in an austere environment. They
have occurred through an inward communion with the physical
body and have taken him through a type of death and rebirth.
Still, I quote this lovely poem for a second reason: because there
are so many examples in it of the perceiving and recording of

singular events for which Bly believes the prose poem possesses such a capacity. As he sharpens our sensibilities by imagining the lives of protozoa our naked eyes can't see, so he trains us to regard carefully, lovingly, what is visible that we often neglect:

> Friend, this body is made of camphor and gopherwood. So for two days I gathered ecstasies from my own body, I rose up and down, surrounded only by bare wood and bare air and some gray cloud, and what was inside me came so close to me, and I lived and died!
>
> Now it is morning. The faint rain of March hits the bark of the half-grown trees. The honeysuckle will drip water, the moon will grow wet sailing, the granary door turns dark on the outside, the oats inside still dry.
>
> And the grandfather comes back inquiringly to the farm, his son stares down at the pickup tire, the family lawyer loses his sense of incompetence for a moment, in the barn the big pail is swung out so as to miss the post.

In poems such as "We Love This Body" and "Wings Folding Up" the results of choosing the right "Road" are disclosed in the acknowledgment of a pervasive, affirming "energy compacted and whirling," which cannot be dissipated, present even in "the forehead bone that does not rot, the woman priest's hair still fresh among Shang ritual things. . . ." Progress on this path brings its initiates or pilgrims to love—of one's body, of another person, of nature in its abundant particulars. Lavishing our affections, we are repaid in kind. Bly offers numerous sections of fine lyrical writing out of this newly wakened spirit:

> We love this body as we love the day we first met the person who led us away from this world, as we love the gift we gave one morning on impulse, in a fraction of a second, that we still see every day, as we love the human face, fresh after love-making, more full of joy than a wagonload of hay.
>
> ("We Love This Body")

> Is this world animal or vegetable? Others love us, the cabbages love the earth, the earth is fond of the heavens—a new age comes

close through the dark, an elephant's trunk waves in the darkness, so much is passing away, so many disciplines already gone, but the energy in the double flower does not falter, the wings fold up around the sitting man's face. And these cucumber leaves are my body, and my thighs, and my toes stretched out in the wind. . . . Well, water-er, how will you get through this night without water?

("Wings Folding Up")

This second passage confirms an abiding unity with and love for self and creation; it is, further, both realistic and prophetic in its assessment of an "age" of difficult transition, when institutions and traditions are losing their once vital hold on human experience, when their explanations for that experience no longer command as much genuine or durable conviction as they did. But Bly has shaped for himself a harmonious bond with nature to serve as a support, and he can now recollect how "the energy in the double flower does not falter."

We learn something of this double flower's significance from the book's penultimate poem, "Snowed In." A Minnesota winter again supplies atmosphere—and more. The poet has re-tired to his writing shack, a setting for other Bly poems. Coming through the door, thick snow flying about him, the first thing he notices on sitting down "is a plant in blossom." In the arrangement of his perception and thought, observation leads to meditation, which in turn takes flight into imaginative vision:

The upper petal is orange-red. The lower petal paler, as if the intensity had risen upward. Two smaller petals, like country boys' ears, poke out on either side.

The blossom faces the window where snow sweeps past at forty miles an hour. . . . So there are two tendernesses looking at each other, two oceans living at a level of instinct surer than mine . . . yet in them both there is the same receiving, the longing to be blown, to be shaken, to circle slowly upward, or sink down toward roots . . . one cold, one warm, but neither wants to go up geometrically floor after floor, even to hold up a wild-haired roof, with copper dragons, through whose tough nose rain water will pour. . . .

So the snow and the orangey blossoms are both the same flow, that starts out close to the soil, close to the floor, and needs no commandments, no civilization, no drawing rooms lifted on the labor of the claw hammer, but is at home when one or two are present, it is also inside the block of wood, and in the burnt bone that sketched the elk by smoky light.

Flower and snow, apparent opposites, thrive on and manifest the same convoluted energies we have seen throughout. The flower's color intensifies as it grows upward, the flakes of snow whirl violently down. Bly identifies both with "oceans," an image recalling the poet's catalogue of things linked with the Mother or feminine consciousness—curving, flowing, rounding things which avoid sharp angles, corners, and logical procedures. Both flower and snow wish in their natures to be driven by this whirling force, this circular "Power of the World" (to use this term from Bly's Black Elk quotation) which exists and functions prior to, aside from, even against, the mathematically calculated ordering of "civilization," "commandments," or buildings laid out in squares and rectangles—we remember "Walking Swiftly." The force does favor unity and relationships between individuals, and has always visited the artist—even the prehistoric, anonymous cave painter—with its presence. In the poem's final section the double flower is, as elsewhere, man and woman, poet and loved one. Bly renders them objectively as he begins, but in the second sentence he alters the distance, applies personal pronouns. This conclusion acquires the strength of intimacy against a background of ageless, ubiquitous cosmic energy; and here, as the cell and the snowflake do in the miniature lyrics about them, this couple knows the joy and grace of accepting their bodies, the tie that unites them, and of living from the profound, balanced center of themselves. "So inside the human body there is the seed," Kabir version 4 says, "and inside the seed there is the human body again."

A man and a woman sit quietly near each other. In the snowstorm millions of years come close behind us, nothing is lost, nothing rejected, our bodies are equal to the snow in energy. The body is ready to sing all night, and be entered by whatever wishes to enter the human body singing. . . .

("Snowed In")

After this paragraph no one will be surprised to learn that the last poem in the collection is even more openly and personally a love poem. "The Cry Going Out Over Pastures" is a lover's declaration—one of both longing and satisfaction—resonating through his natural surroundings, a world of trees, river, birds, pastures, from which, at least partially, he takes his sense of selfhood; and it is a statement of love that is "prudent" and also wild "beyond all rules and conventions." The latter half of the poem roves back in memory to the lovers' first meeting, yet returns at once, in the same sentence, to the immediate moment. There Bly recognizes the unavoidable claim death makes but countenances it with the renewing energies of life, the circling path being follows, bringing with this acceptance a transcending "joy [as] when the bee rises into the air above his hive to find the sun, to become the son, and the traveler moves through exile and loss, through murkiness and failure, to touch the earth again of his own kingdom and kiss the ground. . . ."

Those words apply to more than the poet's elatedness at this instant; they can be said to summarize metaphorically the arduous journey he has undertaken to arrive at this animated condition. Bly's latest prose poems stand as a fine, coherent achievement, a little of the fullness and intricacy of which I hope has been conveyed here. Much can still be discussed about the style of these poems, their employment of assonance, alliteration, internal rhyming—in brief, their music—and other poetic devices; but a watchful reader will discover them. Poem 10 from Bly's Kabir versions seems a very apt concluding comment on the prose poems of *This Body Is Made of Camphor and Gopherwood:*

Between the conscious and the unconscious, the
        mind has put up a swing:
all earth creatures, even the supernovas, sway
        between these two trees,
and it never winds down.

Angels, animals, humans, insects by the million, also
        the wheeling sun and moon;
ages go by, and it goes on.

Everything is swinging: heaven, earth, water, fire,
and the secret one slowly growing a body.
Kabir saw that for fifteen seconds, and it made him a
    servant for life.

VICTORIA HARRIS

"Walking Where the Plows
Have Been Turning"
Robert Bly and Female Consciousness

Our epoch is filled with the resurrection of the woman. In a
variety of disciplines—politics, anthropology, sociology, psychology, linguistics, literature—apartheid features of patriarchy
are giving way to a spirit of *inclusiveness,* the proper context for
the female spirit. In a cohesive gesture, we increasingly mend a
world divided by maps, categories, "objectivity," and a strict
adherence to logic. Cohesiveness results from a participation in
the collapse of a defined bifurcation between masculine and feminine natures. Authentic synthesis occurs as the woman enters a
previously masculine world, and the male taps internal qualities
usually attributed to a woman. Increasingly, one may recognize
this psychic integration in the poetry of Robert Bly. Augment-
ing a new era, and yet recalling an ancient one, Bly's poetry is
invested with a reliance on intuition, a universe of energies, and
an interest in the incorporative nature of a participatory universe. The female rises in his poetry without apartheid features:
no god exists apart from me, no world exists apart from my
perception and participation. Furthermore, Bly recognizes that a
language structured solely by logic is inadequate to communicate intuition, vision, and spirit; that a poem circumscribed by
an inherited form precludes vision that goes beyond the containment of form. In such poetry life evolves beyond its own goals.
Such features suggest reception and gestation beyond intention.
Thus, the female. In a departure from a history of categories and

form, Bly includes intuition, empathy, and reception as bases of female consciousness. By nurturing the woman within the man, Robert Bly portrays a universe the poignancy of which results from a sense of expansion.

Female consciousness is particularly evident in Bly's recent prose poem, "Walking Where the Plows Have Been Turning."[1]

> Some aliveness of the body came to me at five in the morning. I woke up, I saw the east pale with its excited brood. I slipped from bed, and out the back door, onto the sleek and resigned cottonwood leaves. The horses were out eating in the ditch. . . . I walked down the road toward the west.
>
> I notice a pebble on the road, then a corn-ear lying in the grass, then a small earthbridge into the cornfield. It leads to the backland where the plows turn, the tractor tires have married it, they love it more than the rest, cozy with bare dirt, the downturned face of the plow that looked at it each round. . . .
>
> The light gives a cornhusk in one place, a cottonwood tree in another, for no apparent reason. A branch has dropped onto the fence wire, there are eternities near, the body free of its exasperations, ready to see what will come. There is a humming in my body, it is jealous of no one. . . . The cricket lays its wings one over the other, a faint whispery sound rises up to its head . . . which it hears . . . and disregards . . . listening for the next sound. . . .

In the poem, Bly advises that if we listen, we shall hear the earth, the female, whose felt power justifies the departure from Western tradition and form, including traditional poetic and syntactic structure, and finally releases the enclosure of form itself into a universe of energy. Bly perceives, empathizes, hosts a mystical union, takes visionary glimpses of the universe, and yet tells us there is more. A close reading of this poem will reveal his universe—intuitive, integrative, perceptive, empathic: female; the path toward it—tradition and the breaking of it, perception and its expansion into empathy, traditional poetic form relaxed into a more organic synthesis, traditional syntax ignored to suggest departure from structured language, and, finally, words to suggest communion. The integration does not, however, conclude within the poem. Bly reveals, and we witness; he receives, and so do we; he creates, and so do we, a participatory universe, inclusive, female.

"Walking Where the Plows Have Been Turning" depicts a three-paragraph progression. This progression differs from "the leap" which Bly has written about and which occurs in many of his own poems. In this poem, Bly replaces the leap—a startling hurdle from natural progression to universal potential—for a different quality. The three paragraphs here seem to metamorphose into different bodies at a slower pace. In fact, this metamorphosis, like gestation, takes as much time as it needs. The paragraph structure affords a fuller sense of enclosure, while the sentences within intermingle. Without each line breaking off into space, Bly constructs both interiority and fuller development in each paragraph. I suggest that this poem is structured like the three trimesters of gestation. Instead of an insightful leap into the universe—a gesture itself symbolically phallic—this poem evolves through preparation and reception, thus symbolically gestate. The three-part poem mingles centripetal and centrifugal energies until the climax of the poem occurs, when mingling itself is focused upon and even the energies themselves cannot be distinguished as incoming or outgoing. The symbolic sexuality seems both a vehicle toward and a metaphor of mystical vision. Part of this mingling, indeed, involves the male's reaching female resources within and around him.

Bly emphasizes the present moment, relying on continued perception, not photographic and recordable in memory banks, but presently alert, participatory, and deepening; directing attention not only to the traditional poetic concerns of imagery, rhythms, diction, and sounds but also to each turn from regular structure. Bly's use of syntax demonstrates a further effort to go beyond established patterns, suggesting the infinite, for example, by breaking finite patterns of grammatical composition. Such structurally motivated attentiveness also constitutes part of the milieu in this poem, which at first focuses on attention and retention, but then shifts to beatific pleasure in a more encompassing satisfaction of existence that, itself, goes beyond existing parameters. The use of means (such as attention and retention) to go beyond these means (such as into the realm of intuition) parallels Bly's expansion from traditional poetic form or grammatical construction. The prose form of this poem, then, as well as its syntactic construction, is semantically significant. This poem seems to suggest a pattern, then departs from it, only to return again to the pattern. Attention, for example, leads to a sense of insouciance, then back to attention again. These departures and reentries are rhythmically part of a course that changes from models and recollection, even from the dictum of attentiveness itself, to exhilaration at the numinous residing in the physical. Then, an instant later, the numinous evades perception, but the vehicle to that luminous plateau remains.

One part of this progression, itself expansive, is from perception to reception to empathy. An energy pattern—centrifugal, centripetal, and centrifugal—changes not only in direction, but in quality; the last signals both an outward force and a release from parameters. In the first paragraph (reminiscent of *Jumping Out of Bed*),[2] the speaker tingles with an awakening that is explicitly receptive: "some aliveness . . . *came to me*" (italics added). His physical awakening, it will be shown, foreshadows his vision of the life of all surrounding him, and indeed, this comprises a spiritual awakening undergriding this poem. With one exception, "The horses were out eating in the ditch . . . ," the significance of which will be discussed later, the first paragraph, written in recollection (as indicated by past tense), presents the chronology of events apparent to a receptive speaker. After the opening line of the poem, reporting both the time: "Five in the morning," and the speaker's interior response: "Some aliveness of the body," the speaker begins each subsequent thought with the pronoun "I." The words, "I woke up, I saw the east pale with its excited brood," begin the "I" series with a comma spliced construction. Bly has done this before, syntactically suggesting that the additive nature of logic opposes a more holistic response to the universe. Here, language, rooted in logic, is shown to be flawed—the error perhaps existing in the structure of a sentence, but more probably existing in the reliance of a logical mode to communicate this awakening. A turn away from logic may be symbolically indicated by the speaker's position, facing the east, where thoughts need not be validated through an objectivism that serves to dichotomize reality, but where wisdom is gained through more religious sources of Buddha, or reaching the Tao, or maintaining a balance of yin/yang energies. That Bly never avoids one plateau of existence to reach another may be noticed now, when the visceral response to awakening prepares the speaker for going beyond ordinary corporeal enclosure, and when syntactic structure is used as a vehicle for departure from it. By making an unexpected departure, Bly highlights that turn of events; whatever occurs leaps beyond cognitive modes of recognition impelling more involved perception, in fact often necessitating a reception not circumscribed by intention of what is to be portrayed. Bly syntactically suggests going beyond expectation in the opening construction, containing parallel units of "I" with a subsequent verb: "I woke. . . ," "I saw. . . ," and "I slipped. . . ," arousing an expectation of pattern; Bly calls attention to the change from this structure in the following image where "out the back door" is not preceded by the pattern of personal pronoun and verb. Formally arousing this expectation of further repetition in structure, Bly brings the next image into starker relief by departing from this construction. The reader not only notices lack of focus on the speaker and his action, but is simultaneously drawn into the image "out the back door, onto the sleek and resigned cottonwood leaves." This break from repetitive structure changes at the moment when the focus shifts from the speaker and his action to the surrounding scene. Here, Bly begins a centrifugal motion whereby the body does not imprison the vision—neither the corporeal form, the poetic form, nor the syntactic form. This release from formal pattern, in other words, also has semantic significance: an increased scope will result from this gesture of going beyond established boundaries. Thus, visually Bly stops the construction beginning with "I" and verb, and ventures into the scene. Moreover, as in the negative capability of Keats, the speaker noticeably increases sensitivity in his empathic vision of leaves that are "resigned." Now the speaker is not removed from the scene as subject is from object; for, as we have been told, he now is in a scene that he easily "slips" into. Indeed, the following sentence dispenses with the "I" and notes that "horses were out eating in the ditch. . . ." The outgoing consciousness of this speaker, shifting his focus from himself to his landscape, also signifies a departure from dichotomies as suggested by boundaries. This leaning outward prepares the way, and, as will be discussed further, the ellipsis marks suggest that there is more in a vision than finite structure could portray. The strength of structure relents now before the powers of intuition. This power, not brutishly victorious, is a release from boundaries of tradition, rules. Such release, suggesting fluidity of energies instead of restriction of form, empathy rather than recognition, establishes a patina of associations with the female milieu. Bly seems to disregard the entire tradition of history while resurrecting the ancient modes of myth. I suggest a growth in the poet and his speaker of perceptual modes most often attributed to the woman. The receptivity beginning this paragraph prepares the speaker for his outgoing venture concluding the first paragraph.

This paragraph concludes the "I" series: "I walked down the road toward the West," and the next paragraph continues with another sentence beginning with "I." The journey, symbolic in direction: westward, and in time: daybreak, leaves the female milieu of night and dream where images are not based upon physical perception and logical intention. Change is augmented by this centrifugal push from the body-"I" outwardly toward the world. Two sentences in this paragraph that do not begin with "I," along with a change in tense, establish a shift away from both physical enclosure and historic tradition. In the first sentence suggesting "aliveness" and receptivity, the speaker does not control this vitality, and really cannot cognitively prepare for it. Again, logical intention seems irrelevant here, since this preparation is of a different kind—one that does not intend a result, but one that like gestation requires preparation and time. Tense in this paragraph is indeed significant. Recollection, the mind of memory, does not articulate the source of vitality; the shift from a chronology of action does, when sequence, for instance, is interrupted only by the perception that "the horses were out eating in the ditch." This action is not chronological, but endures longer than the catalogue of events before and after this sentence. Furthermore, it implies the speaker's nascent outwardness—by interrupting the "I" sentences with a perception of other things. This gesture is a harbinger of the speaker's spirituality; his aliveness becomes a vehicle not for internalization, but for generation of empathy, and finally communion with the living world. Thus, the paragraph contains an element of life not confined to the first personal "I," and suggests that "some aliveness of the body" may become "some aliveness of the universal body"; the physical body becomes both a metaphor for and a vehicle to the universal body; reception becomes preparatory for generation. (This outwardness, then, like a birth, brings energy from the body out into the world.)

In the second paragraph, a journey occurs from the speaker's body out to a scene that increasingly becomes a female milieu. First, dichotomies are mended through a decreasing sense of enclosure concomitantly with an increase in empathy. Second, the female quality of mythic earth is realized: a decreasing sense of earth as a field of distinctions occurs concomitantly with an increasing intuitive vision. The awakened speaker continues westward—symbolic of a world of logic and dichotomy. But this subject-object dichotomy signalled by the opening of the sentence—again beginning with "I"—relents before a unifying process. Now, the speaker explicitly leans outward, reaching toward the land with which he is familiar, symbolically reaching toward the earth—the great mythical mother, whose harvests are represented by this poem. While empathy grows, this leaning leads to a sense of communion, until familiar objects in the landscape are transformed into personified treasures, thus elevated to the level of conscious life. The magnitude of this evolution may be signalled by the change of verbs and by the change in narrative stance, from self-expression to empathic communion, thereby leaving the aloofness of dichotomy inherent in history for the involved relationship of ritual in the mythic present. This second paragraph, for instance, shifting from memory as indicated by the past tense concluding the first paragraph, begins in the present tense, thus relying on perception. Furthermore, perception changes from the more pedestrian sensory kind to an inseeing capacity. Thus, when speaking as a subject separated from an object, the speaker says, "I notice," connoting rather casual observation by a passerby. These noticed images gain in significance when the focus shifts from a speaker noticing to those elements witnessed in the landscape. Thus, the sentence leads from "I notice a pebble on the road," to "then a corn-ear. . . ," to "then a small earthbridge. . . ." The series of "thens" portrays the speaker's expansion from the enclosed self-contained being inherent in the pronoun "I," to one whose leaning and leaning draws him outward, into close commune with his milieu. Bly here fulfills his own hermeneutics: he has said that good poetry is not self-expression. "What is that?" he inquires. Poetry is the opposite of self-expression.[3] "Being grounded," as he states, is a necessary first step. That grounding does not preclude empathy, but is rather a preparation for having the capacity for venturing out.[4] In other words, the internal resources must be developed to the point that, as in this poem, an "aliveness" occurs allowing harmony with the life of the universe. Now, the realm of intuition, the communion with living powers of earth, the release from parameters of self and other, legitimize an ancient female ambience, born again in this evolving speaker.

This evolution becomes apparent in this series of "then" comments; indicating sequence by its denotation and repetition, Bly intensifies a departure from expectation when the "then" phrases lead, not to further repetition, but to an interiority of vision increasing when the speaker seems released from a self-enclosed milieu. From the casual "notice" of an insular "I," the observer is transformed from one with merely sensory sight to one possessing a deeper capacity. The sequence of images is seen increasingly through intuitive vision: first *on,* then *in,* then *into* the landscape. The first image, of a "pebble on the road," would be available to any observer. Then, as the focus shifts to a field, "a corn-ear" appears lying "in the grass," thereby projecting outwardly and thus portraying less casual observation than implied by "noticing." The third image of a "small earthbridge *into* [italics added] the cornfield," represents the interpenetration of elements. Not only do cornfields admit earthbridges, but the speaker leaving surface manifestations probes beneath, significantly penetrating fields with earthbridges; the earth here changes from horizontal plane into a deeper plateau; such verticality results from a capacity to see beneath surfaces. Rejecting the dichotomy of subject and object is also a symbolic departure from cultures of positivism, scrutiny, and category. The speaker intuits depths of earth, in earth, entering finally into the earth—spiritually joining the symbolic woman.

A study of Bly's syntax reveals that the interpenetration of elements is also symbolically rich in this paragraph. A rush of events is implied through repetition; "I notice" is followed with "a pebble," "then" a "corn-ear," "then" "a small earthbridge." Bly changes grammatical gears, however, in this construction that ostensibly contains repetition but goes increasingly from the speaker's action to the image. "I notice" describes "a pebble on the road," the action here occurring in the speaker who notices the pebble; then, with a verbal, "a corn-ear lying in the grass," more pointedly centers on the corn-ear, and finally "a small earthbridge into the cornfield" noticeably departs from the portrayal of the speaker and of natural observation. "I notice" could not semantically be the antecedent verb of "an earthbridge *into* the cornfield" (italics added). The concluding image does not focus on the speaker or the object in the landscape. Rather it unites apparent divisions by portraying an image as invested with the speaker's intuition. Focusing on an image while leaving the source of the action has the effect of making that image more pictorial. Thus, through verb-omission, Bly offers this picture of deep interpenetration and holds this picture still for a moment.

This pause on interpenetration leads to a visionary glimpse more sublime than recordable through a grammar of logic. Grammatical inadequacy in the subsequent sentence, which contains comma splices, a fragment, and ellipsis marks implies a theory that grammatical logic is inadequate, symbolically responding to the inadequacy of a historical world that spawned such structures. "It leads to a backland where the plows turn, the tractor tires have married it, they love it more than the rest, cozy with bare dirt, the downturned face of the plow that looked at it each round. . . ." The referent of "it" is presumably that earthbridge whose unity with the cornfield provides the vehicle for a vision into universal harmony. The comma splice following this image utilizes a grammatically incorrect connecting device. Here, the joining of two things is not as harmonious in language as it is through vision. Again, joined by comma-spliced connections, the next two images increasingly envision a speaker in harmony with his landscape at the same time that the punctuation is flawed. It appears that by this very combination, Bly portrays a vision too large for logical modes. Masculine and feminine symbolism seem appropriate here when connection is made with the earth and fault is found in the written language. And indeed the content of the lines affirms this suspicion of connecting with female forces; the mingling of tractor tires with the earthbridge is portrayed as a marriage; then contiguity is further portrayed as love. The landscape is not only personified, but alive with the emotion of love in union. Union is first depicted as "cozy"; then Bly increases the sexuality with the image of "the downturned face of the plow that looked at it each round. . . ." Not only has the landscape become alive with love and sexual harmony, but this sexuality may be the vehicle to an epoch of more spiritual harmony. Ellipsis marks, I suggest, syntactically represent this notion that physical contiguity-becoming-love-becoming-sexual union is preparatory to more spiritual union, and this, in turn, preparatory to a vision of correspondences. This suspicion will be confirmed later, when the implied notion of ellipsis—that there is more—increases with the depiction of the speaker's spiritual awakening, including his awareness of aliveness in the earth.

Like vision that penetrates surfaces, "aliveness of the body" seems a resource allowing this speaker to leave his body. Deadness of the body, accordingly, would lock the energy in the frame stillborn. This paragraph concludes not only with portrayal of a series of images changing from photographic to insightful, but this inseeing vision augurs an intuition of earth itself brimming with life, and thus brings life into the scene. The second sentence does not begin with "I" but with "it," referring to the earthbridge. Furthermore, the speaker not only centrifugally journeys outward, but the "it" of earthbridges shifts from its inanimate state to one containing a more personified aspect. Earthbridges lead "to the backland," perhaps further away from sensory sight, but seen with intuitive vision, as a place "where the plows turn," and then, in combination with other natural objects, the juncture becomes marriage: "the tractor tires have married it." Union in marriage is underscored in three ways: First, the personification attributes consciousness to the farmland scene. Second, the marriage suggests the quality of life involved in this scene. Third, Bly formally connects this image of conscious unity to "love," the emotion undergirding marriage, in a comma spliced construction. Thus, logic, the logic of syntax and grammar, is inadequate for this intuitional vision of unity; a coupling of two sentences with a comma seems merely additive, while the vision of unity requires a more integral connection. Unity of subject and object, then, becomes communion in marriage. Such communion is depicted by "I" reaching "it," thereby leaving an enclosed speaker in order to enter the living milieu. "It" becomes "they" as singular joins into plural and the "they," although referring to tractor tires, is given the passion of love. "They love it more than the rest" personifies and qualifies this commingling quality as that which fosters love. The significant prerequisite, then, is unity—leaving the enclosure of "I" in a gesture of universal harmony.

Symbolically, the speaker departs from the dichotomized atmosphere of subject and object. Bly eschews the constructions of history—its patriarchal forms of logic, grammar, and tradition—while offering the more matriarchal forms of the mother herself, receiving and bearing, intuitive and fluid. The rewards are reaped in a scene symbolically harvesting love; love fosters a "cozy" event suggestive of intimacy when joined to the next image of "the downturned face of the plow that looked at it each round. . . ." This sexual metaphor, used to express intimate mingling, changes the more casual "cozy" into a more passionate mingling, much as the more casual "notice" changed to the more intense intuitional vision. This instant of personification reaches a visionary plateau, yet the poet implies no stopping place. Grammatically, Bly cannot depict this harmony except by portraying the inadequacy of grammatical logic. Though the mark of a visionary has been made—the tingling body, the leaving of it, the reaching outward, the union made—Bly leaves sllipsis marks signifying there is more. In such a fluid milieu, categorization of "what is" becomes pedestrian. There is always more; the aliveness beginning the poem and the humming concluding the poem suggest this sensitivity of body awakened by spirit. This spiritual birth is central to the second paragraph in which envisioned correspondences cannot be transmitted through logical discourse.

By the conclusion of this poem, Bly brings the reader closer to the nurturing earth, close enough to hear tiny crickets. Bly emphasizes harmony, reception, intuition, sensitivity, and sexuality, while discarding the authority of rule, logic, parameters, and tradition. It seems no accident that these characteristics clearly depict the mythic matriarchal cultures as opposed to the historical patriarchal times. Indeed, holism associated with matriarchy and myth seems inestimably more valuable than the rational dimension of splitting the universe into categories. The concluding paragraph goes beyond the natural ordering of the mind; Bly seems to suggest a setting for receptivity as opposed to selectivity. Shafts of light, for example, yield "a cornhusk in one place, a cottonwood tree in another, *for no apparent reason*" (italics added). Images perceived by the speaker seem offered by the light in a natural correspondence, unordered by will, or intention. "Apparent" takes on the same casual quality as "notice" did in the previous paragraph. Bly does not dispute whether or not a reason exists, but maintains that the reason is not apparent. Indeed, the world of appearance, afforded the objective eye, seems ordinary compared to the vision of a universe of connections glimpsed in this poem. In the following sentence, for example, temporal and eternal time join in a conception too large for logical apprehension. The additive nature of a logical mind is again indicated in syntax containing comma splice and fragment. The beginning of the sentence, "A branch has dropped onto the fence wire," is a natural, temporal image. The subsequent meditation, "there are eternities near," is a Wordsworthian response too large for logic. Since language seems bereft of the capacity for containing intuition, this line, added to the previous sentence with a comma splice, indicates not the lack of intuition but its magnitude—too grand to be contained in a grammar of logic. Indeed, the intuition is a given, presented with the certitude implied in a state-of-being construction. Intuition joins the concatenation of values revealed in this poem to suggest clearly by now that a female psyche permeates this earth.

In this paragraph, Bly goes from natural image to natural image; observation changes to vision when it becomes clear that a synthesis exists among these elements. The reader also is compelled to make the connection, one more harmonious than logically decipherable. Moreover, this harmony encompasses aesthetic response in general, the reader no longer removed from the poem as subject is from object. Thus, Bly structurally indicates logical inaccuracies at the moment when the vision enlarges, and this enlargement, furthermore, enforces the envisioned harmony by drawing the reader into the poem. Bly strengthens the poet-poem-reader relationship through intuition.

Intuition—a holy thing—is not removed from the physical being. In fact, the body may be a vehicle for intuition. With no transition from eternity to the body, Bly quickly flashes from one to the other, perhaps indicating connection through contiguity. "Exasperations" may imply petty quarrels of the physical life, such as are resolved through a vision of eternity. Thus, the body, becoming "free of its exasperations," has symbolically given birth. Intuitions are born as a release from containment. In this poem its especial interpenetrating characteristic also symbolically mends dichotomies of subject and object, memory and perception, even male and female. "Eternities are near" articulates these visionary correspondences.

Such freedom suggests evolution from restraints, and leaves the speaker "ready to see what will come." This stage is signalled again by an aliveness in his body. Now, "there is a humming in my body." Auguring a birth, the physical humming becomes metaphoric of spiritual revival. Through his use of punctuation, Bly implies that physical becomes more than physical: first, a comma splice and then ellipsis marks occur in this construction when the humming body precedes "it is jealous of no one." The antecedent of "it" is presumably humming, since humming seems to be the alert, alive aspect of the speaker, such in quality that "it is jealous of no one." Bly indicates a life (humming) not restricted to ownership (jealousy). Furthermore, there is more, perhaps too grand for language; thus, the ellipsis marks.

Bly calls upon the tiny cricket once again to indicate spirituality at the conclusion of this poem: "The cricket lays its wings one over the other, a faint whispery sound rises up to its head . . . which it hears . . . and disregards . . . listening for the next sound. . . ." Again a comma splice and ellipsis mark indicate intuition bursting grammatical boundaries; just as the vision supercedes eyesight, and the humming declares more than physical body, the message requires more than grammatical logic. Thus, more is needed as is additively indicated by the comma splice insistence that this too should be said. But the essence of this perception does not transmit through one sentence, then another. The comma spliced arrangement turns out to be a redundancy of an arrangement, each, in itself, inadequate; the combination, cumulatively inadequate—a repetition rather than a clarification. Then, Bly uses ellipsis marks for opposite purposes. Sentence upon sentence suggests repetition, each in itself inadequate singularly and cumulatively. If the whole grammatical structure seems inadequate, then how could the perception be transmitted? Intuition broke the boundaries of the body; distinction of separate natural objects joined through their correspondences; limitation of grammatical logic is overcome through portrayal of its inadequacy. Now, Bly turns to ellipsis marks—a positive rejection of incapacity. Instead of silence as a response to the ineffable, Bly offers words, and then asserts over and again that there is more. A poet whose wisdom is more than words, Bly reaches into the life surrounding him and provides images, correspondences, and then teaches—saying these are the vehicles; there is more. As a guide, Bly notes humming in a body; as a visionary he describes not only the cricket's "faint whispery sound," which corresponds to this humming body, but with empathic sensitivity notes that "it hears . . . [and there is more] and disregards . . . [and there is more] listening for the next sound . . ." [and there is more]. In other words, we too are "walking" and must not stop our journey.

Thus, "Walking Where the Plows Have Been Turning" is a three-part metamorphosis in which Bly constructs a mythology of human experience through reception, expansion, and generation. He clearly values incorporative functions, elevating sensitivity and empathy over observation and detail; receptivity and sexuality over aggression and submission; fluidity of form over tradition and pattern; and a world of correspondence and intuition over a land of rules and order. Finally, Bly mends a world torn into parts through his construction of a more fluid ambience of interacting energies. Intuition, sensitivity, empathy, reception—usually characterizing the female—permeate this creation. We witness, I suspect, one of the creators of a new epoch, in which the mythic woman powerfully rises also within a male. There will be more to witness Bly tells us, if, receptive, intuitive, and attentive, we too listen "for the next sound. . . ."

NOTES

1. Robert Bly, "Walking Where the Plows Have Been Turning," *Georgia Review,* 32 (1978):513. Revised and included in *This Tree Will Be Here for a Thousand Years* (New York: Harper & Row, 1979), p. 49. Reprinted here by permission of Harper & Row, Publishers, Inc.

2. Robert Bly, *Jumping Out of Bed* (Barre, Mass.: Barre Publishers, 1973).

3. Bly stated this idea at a poetry reading at Western Illinois University, November 2, 1978.

4. Bly discusses "grounding" in "On Gurus, Grounding Yourself in the Western Tradition, and Thinking for Yourself," *East-West Journal,* August 1976, pp. 10–15.

WAYNE DODD

Back to the Snowy Fields

Go back now twenty years later and you will still find it, lying silently in ditches beside the road, drifting noiselessly in with the snow at nightfall, standing dry and bristly in a field of weeds: *the spirit of the American prairie*. For that's what Bly discovered for us in *Silence in the Snowy Fields:* the spirit of the American (prairie) landscape. Nowhere a trace, not one blurring linger, of language or perception from another culture or geography (all influences of Spanish, Chinese, Latin American—and other—poets not withstanding). Just the American land, breathing into and through Bly. And us. I would even go so far as to say, if pressed, that however much else Bly may have contributed to the ferment of American letters, this has been perhaps his most important contribution—aside from the rich offering of the poems themselves. Once we had experienced *Silence in the Snowy Fields,* the body of America was never again the same to us—never again "merely" there, never again *external* to our own locus of spirit, no longer obedient to even the most carefully translated commands from "English" poetry. Since *Silence,* a developing generation of new young poets has been able to take for granted the subtle and important knowledge of our geographical lives these poems provide. It has come to be a given, something which, once gained, one can never go back from. Like self-consciousness. It has become a fundamental fact of not just a *way* of knowing, but also a *what*.

But perhaps *consciousness* would be a more useful comparison, because it is *consciousness* these poems are concerned with, consciousness of the world of solitude, of darkness, of isolation, of silence: the other world—sleep, the hidden or unseen, *the rest of it*. That's what the silence is filled with, what it frees us for: the

Previously unpublished, 1982.

other half, the realm of dark knowledge, night. The fields and rural buildings here open out into this large dimension of (our) being. "We are all asleep in the outward man," Bly quotes Boehme, as an epigraph for the book, then goes on to offer poems which, taken all together, call to us, *Wake up! Wake up!* in (and through) the inward man. This is the persistent urge one feels in *Silence in the Snowy Fields:* the urge to spiritual perception. We sense the need to discover the other-dimensionality of being. "There is unknown dust that is near us," the poem "Surprised By Evening" begins, "Waves breaking on shores just over the hill, / Trees full of birds that we have never seen, / Nets drawn down with dark fish."

> The evening arrives; we look up and it is there,
> It has come through the nets of the stars,
> Through the tissues of the grass,
> Walking quietly over the asylums of the waters.

Everything, we sense, is fraught with incommensurably greater meaning. In a substantial number of these poems we have the overwhelming sense that somehow we have suddenly broken through a thin covering into a purely subjective landscape. And yet *it* is the one that seems more real; indeed, in those moments we believe that it is *the* real:

Now we wake, and rise from bed, and eat breakfast!—
Shouts rise from the harbor of the blood,
Mist, and masts rising, the knock of wooden tackle in the sunlight.

Now we sing, and do tiny dances on the kitchen floor.
Our whole body is like a harbor at dawn;
We know that our master has left us for the day.

("Waking From Sleep")

> It is a pleasure, also, to be driving
> Toward Chicago, near dark,
> And see the lights in the barns.
> The bare trees more dignified than ever,

Like a fierce man on his deathbed,
And the ditches along the road half full of private snow.

("Three Kinds of Pleasures")

And in a poem such as "Return to Solitude" there is the implication that entire histories go on in a kind of subjective isolation, a place of solitude:

> What shall we find when we return?
> Friends changed, houses moved,
> Trees perhaps, with new leaves.

There is an urgency about the moments and events in these poems. Everything is darkly radiant with something which, Bly manages to suggest, we need urgently to know.

> The dusk has come, a glow in the west, as if seen through the isinglass on old coal stoves, and the cows stand around the barn door; now the farmer looks up at the paling sky reminding him of death, and in the fields the bones of the corn rustle faintly in the last wind, and the half moon stands in the south.
>
> Now the lights from barn windows can be seen through bare trees.

("Fall")

And at such times as these we don't know whether we fall, or rise, into greater awareness.

But of course the physical details, in Bly, are the essential ingredients, for they are the windows we see through, they are the doors we fall through, the vessels we find ourselves in.

TAKING THE HANDS

> Taking the hands of someone you love,
> You see they are delicate cages . . .
> Tiny birds are singing
> In the secluded prairies
> And in the deep valleys of the hand.

The poems continually plunge inside: ourselves, the landscape, the face of the American prairie. The spiritual content, we feel, does not exist as some detached or detachable "significance"; it is the content of *this* body (or bodies): *these* places, *these* moments, *these* people. And if one should have a sudden epiphany, a plunge to an unconsciousness knowing of the gestalt of wholeness in a moment, it will likely be while driving toward the Lac Qui Parle River, through small towns with porches built right on the ground. Or while walking in a corn field. Or among odorous weeds. Authentic language, Bly says elsewhere, arises out of a depth, "coming up from . . . every source." And what Bly offers, in the images and language of these poems, is not an excess of originality, but an ecstasy of appropriateness and recognition.

A successful poem, it seems to me, can profitably be talked of as if it were a living thing, through and in whose body we find beauty, density, grace, *further* life. All bodies are different of course, as all persons, all poems, all experiences. But even the most limited glimpse of a person's physical presence, the merest hint, can bring the whole of it rushing into our consciousness: the line of a neck, the sound of a familiar footstep, the lovely curve where hip rounds down into flank—suddenly we know the whole of it: person, poem, place. In *Silence in the Snowy Fields* the *whole* Bly is reaching for is that insistent sense of spiritual reality which the *family* of poems must identify. And we know what the family, individual in their bodies, will look like: clear-eyed, blond haired, physically alive to the dark winters inside them.

The light was dawn. Like a man who has come home
After seeing many dark rivers, and will soon go again,
The dawn stood there with a quiet gaze;
Our eyes met through the top leaves of the young ash.

Dawn has come. The clouds floating in the east have turned white.
The fence posts have stopped being a part of the darkness.
The depth has disappeared from the puddles on the ground.
I look up angrily at the light.

("Getting Up Early")

Poem after poem in this remarkable book successfully enlarges a bare-bones narrative, exemplumlike in its simplicity, with an incomparably greater sense of existence, a complex presence of life. We come to be aware, as Bly is aware, of the abiding presence of a hidden order, the sacred masked by the ordinary. Poems arrive to suddenly opened vistas:

> We know the road; as the moonlight
> Lifts everything, so in a night like this
> The road goes on ahead, it is all clear.
>
> ("After Working")

or to vague, indefinable threats:

> The barn is full of corn, and moving toward us now,
> Like a hulk blown toward us in a storm at sea;
> All the sailors on deck have been blind for many years.
>
> ("Snowfall in the Afternoon")

For there *is* threat in *Silence*. Water:land, dark:daylight, waking:sleeping—these are the antinomies of our life the poems embody. And within the antinomies lies, often, a susceptibility to the forlornness in "Silence":

> Something homeless is looking on the long roads—
> A dog lost since midnight, a small duck
> Among the odorous reeds,
> Or a tiny box-elder bug searching for the window pane.
> Even the young sunlight is lost on the window pane,
> Moving at night like a diver among the bare branches silently lying
>   on the floor.

Indeed there are times when it is impossible to tell whether the waking is a source more of gain or of loss. Even the beautiful and brilliant (and oft-quoted) "But, at last, the quiet waters of the night will rise, / And our skin shall see far off, as it does under water"—even this is, finally, ambiguous (I think richly so) in its emotional implication. There is a sense of *duende* about the darkness, "like a paling sky reminding [us] of death." So

227

much happens in these poems at the very moment of shift—
from day to night, from sleeping to waking, etc. Events suddenly open up like doors, and a world walks strangely and disturbingly in.

AFTERNOON SLEEP

I

I was descending from the mountains of sleep.
Asleep I had gazed east over a sunny field,
And sat on the running board of an old Model A.
I awoke happy, for I had dreamt of my wife,
And the loneliness hiding in grass and weeds
That lies near a man over thirty, and suddenly enters.

II

When Joe Sjolie grew tired, he sold his farm,
Even his bachelor rocker, and did not come back.
He lfet his dog behind in the cob shed.
The dog refused to take food from strangers.

III

I drove out to that farm when I awoke;
Alone on a hill, sheltered by trees.
The matted grass lay around the house.
When I climbed the porch, the door was open.
Inside were old abandoned books,
And instructions to Norwegian immigrants.

The movement back and forth between dreaming and waking, between unconscious and conscious is a fundamental one in
these poems, as in "Remembering in Oslo the Old Picture of the
Magna Carta":

The girl in a house dress, pushing open the window,
Is also the fat king sitting under the oak tree,
And garbage men, thumping their cans, are
Crows still cawing,

And the nobles are offering the sheet to the king.
One thing is also another thing, and the doomed galleons,
Hung with trinkets, hove by the coast, and in the blossoms
Of trees are still sailing on their long voyage from Spain;
I too am still shocking grain, as I did as a boy, dog tired,
And my great-grandfather steps on his ship.

Here is a move not only to unconscious knowing, but almost to
a kind of *racial* knowledge, sweeping away differences of both
time and space in the identification offered in the last two lines.
And in a poem such as "Getting Up Early" we experience a
form of double existence in ourselves. The poem has a sort of
commutative effect, causing us suddenly to experience the potent flow of spiritual energy back and forth between the two
poles, conscious and unconscious. Or the movement can lead to
the momentary experience of pure timelessness, the extension of
a perception into endless duration, as in "A Late Spring Day in
My Life":

> A silence hovers over the earth:
> The grass lifts lightly in the heat
> Like the ancient wing of a bird.
> A horse gazes steadily at me.

Needless to say, the duration is achieved through the induction,
via the images used, of a flow at once into and outside of the
speaker, as well as backward and forward in time, so that in the
experience itself, inside and outside become one, as do past and
present. Indeed, it might be worthwhile to note that a sort of
reverie, a dreaming recovery, is frequently an effective instrument in these poems for evoking the unconscious.

> We want to go back, to return to the sea,
> The sea of solitary corridors,
> And halls of wild nights,
> Explosions of grief,
> Diving into the sea of death,
> Like the stars of the wheeling Bear.
>
> ("Return To Solitude")

Memory (Mnemosyne) was, it should be remembered, long ago identified as the mother of poetry. And rightly so. Surely a primary force in the impulse to poetry is the need to rescue the life of the individual spirit from the constant fall into unawareness, to recover, in M. L. Rosenthal's words, "past states of existence, isolated and framed and glowing with their own life as well as with the emotion that has recalled them—something in the present moment that is shared with the past state." Memory, reverie, the unconscious—they share, in some close, symbiotic way, a common, if at times dark, area of the human mind. Memory is perhaps like a heretofore missing conductor, now suddenly completing the circuit that makes possible the flow further into, and out of, ourselves—and our world. It provides in some way, I would guess, the emotional force field that makes possible a sense of temporal simultaneity and spatial diffusion. If poetry depends absolutely on its idiosyncratic truthfulness to the poet's own sense of reality, it depends equally on a powerful stroke of memory, memory of the living quality of an experience that in part was not a *conscious* experience. For Bly, in *Silence,* this is memory of experience irradiated by meaning and significance—always in danger of being lost. And the poems continually put us in contact with an urgent sense of the numinous, out of which we wake (or fade) into *mere* being. The second (or middle) section of *Silence* is entitled "Awakening," but the poems there lead one to an awakening that is more an awakening into, than out of, sleep. Here—in dreams, in reveries, in dark descents, in flights into the unconscious—we wake, paradoxically, into the other dimension of ourselves.

And always we are aware of our bodies—stiff-fingered and clumsy with cold, or alive like a harbor at dawn, or alert to the sound of corn stalks in the wind, to the dark pull of a spot of earth we could be safe in, to the odor of leaves on the wet earth, to the feel of moonlight on our branches. And then we are, at last, fully inside the land of ourselves. "If I reached my hands down, near the earth," we say,

> I could take handfuls of darkness!
> A darkness was always there, which we never noted.

So after *Silence in the Snowy Fields* we were never quite the same again, either. The darkness in us was never the same again. Nor the snow that covers the bare fields waiting always behind our eyes. Nor the barns we hold ourselves to the remembered earth by. Nor the houses we are adrift in—in Minnesota, Ohio, Michigan, Illinois, and elsewhere all over the great body of the land our breath freezes, and warms, in. Sometimes, now, a cowbell sounds from so deep within us, or the eyes of a horse gaze so clearly into our consciousness, that we wake into a present which *Silence in the Snowy Fields* seems always to have been a bright, and dark, part of.

DONALD WESLING

Sentences as Measures in
Two of Robert Bly's Prose Poems

Bly's is a poetics of ecstasy. The writer has to use images of the ordinary to get beyond the ordinary, has to use language to get beyond language. The prized conditions are Not Understanding and Not Saying. Dreaming or sitting, the latter Bly's term for meditation, will open the doors of perception to such states of full presence. The body, because it is made of camphor and gopherwood, may be trusted to protect us, connect us with what is deep in us, correct what is overly theoretical. The use of the prose poem in such a poetics, I would imagine, is to call us "into what is possible, into what is not said"—into the depth which is always under our familiar conversation. I have been quoting from a poem which seems to be a manifesto for Bly's poetics, "Falling into Holes in our Sentences,"[1] where Bly says that every day "we take out first step in words . . . and instantly fall into a hole in the sounds we make." That is, if we are sensitive to what is going on, we are continuously dropping into the depth, returning, dropping. By implication the prose poem is a method of training our faculties so that we can more easily drop into the holes in our sentences and sounds. Apparently for Bly there is no presence in language, but we have to begin with language in order to leap into presence through big gaps in the floorboards of language.

   In this brief study, I will consider some of the ways in which Bly's sentences strive (through sequence) to drop the reader into deeper levels of personality. Much in Bly seems to be determined by an originary premise that such deeper levels might be

Taken from a longer essay, "Image and Measure in the Prose Poems of Robert Bly," in *The New American Prosody,* ed. Norma Procopiow (College Park. Md.: Sun & Moon Press, 1983). Reprinted with permission.

reached by acts of writing and reading, but a commentator on image and measure in his prose poems need not share this premise. For me there are many difficulties with his opposition between surface and depth, not least in the way rationality, ordinary perception, wit, and sound-values are too easily dismissed. Yet I am grateful for Bly's explicit emphasis on the category of the sentence, because sentences are the scissors of poetry. The convergence of grammar and metrics is most obvious and accessible in the prose poem, where (except in those texts constructed by the *verset*) the coincidence or noncoincidence of sentence and line is not a factor, and where we are thus left with sheer sentencing as the main method of construction. The prose poem is no less literary than any other poetic form, but because of the lack of line-breaks it offers a privileged context for the isolation of styles of sentencing.

Sentences are very curious measures in a text. They are not standard building blocks but highly, if not infinitely, various in content, internal structure, and length. The disadvantage of considering them as artistic measures is that they resist formalization. The advantage is that as complete units of meaning, complete thoughts, they are, as measures, already intrinsically semantic: not abstract theoretical entities, but rather formal semantic entanglements. Let us read sentences as formal devices by inspecting their internal structures, their relations one to another in the sequence of the prose poem, and their role in stanzalike paragraphs in the poem as a whole.

Here is a single sentence typical of Bly in his more urgent, oratorical frame of mind. It is the fourth of five sentences in "Falling into Holes in Our Sentences," the longest and most image-packed sentence in the poem:

> . . . Overly sane afternoons in a room during our twenties come back to us in the form of a son who is mad, every longing another person had that we failed to see the body returns to us as a squinting of the eyes when we talk, and no sentimentality, only the ruthless body performing its magic, transforming each of our confrontations into energy, changing our scholarly labors over white-haired books into certainty and healing power, and our cruelties into an old man with missing fingers.[2]

The passage affords evidence for Bly's assertion, earlier in the poem, that "the body watches us, calling us into what is possible, into what is not said," and does so by giving four examples of how disparate events are connected. Apparently no slightest gesture is without consequences in either healing power or cruelty. The agent of transformation is not consciousness or conscience but the body itself, "the ruthless body." In this sentence, the body is both object and agent of the action. To a composition instructor the sentence must seem a case study in the proliferation of the comma splice; to a linguist it would exemplify failures of cohesion, particularly in the sequence

> . . . every longing another person had that we failed to see the body returns to us . . .

But just these deviant qualities of syntax give the passage charm for the reader of prose poems, who apprehends the sentence in the form of a double parenthesis around a kernel center ((O)):

- Instance (Physical into Moral)
- Instance (Moral into Physical)

- Three Claims about the Body as Transformer of Energies

- Instance (Physical into Moral)
- Instance (Moral into Physical)

This may be diagrammed more specifically:

$$
\begin{array}{l}
\text{Overly} \rule{5cm}{0.4pt} , \\
\text{every} \rule{5cm}{0.4pt} , \\
\qquad \text{and} \rule{4cm}{0.4pt} , \\
\qquad\qquad \text{only} \rule{3.5cm}{0.4pt} , \\
\qquad\qquad \text{transforming} \rule{2cm}{0.4pt} , \\
\text{changing} \rule{4cm}{0.4pt} , \\
\text{and} \rule{5cm}{0.4pt} .
\end{array}
$$

Tucked into the third of the inset relative clauses, "transforming each of our confrontations into energy," is the major claim of sentence and poem. We may have our reservations about the validity of this claim, and about the cliché phrasing in "magic" and "white-haired books," but I do not think we feel the sentence is careless. For its purposes it is scrupulously and excitingly made.

"How the Ant Takes Part" strings seven sentences, the last of which uses this same comma-splice syntax of ecstatic listing:

> Smoke rises from mountain depths, a girl walks by the water. This is the body of water near where we sleep. And the mountain climber picks his way up the rocky scrap. How far up on the mountainside he is! As he disappears over the pass, an ant in the village below hurries up his mound of dirt, a woman turns her face back to the stove. Her man at that instant feels some mistake in his heart. The girl moves her hands, all the images rearrange themselves, the bacteria go in swarms through the ocean-salted blood.[3]

Divided by slashes that represent sentence periods, here is the line of images: smoke-mountain-girl-water / body of water-sleep / mountain climber / mountainside / ant-mound of dirt / woman-stove / man's heart / girl-bacteria-"ocean-salted blood." The connections between these items are not causal but analogical: a chain of being stretching from the rocky scrap through large and small bodies of water through the bacteria and the ant through to woman, man, and the ocean-salted blood. Whatever affects one part of this ecology has obscure analogies to and in the other parts. The images line up this way, by categories:

- The Mountain Grouping: mountain; rocky scrap; climber; ant; mound of dirt
- The Feminine Grouping: woman at stove; girl (twice)
- The Water Grouping: water; body of water; "ocean-salted blood"

It is unnecessary to show how all these groups are interrelated. I would single out "ocean-salted blood" as the culminating and most explicit of the ecological analogues whereby Bly interfuses the body and the earth, making the man's heart attack seem not a disaster but part of naturing nature. Perhaps it is not a heart attack; perhaps it is a love attack, an unfaithful feeler of thought sent out toward the girl and away from the man's wife; but whether the "mistake in his heart" is read as a physical or a moral event, surely this is the crisis of the little poem which makes (Bly comments on his method) "all the images rearrange themselves." A return to the title of the poem evokes a final rearrangement. The ant takes part by being the tiny analogue of the mountain climber and, I imagine, the larger cousin of the bacteria which swarm through the man's heart. The ant is thus placed in the middle of the scale of the created world, and in the middle of the poem. To think about his role rearranges our image of ourselves by diminishing our self-importance.

NOTES

1. Robert Bly, *This Body Is Made of Camphor and Gopherwood* (New York: Harper & Row, 1977), p. 29.

2. *This Body*, p. 29.

3. *This Body*, p. 43.

WILLIAM V. DAVIS

"Still the Place Where Creation Does Some Work on Itself"

Robert Bly's Most Recent Work

The Man in the Black Coat Turns (1981), Robert Bly's most recent book of poems, will inevitably be paired and compared with his first book, *Silence in the Snowy Fields* (1962). This is entirely appropriate since these two books come from the same source and have a similar form as well as the same central tone, mood, and theme. There is, however, one conspicuous difference between them, and since they speak of the same journey in essentially the same way this difference is crucial: *Black Coat* describes the end of the journey which *Silence* began. As such, *Black Coat* is Bly's symbolic turn toward home, the self-referential elegy so many writers come to, whether they are aware of it or not. Bly is, I think, clearly aware of it and, as is his way, moves toward it directly. Just as typically, his turning back here in *Black Coat* is more than a simple return. It is not an end but another new beginning—"still the place where creation does some work on itself," as Bly has translated a line from Tranströmer.[1] Thus, this return is a turning from which he can go forward again. It may well be the beginning Bly has been seeking for some time. But it is also the beginning of the end for him, and he knows it.

In "Eleven O'Clock at Night," the first prose poem in the central second section of *Black Coat,* Bly says: "Many times in poems I have escaped—from myself. . . . Now more and more I long for what I cannot escape from."[2] What is this inescapable residue, so long avoided, and now so conspicuously sought after? If a poet is honest with himself, and Bly is, he knows it is

Previously unpublished, 1982.

himself he seeks, the very self which seeks and has sought him out in the lines of his most authentic poems. In the sense that the poems in *Black Coat* are some of the most authentic poems Bly has written, they tell us a good deal about him, man and poet. They tell us where he has been, where he has gone, and what he returns to.

Paul Tillich has said:

Whenever man has looked at his world, he has found himself in it as a part of it. But he also has realized that he is a stranger in the world of objects, unable to penetrate it beyond a certain level of scientific analysis. And then he has become aware of the fact that he himself is the door to the deeper levels of reality, that in his own existence he has the only possible approach to existence itself.[3]

In *Black Coat* we watch Bly opening the door of the self in a way he has never quite done before. This book is private, personal, in a way Bly has never been. In the metaphor of the man in the black coat Bly adds a major additional element to his thinking and to the scope of his poetry: he becomes the man who "has lived his whole life to create something dark" (19), seeing now how the dark is the core around which the light shines. In terms of the metaphor of *The Light Around the Body,* the dark is here illuminated as that light which must be "risen to," the light "Through which the body moves like a sliding moon."[4]

In *Black Coat* Bly returns again to Boehme, the one thinker he has never abandoned, and adds Boehme's third division of reality to the two he has already developed at considerable length elsewhere. Boehme believes that reality is based on a trinity of emanations through which God realizes his generation and revelation. These three emanations are the fire-world, the light-world, and the dark-world. In rough parallel to this Boehmean system, Bly has developed the first two of these emanations in his earlier work, most specifically in *Silence* and *Light*. Although Bly is as unsystematic and, often, as confusing as Boehme is, it is clear that Boehme's early influence on him has been continuous.[5]

Boehme describes the *Ungrund* in terms of a threefold sequence of emanations which result in the full and final self-revelation of the deity to man. Now, while Bly is not interested in the same ends, he has always found Boehme's thinking suggestive and metaphorically illuminating. In *Black Coat* Boehme's basic notion of the Freedom of the *Ungrund* is crucial to an understanding of Bly's poetic philosophy. For Boehme, the *Ungrund is* Freedom. Further:

Freedom is and resides in darkness, it turns away from the desire for darkness toward the desire for light, it seizes the darkness with its eternal will; and darkness tries to seize the light of freedom and cannot attain it, for darkness closes in again upon itself with its desires, and transforms itself back into darkness.[6]

As Berdyaev indicates:

Boehme was perhaps the first man in the history of human thought to recognize that the foundations of being, prior to being, are unfathomable freedom, the passionate desire of nothing to become something, the darkness in which fire and light are burning. . . .[7]

And since it is the case that light, for Boehme, presupposes the existence of darkness, we can see how the darkness in Bly's *Black Coat* associates itself *as source* with much of what has gone before, developed around the metaphor of light—just as Bly's notion of "leaps" owes something to Boehme's "flash" (*Blitz*), just as his interest in Jungian psychology has its source in Boehme's "mythological consciousness." These continuing associations with Boehme provide the crucial connection between *Black Coat* and Bly's earlier work. As Bly says in the prose poem "The Ship's Captain Looking over the Rail," "When a man steps out at dawn, and breathes in the air, it seems to him that he has lived his whole life to create something dark!"(20). In this sense, the "treasures of darkness" (Isaiah 45:3) prophesied by *Silence* and *Light* are here finally, fully fulfilled.

Jung, another of Bly's major influences, and, like Boehme, one he has also been faithful to from the beginning, describes the development of consciousness this way:

> For the most part our consciousness, in true Western style, looks outwards, and the inner world remains in darkness. But this difficulty can be overcome easily enough, if only we will make the effort to apply the same concentration and criticism to the psychic material which manifests itself, not outside, but in our private lives.[8]

This concentration on private life, more specific now than ever before, is what Bly focuses on in *Black Coat.* And what is even more interesting is that the concentration, now, here, is on the masculine, the fathers and the personal father, where earlier it had been on the mothers and on mother consciousness. Having "righted" the "spiritual balance" toward the feminine in *Sleepers Joining Hands* and elsewhere,[9] Bly now turns back (a man in a black coat turning) to the masculine, in order to, as Stevens would have it, let the fathers fetched "muse much on the tales" that need now to be told.[10]

"So the darkness enters" (21) here, in *Black Coat,* not as something new but as meaning deferred, present always already and prepared for in what has gone before. This mystery at the core of Bly's meaning is celebrated in one of the seminal poems of *Black Coat,* "Fifty Males Sitting Together," which begins/ends:

> After a long walk in the woods clear cut for lumber,
> lit up by a few young pines,
> I turn home,
> drawn to water. A coffinlike shadow
> softens half the lake,
> draws the shadow
> down from westward hills.
> It is a massive
> masculine shadow,
> fifty males sitting together
> in hall or crowded room

lifting something indistinct
up into the resonating night.
. . . .
The dark comes down slowly, the way
snow falls . . . or herds pass the cave.
I look up at the other shore, it is night.

(55, 57)

This dark light has been explicitly available, recently, in Bly since at least the first poem in *Sleepers* where "the darkness appears as flakes of light" (3) but, essentially, it goes back to Bly's beginnings as a poet where it is as pertinent poetically as it has always had to be personally. In "Snowfall in the Afternoon," Bly describes how "a darkness was always there, which we never noticed" and in the "thin man with no coat" riding "the horse of darkness . . . fast to the east" ("The Clear Air of October") we find perhaps the first prefiguration of the man who has now donned the black coat and speaks in the most recent poems.[11] Further, it is conspicuously the case that the obsession with "awakening" so constant in *Silence* occurs inevitably in sleep and death, both darknesses. What Jung calls "the paternal principle, the Logos, . . . eternally struggles to extricate itself from the primal warmth and primal darkness. . . ."[12] As Bly's epigraph to *Silence,* from Boehme, has it: "We are all asleep in the outward man."

What, in one way, and that perhaps the most important one, *Black Coat* seeks to do then is to find out the father(s) so long lost—at least to the dominant metaphor of Bly's poetry (and not, I think, to his life) in the last few years. In this sense, *News of the Universe* is the inevitable historical rediscovery of the poetic fathers, somewhat repressed, just as *Black Coat* is the personal rediscovery of the literal personal father(s). What we have then, in *Black Coat*, is a return, psychologically, to an earlier obsession, that of finding the father. The most explicit poem, before *Black Coat*, to suggest this quest is to be found in *This Body Is Made of Camphor and Gopherwood* and is entitled, appropriately enough, "Finding the Father":

This body offers to carry us for nothing—as the ocean carries logs—
so on some days the body wails with its great energy, it smashes up

241

the boulders, lifting small crabs, that flow around the sides. Someone knocks on the door, we do not have time to dress. He wants us
to come with him through the flowing and rainy streets, to the dark
house. We will go there, the body says, and there find the father
whom we have never met, who wandered in a snowstorm the night
we were born, who then lost his memory, and has lived since longing for his child, whom he saw only once . . . while he worked as a
shoemaker, as a cattle herder in Australia, as a restaurant cook who
painted at night. When you light the lamp you will see him. He sits
there behind the door . . . the eyebrows so heavy, the forehead so
light . . . lonely in his whole body, waiting for you.[13]

This kind of "male energy that disappears" (*Body,* 31) first
comes to the speaker of the poem which precedes "Finding the
Father," entitled, interestingly enough, "The Sleeper." Here, in
a dream, we read, "He came in and sat by my side, and I did not
wake up. . . . Because I am asleep, and the sleeping man is all
withdrawn into himself" (17). If that has been the case with Bly
in the past, it is no longer.[14] In *Black Coat* the speaker is himself
awake, and he is also aware of what he has repressed or, better,
what has been deferred.

In order fully to understand the significance of Bly's accomplishment in *Black Coat* and to appreciate its importance in terms
of his past work it may be helpful to recall Freud's crucial idea of
Nachträglichkeit as well as Heidegger's conception of Dasein's
"thrownness." These two notions provide us with a way of
seeing in Bly's work to date a continuum of accomplishment not
usually noticed and not yet adequately described.

Freud's clearest definition of *Nachträglichkeit* occurs in one of
his letters:

I am working on the assumption that our psychical mecha-
nism has come into being by a process of stratification: the
material present in the form of memory-traces being sub-
jected from time to time to a *rearrangement* in accordance with
fresh circumstances—to a *retranscription*.[15]

Heidegger discusses "the coming [*Kunft*] in which Dasein, in
its ownmost potentiality-for-Being, comes toward itself." He
continues:

. . . taking over thrownness signifies *being* Dasein authentically *as it already was*. Taking over thrownness, however, is possible only in such a way that the futural Dasein can *be* its ownmost "as-it-already was"—that is to say, its "been" [*sein 'Gewesen'*]. Only in so far as Dasein *is* as an "I-*am*-as-having-been," can Dasein come towards itself futurally in such a way that it comes *back*. As authentically futural, Dasein *is* authentically as *"having been."* Anticipation of one's uttermost and ownmost possibility is coming back understandingly to one's ownmost "been." Only so far as it is futural can Dasein *be* authentically as having been. The character of "having been" arises, in a certain way, from the future.[16]

In the directions which these suggestions lead us, *Black Coat* is both the "deferred meaning" of Bly's work (picking up his beginnings) and it is also that which is arising "from the future" in the work he will yet do. Here then, in *Black Coat,* in the most personal and powerful poems he has written, Bly brings past, present and future together. It is no accident that the climatic poem of the book, the one which ties these threads inseparably together, is "My Father's Wedding 1924":

> On my father's wedding day,
> no one was there
> to hold him. Noble loneliness
> held him. Since he never asked for pity
> his friends thought he
> was whole. Walking alone, he could carry it.
>
> He came in limping. It was a simple
> wedding, three
> or four people. The man in black,
> lifting the book, called for order.
> And the invisible bride
> stepped forward, before his own bride.
>
> He married the invisible bride, not his own.
> In her left
> breast she carried the three drops

that wound and kill. He already had
his barklike skin then,
made rough especially to repel the sympathy

he longed for, didn't need, and wouldn't accept.
They stopped. So
the words are read. The man in black
speaks the sentence. When the service
is over, I hold him
in my arms for the first time and the last.

After that he was alone
and I was alone.
No friends came; he invited none.
His two-story house he turned
into a forest,
where both he and I are the hunters.

(49–50)

There is no more fitting or appropriate way to describe the
scope of Bly's career to date than to recall the words of Jacob
Boehme when he said that "all beings move onward until the
end finds the beginning" and "the beginning . . . swallows the
end" and thus "beginning and end turn back into unity."[17] In
The Man in the Black Coat Turns we see Robert Bly turned thus,
back into unity.

NOTES

1. Robert Bly, trans., *Friends, You Drank Some Darkness: Three
Swedish Poets* (Boston: Beacon Press, 1975), p. 255.

2. Robert Bly, *The Man in the Black Coat Turns* (New York: The
Dial Press, 1981), p. 18. Further page references to *Black Coat* will be
included in parentheses in the text.

3. Paul Tillich, *Systematic Theology*. vol. 1 (Chicago: University of
Chicago Press, 1951), p. 62. Bly has recently noted the significance, for
contemporary poetry, of the "new poem," the "object poem, or thing

poem" in his anthology of "poems of twofold consciousness," *News of the Universe* (San Francisco: Sierra Club Books, 1980), pp. 210–14. See below.

4. Robert Bly, *The Light Around the Body* (New York: Harper & Row, 1967), p. 53. Cf. Tertullian: "Resurget igitur caro, et quidem omnis, et quidem ipsa, et quidem integra" (*De Carnis Resurrectione*). Here, of course, Bly has been influenced by Jacob Boehme (see note 5).

5. I have tried to show something of the essential significance of Boehme's thinking on Bly's work in my " 'Hair in a Baboon's Ear': The Politics of Robert Bly's Early Poetry," *Carleton Miscellany,* 18 (Winter 1979–80):74–84.

6. Quoted in Nicolas Berdyaev, *Six Theosophic Points and Other Writings by Jacob Boehme* (Ann Arbor: University of Michigan Press, 1958), pp. xix–xx.

7. Berdyaev, *Six Theosophic Points,* p. xx.

8. C. G. Jung, *Two Essays on Analytical Psychology,* trans. R. F. C. Hull (Princeton: Princeton University Press, 1966), p. 198. Cf. Julian Jaynes's treatment of the development of consciousness in *The Origin of Consciousness in the Breakdown of the Bicameral Mind* (Boston: Houghton Mifflin, 1976).

9. Robert Bly, *Sleepers Joining Hands* (New York: Harper & Row, 1973), p. 50. Further page references to *Sleepers* will be included in parentheses in the text. For my reading of this phase of Bly's work see my " 'At the Edges of the Light': A Reading of Robert Bly's *Sleepers Joining Hands,*" *Poetry East* no. 4/5 (Spring/Summer 1981):265–82. (This essay is also included in *Of Solitude and Silence: Writings on Robert Bly,* ed. Richard Jones and Kate Daniels (Boston: Beacon Press, 1981), pp. 250–67.)

10. Wallace Stevens, *The Collected Poems* (New York: Alfred A. Knopf, 1971), p. 415. Bly has said of Stevens that he "is one of the few American poets whose work carries the values of an entire clan" (*Missouri Review* 5 [Fall 1979]:190). Bly has long been interested in Stevens, in several ways, as is indicated by the fact that the sixth poem of *Silence* is entitled "Thinking of Wallace Stevens on the First Snowy Day in December."

11. Robert Bly, *Silence in the Snowy Fields* (Middletown, Conn.: Wesleyan University Press, 1962), pp. 60, 52.

12. C. G. Jung, *Four Archetypes,* trans. R. F. C. Hull (Princeton: Princeton University Press, 1970), p. 30.

13. Robert Bly, *This Body Is Made of Camphor and Gopherwood* (New York: Harper & Row, 1977), p. 19. The ellipses here are Bly's. Further page references to *This Body* will be included in parentheses in the text.

14. I have dealt with the metaphor of sleep and awakening in my article "'Hair in a Baboon's Ear': The Politics of Robert Bly's Early Poetry" referred to earlier (see esp. pp. 78ff.).

15. Letter to Wilhelm Fliess, December 6, 1896, in Sigmund Freud, *The Standard Edition of the Complete Psychological Works of Sigmund Freud,* vol. 1, trans. James Strachey (London: Hogarth Press, 1966), p. 233. Cf. Freud, *Standard Edition,* vol. 2, pp. 161 ff.; vol. 3, p. 167; vol. 17, p. 45, *passim.* Commenting on this Fliess letter Harold Bloom suggests that "Freud seems to imply that *Nachträglichkeit* rises in response to situations where impulses and impressions sense that they must reserve themselves for another time . . ." (*Poetry and Repression* [New Haven: Yale University Press, 1976], p. 288.)

16. Martin Heidegger, *Being and Time,* trans. John Macquarrie and Edward Robinson (New York: Harper & Row, 1962), p. 373.

17. See Jacob Boehme, *Psychologia Vera,* in *Sämmtliche Werke,* ed. K. W. Schiebler, vol. 6 (Leipzig: J. A. Barth, 1846), pp. 18–19.

PART TWO   *Reviews, Conversations,*
Memoirs, Poems

DONALD HALL

From the Introduction to
Contemporary American Poetry

One thing is happening in American poetry, as I see it, which is
genuinely new. In lines like Robert Bly's:

> In small towns the houses are built right on the ground;
> The lamplight falls on all fours in the grass.

or Louis Simpson's:

> The clouds are lifting from the high Sierras,
> The Bay mists clearing;
> And the angel in the gate, the flowering plum,
> Dances like Italy, imagining red.

there is a kind of imagination new to American poetry. The
vocabulary is mostly colloquial, but the special quality of the
lines has nothing to do with an area of diction; it is a quality
learned neither from T. S. Eliot nor William Carlos Williams. It
is a quality closer to the spirit of Georg Trakl or Pablo Neruda,
but it is not to be pigeon-holed according to any sources. This
imagination is irrational, yet the poem is usually quiet and the
language simple; there is no straining after apocalypse. There is
an inwardness to these images, a profound subjectivity. Yet they
are not subjective in the autobiographical manner of *Life Studies*
or *Heart's Needle,* which are confessional and particular.

The movement which seems to me *new* is subjective but not
autobiographical. It reveals through images not particular pain,
but general subjective life. This universal subjective corresponds

From *Contemporary American Poetry,* edited by Donald Hall (Baltimore: Penguin
Books, 1962; 1969), pp. 24–25. Reprinted with permission.

to the old objective life of shared experience and knowledge. People can talk to each other most deeply in images. To read a poem of this sort, you must not try to translate the images into abstractions. They won't go. You must try to be open to them, to let them take you over and speak in their own language of feeling. It is the intricate darkness of feeling and instinct which these poems mostly communicate. The poems are best described as expressionist: like the painter, the poet uses fantasy and distortion to express feeling. The poet may hesitate, when he is looking for a word, between opposites; would "tiny" or "huge" be better here?, "mountain" or "valley"? Such hesitation shows the irrationality and the arbitrariness of this method, but it does not imply that one of the alternatives is not enormously more appropriate than the other—only that neither is literal. The reader or the poet cannot go to the outside world and *check*—Ah, yes, the Empire State Building is "huge" not "tiny"—but we are not concerned with accuracy to externals; he can only make a subjective check with his inward world.

NORMAN FRIEDMAN

From "The Wesleyan Poets—III:
The Experimental Poets"

Silence in the Snowy Fields (1962) is characterized by sharp images, abrupt juxtapositions, loose rhythms, and natural diction. These poems are spoken by a man who is quizzically observant, deeply responsive, and restless and dissatisfied. Techniques and style, therefore, embody poetic vision. Curiously, we are in a world very much like [James] Dickey's—that of the Middle West—and imagery of horses, moonlight, and water predominates, but nothing can be further from Dickey's diffuse wooliness than Bly's concentrated clarity. The influence of Williams appears once again, but it is more real here than in Tram Combs. And yet there are similes in Bly, and more than an echo here and there of the complex richness of Dylan Thomas. Take, for example, "Waking from Sleep," which I quote entire:

Inside the veins there are navies setting forth,
Tiny explosions at the water lines,
And seagulls weaving in the wind of the salty blood.

It is the morning. The country has slept the whole winter.
Window seats were covered with fur skins, the yard was full
Of stiff dogs, and hands that clumsily held heavy books.

Now we wake, and rise from bed, and eat breakfast!—
Shouts rise from the harbor of the blood,
Mist, and masts rising, the knock of wooden tackle in the sunlight.

Now we sing, and do tiny dances on the kitchen floor.
Our whole body is like a harbor at dawn;
We know that our master has left us for the day.

Chicago Review 19 (1967):52–73. Reprinted with permission of the author.

The poem beings with suggestions of Thomas, and ends with suggestions of Williams, but the whole is entirely Bly's, with its characteristically understated yet fully realized energy.

The book is divided into three titled sections. The first is called "Eleven Poems of Solitude," and in stanzalike groups of irregular lines it presents hard images of night and winter in the Midwest: bare stalks of corn, snow, denuded trees, solitary barns, and so on. And yet the mood is not of a waste land but rather of earth's cycles and man's durability. Light from barn windows can be seen through bare trees ("Three Kinds of Pleasures," "Fall"); leaves will return to the trees after absence ("Return to Solitude"); spring will come back ("Waking from Sleep"); and the coming snow will be beautiful, "like jewels of a murdered Gothic prince" ("Approaching Winter").

Bly is not a formal poet for more reasons than that he eschews conventional rhyme and meter. More basically it is because his is not only an outdoor world but also a world which the speaker lives in and responds to directly—not as a tourist, landscapist, or dilettante, but as a man in the agony of searching for himself, and for whom the external world has real and objective existence. And he is an experimental poet not simply because he writes in free rhythms and easy diction, but more because of the way in which his imagination releases startling perspectives from a bright perception of the ordinary. Here is "Poem in Three Parts," for example, which I give in full:

I
Oh, on an early morning I think I shall live forever!
I am wrapped in my joyful flesh,
As the grass is wrapped in its clouds of green.

II
Rising from a bed, where I dreamt
Of long rides past castles and hot coals,
The sun lies happily on my knees;
I have suffered and survived the night
Bathed in dark water, like any blade of grass.

III

The strong leaves of the box-elder tree,
Plunging in the wind, call us to disappear
Into the wilds of the universe,
Where we shall sit at the foot of a plant,
And live forever, like the dust.

The sequence of moods and images here is not smooth, but neither does this disjunction become incoherent, as it does in Ashbery. The second section does follow from the first, both in action and in image (he awakens happily after a difficult night, and the grass serves intelligibly as a symbol of each mood), but there is nevertheless a strangeness developing in these sections which will be consummated in the third. To be "wrapped" in his flesh, for grass to be "wrapped" in "clouds of green," to dream of castles and hot coals, to have the sun on his knees, to have suffered as a blade of grass bathed in dark water—all this is to create a world which is at once surrealistic and yet objectively convincing, for the experience out of which it arises is a common and significant one, and it arises from it in a natural and inevitable way.

But the third section seems to jump entirely out of the realm of the familiar. Yet taking the happy awakening and the night of suffering—seeing the one in terms of the other, as it were—it does project the whole mood appropriately into mystery, suggesting the speaker's sense of merging with rocks and stones and trees, a merging which promises, although it suggests death, eternal life in the release from the cycles of human anguish and joy. The speaker's survival from nightmare to ecstasy has released him from both, and the overlapping and abrupt images embody effectively the quiet wildness of the experience.

The second section is called "Awakening," and the speaker's search comes closer to the surface. Here are even more surrealistic images of disquiet, where to be awake is to be asleep, and to be asleep is to be awake. Poems of the restless self, a sense of social protest appears together with images of history and of the impingement of the world at large on the Midwest. Love and death mingle, and the peace and pleasure and anger of moments of illumination emerge. Self-questioning and self-confrontation are portrayed directly, as in Simpson and faintly in the later Dickey: "Having accomplished nothing, I am travelling somewhere else" ("On the Ferry Across Chesapeake Bay"); the wonderfully effective "A Man Writes to a Part of Himself"; "My body was sour, my life dishonest, . . . / Now I want to go back among the dark roots" ("Depression"); in the brief but marvelous "Watering the Horse":

> How strange to think of giving up all ambition!
> Suddenly I see with such clear eyes
> The white flake of snow
> That has just fallen in the horse's mane!

In the third section, "Silence on the Roads," the imagery of moonlight, animals, water, and ships begins to accumulate, and the speaker's recovered self seems more at ease in a more humanized world: "After many strange thoughts, / Thoughts of distant harbors, and new life, / I came in and found the moonlight lying in the room" ("After Working"); "The human face shines like a dark sky / As it speaks of those things that oppress the living" ("Late at Night During a Visit of Friends"); and so on.

What, then, is lacking? For all its pleasures, the poetry of Bly is too taut, too tight, and too economical for comfort. Aiming at deep, hard, direct, and clear presentation, he succeeds only too well. Wanting to avoid the fuzzy, the verbose, and the prosaic, he evades ideas and feelings, creating a world that is too hokkulike, too cameolike, too Imagistic. And too self-absorbed: there are almost no other realized people in this book, and the speaker's moody brooding is indeed silent, conducted in solitude, and uncomfortably muted. There is a point beyond which intensity becomes suffocating, and it's as if the poet were hoarding a too-meager gift. The spaciousness and mystery of his best poems are too often defeated by the smallness and closeness of his average work. What Bly needs is something to fire him to risk more sustainedly passionate work—but without costing him his precious and hard-won intensity—and I am not sure his recent protests against the war in Vietnam are what I have in mind.

From *Spinning the Crystal Ball*

The other "movement" around is the one headed up by Robert Bly, out of Madison, Minnesota. As professional soldiers say of the particular war they're fighting in at the time, "It ain't much, but it's the only one we got." Bly believes that the salvation of English poetry is to be found in non-English poetry, particularly in Spanish and French and German, understood as badly as possible. One does translations, taking as many liberties as one wants to take with the original, it being understood that this enables one somehow to approach the "spirit" of the poet one is translating. If I had time I would talk some about surrealism, for the French and Spanish surrealist poets are very much the bell-wethers of the Bly faction. But it might be better to quote a couple of things to show you the end results. This is Bly's "Approaching Winter."

I
September. Clouds. The first day for wearing jackets.
The corn is wandering in dark corridors,
Near the well and the whisper of tombs.

II
I sit alone surrounded by dry corn,
Near the second growth of the pigweeds,
And hear the corn leaves scrape their feet on the wind.

III
Fallen ears are lying on the dusty earth.
The useful ears will lie dry in cribs, but the others, missed
By the picker, will lie here touching the ground the whole winter.

Spinning the Crystal Ball (Washington, D.C.: Library of Congress, 1967), pp. 8–10.

IV
Snow will come, and cover the husks of the fallen ears
With flakes infinitely delicate, like jewels of a murdered Gothic
    prince
Which were lost centuries ago during a great battle.

Here is another poem, called "Thinking of Robert Bly and James Wright on the First Hot Day in April After Having Stayed up Late All Night Drinking and Singing With a Gang of Old Norwegian Trolls." (Bly is Norwegian.)

> Whenever I think of you,
> Tiny white horses gallop away in darkness.
> I am lulled by the sound of old guitars
> Strummed by ghostly fingers of the wind.
>
> Your gentleness is like beautiful white snow
> Drifting down on ancient homesteads
> Over lonely prairies in Tennessee;
> And you are falling, falling softly down.
>
> America is falling also
> Into dark cathedrals of the sea.
> But what is that to me?
> I am oblivious to missile siloes in Minnesota.
>
> I lie here in the holy darkness
> Listening to cornstalks creaking,
> Thinking I have ruined myself
> Climbing over a pale barbed-wire fence.

Now, though this latter poem is a conscious parody—it came to me in the mail the other day—the writer said he turned it out, without changing a word, as fast as he could type. Though, as I say, it is a parody, it really isn't, for it is completely undistinguishable from the seriously intended poems it models itself on. It has the same particular faults and characteristics as its model: the sentimentality, the attempt to link up all sorts of disparate items—snow, corn, jewels of murdered princes, missile siloes, and so on—in a kind of loose emotional mental drifting having a bogus, unearned conclusion. The parody is as good and as bad as the original. Above all, it is as arbitrary. This is essentially a derivative, imitative, extremely lazy, unimaginative poetry: small, static, and very easy to write. It lacks *necessity* of statement; it cannot sustain narrative. If the salvation of American poetry is to write imitation Spanish poems, even that will have to be done better than this. But no such salvation is indicated, even if it were possible. We have a lot more going for us than that.

ROBERT MAZZOCCO

From "Jeremiads at Half-Mast"

The Light Around the Body is a meditation on politics, fatigue, failure, war, where we are now. In its theme and sensibility, its eerie passivity and suppressed anguish, it is, I suppose, a jeremiad at half-mast.

> The President dreams of invading Cuba.
> Bushes are growing over the outdoor grills,
> Vines over the yachts and the leather seats.
>
> ("The Great Society")

All of the poems in Robert Bly's second collection spread themselves in the same sad, gray, moonlit language, the emotions deceptively bedded deep below the surface, a sort of postcontemplative, postsurrealist style, the mind drained of its data, possibility wrung dry. Yet, too, the poems seem ennobled by the small rightness of tone, images, indictment, and modest urgency of the poet's response.

Like Thoreau and Tolstoy, Robert Bly is a Puritan at heart. I think he would renounce art for truth, the imagination for "reality," and both, should he be forced to do so, for morality— perhaps an unappealing middle-western morality, thin-lipped, reedy, self-righteous. In Bly's America, an America very much of the moment, everything's a cheat, or everything's *ersatz,* or everything becomes so, even, at times, Nature. The silence in the snowy fields (the title of the poet's first collection) becomes here the official silence of injustice, or the babble of the insane.

New York Review of Books, June 20, 1968, pp. 22–25. Copyright © 1968 *New York Review of Books.* Reprinted with permission.

> Bishops rush about crying, There is no war,
> And bombs fall,
> Leaving a dust on the beech trees . . .
>
> ("War and Silence")

The good Germans drink cokes and watch the hockey match, dressed in different suits, different roles, but aimless, apprehensive. The swinging society swims into sight like some barren planet tufted with tokens of USA today: "Tiny loaves of bread with ears lie on the President's table." The President is the great devourer, the smyler with the knyfe beneath the cloke, everyone's monster. . . .

Bly is a strange poet, austere yet tender. A sense of distaste or personal disquiet haunts much of his work: the poet himself, in his wayward, intensely musing way, drawn close to disintegration. But he is also strong-willed, carefully armored, defensively settled in his beliefs and sense of place or of history. He is tremendously subjective, but his subjectivity has always been pitted against objectivity. In *Silence in the Snowy Fields* the contrast was between his self-enclosure and his everyday existence, his Minnesota farm, horses, hunting. In *The Light Around the Body* the dramaturgy is that of the poet's interior journey through Vietnam, imperialism abroad, materialism at home. The new poems are political, but not agitprop.

Very likely all of these poems should really be read as one poem, or as a set of variations on a single complaint. "Merchants have multiplied more than the stars of heaven," a sardonic echo of Kant's "the moral law within and the starry heavens above," is the first line of the first poem. Luxury, indolence, boredom, the TV set, the Chase National Bank, Johnson's cabinet, people existing in an affectless calculating well-fed indifference—these thematic properties appear again and again, giving an air of noxious confinement. "Accountants hover over the earth like helicopters / Dropping bits of paper engraved with Hegel's name"—system-building estrangement, decision-making machinery all about man, beyond man.

Throughout, the tendency is to present a fantasylike landscape of drift and disjunction, or scenes from our day in a more or less newsreel setting:

The saint is born among tin cans in the orchard;
....
Black beetles, bright as Cadillacs, toil down
The long dusty road into the mountains of South Dakota.

>   ("The Current Administration")

Narrow-eyed pitiless montages. The indifferent voice of the
news media tripping over the wires, the bulletins, antiseptic,
caressing: "We have violet rays that light up the jungles at night,
showing / The friendly populations . . ." Figures from the past
(Jackson, Theodore Roosevelt, Kennedy) are introduced, democratic institutions seen as another form of deceit or detachment,
the American dream disappearing in conquest, avarice, recriminations:

Last night we argued about the Marines invading Guatemala in 1947,
The United Fruit Company had one water spigot for 200 families,
And the ideals of America, our freedom to criticize,
The slave systems of Rome and Greece, and no one agreed.

>   ("Sleet Storm on Merritt Parkway")

The focus is the Vietnam War, though many of the poems
dealing with it are among the least successful in the collection.
Here the psychological and political footholds grow deeper and
duller, a drudging back and forth, the tone hardening. Often
Bly's imaginative resources get lost in the purity of his appeal,
the sensitivity seeming secondary to the Jacobian effects. The
particulars themselves become abstractions, like the titles:
"Asian Peace Offers Rejected without Publication." Beyond
that, an amorphous lament, suggesting the smash up of the great
society in slow motion, with the poet as the dying commentator, recording the split in man and his two worlds, identity
and environment, the inner and the outer, and in another part of
the morass, history thrashing about fatalistically, intent on a
wrong turning, a cornered beast. . . .

Let me present a typical poem:

> There is another darkness,
> A darkness in the fences of the body,

And in moles running, and telephone wires,
And the frail ankles of horses;
Darkness of dying grass, and yellow willow leaves;
There is the death of broken buttonholes,
Of brutality in high places,
Of lying reporters,
There is a bitter fatigue, adult and sad.

The poem is called "Listening to President Kennedy Lie about the Cuban Invasion." But it seems to me it could just as well have been called "Watching Television" or "Turning Away from Lies" or "The Hermit" or practically any of the other titles in Robert Bly's collection. Like most of Bly's work, the poem is distinctive and arresting, with its own sort of spiraling queerness ("the fences of the body," "the death of broken buttonholes"), but many of its lines could be transplanted quite easily into neighboring poems, and lines from neighboring poems transplanted right back into the empty spaces, with few readers the wiser.

Bly has arranged his volume in five sections, with each of the sections repeating some theme, some nuance from every other section. Demarcations are made only to evaporate or overlap. So the most damaging remark to be leveled against *The Light Around the Body,* even while granting its necessarily oppressive or "alienated" atmosphere, is that there's still something monotonous in the cumulative effect, and something a little arbitrary in its aesthetic strategy. After a while, too, the political content, I'm afraid, seems predictable, even pious. Some of the poems, for instance, suggest hapless mutations, an "ironic" cross between *The Other America* and *Thinking About the Unthinkable,* or copy from the *National Guardian* and the *National Review* inexplicably entangled—an all-too-easy, and currently all-too-familiar, juxtaposition of the Left and Right, the angelic and satanic, the pop apocalyptic. "Tonight they throw the firebombs, tomorrow / They read the Declaration of Independence." "Rusk's assistants eat hurriedly / Talking of Teilhard de Chardin." The anger in the first statement, and the satire in the second, come across as purely perfunctory, or as wasted gestures.

No doubt, it is easy enough to assent to Bly's political commitments. Certainly they are warranted by the times. But time is fickle. Auden on the Spanish Civil War, some of Brecht, some of Neruda, Aragon's *Front Rouge*—you can't really say there have been many lasting marriages between politics and poetry, not in our culture, probably not in any culture.

Actually, the one instance that I know of where the individual imagination and what Marxists call a revolutionary consciousness do *naturally* engage each other, is in the work of Cesar Vallejo, the comparatively unheralded Peruvian poet and Loyalist fighter who died in Paris in the late thirties and whose grave and beautiful poems have, not surprisingly, influenced Bly. Also, I believe, through Bly's example, others such as James Wright ("Eisenhower's Visit to Franco, 1959") and W. S. Merwin ("The Asians Dying"). What Bly seems to share with, or has taken over from, Vallejo, aside from technical models (the Peruvian's singular metaphors, dry lyricism, the movement from the colloquial to the obscure and vice versa), is a feeling of loss or isolation so pervasive, or so famished by, or for, experience, that surrender to it is all: a new sort of stoicism, a new humility arises.

Paradoxically, too, there's the creation of an underlying communion with man and nature and the pressure of the times— especially in Vallejo, who knew poverty and imprisonment. No thunderous statements are made. Instead, the poetry presents an accretion of small illuminations, sunken images, memories, contacts, a dream world, but without the flamboyance and libidinal extremity of dreams—with the impenetrability of dreams, but more earthy, lifelike, Vallejo, undoubtedly, is an important figure, piercingly human, full of blindingly right moments or accents which once heard, even if the reader's understanding of Spanish is rudimentary, he does not forget:

> Cesar Vallejo ha muerto, le pagaban
> todos sin que el les haga nada . . .

Bly is more ascetic, thinner in texture and ideas, a little edgy and evangelical. Bly is always seeking to atone:

Therefore we will have
To go far away
To atone
For the sufferings of the stringy-chested
And the small rice-fed ones, quivering
In the helicopter like wild animals,
Shot in the chest, taken back to be questioned.
("Driving through Minnesota during the Hanoi Bombings")

In the concluding poems the poet retreats to a private demesne, robbed of growth and purpose, becoming an analogue of contemporary disrelation and affluence: melancholic interior mutterings, new fallen snow, a funeral, waters rising, wind "rising, swelling, / Swirling over everything alive," a ship sinking. Later, the dying bull "bleeding on the mountain" till the "mountains alter and become the sea." "The Executive's Death," the opening poem of the collection, is a mosaic of decay; the final poem, "When the Dumb Speak," a muted celebration of innocence. As prefaces to four of the sections there are quotations from Jacob Boehme, pretty much the Boehme of *Life Against Death,* the chapter entitled "The Resurrection of the Body."

The remarkable quality in Robert Bly's work is the detail: it is clear cut, disturbingly imagistic, at times cunningly evocative, with rarely a word produced by sloth or insensitivity, as in "Opening an Oyster." Still, unlike Vallejo, unfortunately, little on the whole really quickens, really develops, little's revelatory. More than anything, there's always that sense of movement across vast stretches of waste, or a sense of sequences and impressions enacted in double focus: the sociopolitical notations of condemnations, and a series of mystical redemptive rendezvous, *pro remedio animae* à la Boehme. With Bly, the politics of concern, however heartfelt, tend to sound somewhat hortatory, nagging, secondhand. With Vallejo, both the political temper and the particular psychology are indelibly inscribed: instinct, indictment, vision are one, sans any intimation of posture at all. . . .

LOUIS SIMPSON

From *North of Jamaica*

Robert Bly grew up on a farm in Minnesota and went to St. Olaf's College—the only other person I knew of who had gone to St. Olaf's was the Great Gatsby—then to Harvard, and had spent a few years thinking for himself. When I met him in New York his outer garment—the blue or grey business suit that even poets were wearing in the fifties—disguised a seething mind. He bought a Viking helmet with horns and contemplated wearing it to poetry-readings.

Bly was dissatisfied with nearly everything that had been taking place recently in American poetry and was looking for new ideas. He had been reading modern Spanish poets in particular. His own writing up to this point was typical of the 1940–1950 younger poets; he had been as able as anyone to write rhymed stanzas in literary language, but now he was growing irritated with this and searching for new ways of poetry in the writings of

> Pablo Neruda . . . Garcia Lorca and Cesar Vallejo; in the Swedish tradition, Ekelof, in the French Char and Michaux, in the German Trakl and Benn—all of them writing in what we have called, for want of a better word, the new imagination, and making contributions to that imagination as enormous as Eliot's or Pound's and with a totally different impact, and on totally different roads.

Bly wanted poems that would not explain everything in the plodding, rationalistic way of the poetry of the forties. The new

---

North of Jamaica (New York: Harper & Row, 1972), pp. 208–16. Copyright © 1972 by Louis Simpson. Reprinted by permission of Harper & Row, Publishers, Inc.

poems would be based not on English tradition, nor upon the—in Bly's opinion—exclusive, snobbish, psychically crippling ideas of critics such as T. S. Eliot and Allen Tate. Away with abstract language! Down with literary writing! Bly wanted writings in images, and the images must be new.

His description of the new images, however, was vague. He thought that the Imagists had been merely making pictures, and the images of the French Surrealists came out of trivial associations, they lacked depth. The new image would be "deep." Bly found the Spanish Surrealists more to his taste.

> An imagination, a content, a style exists that has a magnificence of suggestion and association. I think it is mistaken to think that if we work in this style our works will resemble Eliot's or Pound's. Two things make me think different. First, some profundity of association has entered the mind since then. Freud's ocean has deepened, and Jung's work on images has been done. To Pound an image meant "Petals on a wet black bough." To us an image is "death on the deep roads of the guitar" or "the grave of snow" or "the cradle-clothes of the sea."

What would be the difference between Bly's use of surrealistic images and the old kinds? It was easy to see what he was against, but not so easy to see what he would make that would be new. That would depend on the quality of the life of the poet himself. If this surrealism were new, it would be so because it was written by men who were not French or Spanish, but American. So, at the same time that Bly's new magazine *The Fifties* spoke of neglected avant-garde traditions in Europe, South America and China, it was furiously American, printing poems that spoke of American earth, farm landscapes and highways. It was a curious, and at times awkward, combination of eclectic theorizing and local colour.

In his own poems Bly seemed to be trying to reconcile the irreconcilable.

> the gold animals, the lions, and the zebras, and the pheasants,
> Are waiting at the head of the stairs with robbers' eyes.
>
> ("The Clear Air of October")

He asked for a poetry that would include "the dark figures of politics, the world of street cars, and the ocean world"—by the ocean he meant "this profound life," a life of the spirit. It is easier to call for spiritual life than to represent it in poems, and yet he was beginning, in certain poems about Minnesota, to give the sensation of his ideas.

> How strange to think of giving up all ambition!
> Suddenly I see with such clear eyes
> The white flake of snow
> That has just fallen in the horse's mane!
>
> ("Watering the Horses")

My tastes in poetry were frequently different from Bly's. I thought that some of the South American poems—maybe as a result of translation into English—were just a series of ecstatic exclamations. The poem was in a rapture with itself; it would finish abruptly and seem to be waiting for the reader to say, "Astonishing! Fantastic!" The reader was expected to be continually in a posture of amazement.

> The eye of a pistol wept dark tears,
> And smiles came from the ocean.

Maybe there was some resonance to the images, but I thought you would have to be in Chile to feel it. You couldn't just transplant objects or turns of speech from one culture to another—they didn't take. South American Surrealists might be deep, but translated into English they were not interesting.

Also, poetry is an experience rather than a statement—prose is for statements—and some of the poets Bly recommended seemed to be merely talking.

> Grief, my great laborer,
> Grief, be seated,
> Be still,
> Let us be still a little you and I,
> Be still,
> You are finding me, you are proving me . . .

But the ideas brought forward in *The Fifties* were stimulating—at least they were more useful to poets than what you could find in the *Hudson Review* or the *New Yorker*. Though I would never write in the manner of the Spaniards, Germans or Scandinavians Bly was publishing, my writing was sharpened by our talks. Besides, the iconoclasm was refreshing; we agreed vehemently about things we did not like.

While praising the poets he admired, some of whom were obscure, Bly attacked the poets he disliked, especially those who were entrenched, and so he made enemies. Also, as an editor he seemed unable to play the game according to the rules agreed upon by editors of literary magazines. It is practically unheard of for one editor to criticize another's magazine, for all have to make a living. This is particularly true in New York. Not only do they agree not to criticize one another for practical reasons, but also they are linked by friendship and even by marriage. If an editor has a wife with literary ambitions, her name will soon appear on the masthead of another magazine as one of their editors. This is the Liberal Establishment, and it resembles the foreign policy of the United States—as they are Liberal, whatever they think must be right. These Liberals pride themselves on having independent opinions about Civil Rights, foreign movies, the war in Vietnam, hard-edge painting, et cetera—but they all have the same ideas. The article that appears in *Commentary* could just as well have appeared in the *New York Review of Books,* and they do not print anything of which they would not all approve.

This, on the other hand, was Bly's style:

AWARD

The Order of the Blue Toad is herewith awarded to Norman Cousins, editor of the *Saturday Review,* for putting out a boring, stupid magazine. His list of reviewers is enough to make anyone die of boredom—Granville Hicks, Doris Betts, Ben Ray Redman, Alma Lutz, Vincent Sheean, Lynn Montross, Stanley M. Swinton, *et al.* Why waste paper on such junk? The only good things *Saturday Review* has published in the last five years were Schweitzer's atom-test appeal, and Ciardi's blast against Anne Morrow Lindbergh. However, someone soon quenched Ciardi's ardor; and his department has now settled down to the same level of mediocrity as the rest of the magazine.

Such remarks were insulting, and Bly's habit of mentioning the social or political implications of a poem struck some people as being in very poor taste. Writing was a game played by gentlemen, and to bring in personalities or to argue about politics was as unwelcome as a serious discussion at a cocktail party.

Poets who published in *The Fifties* were soon thought of as a group, for people are not happy unless they can label everything. I do not think that the *Fifties* poets—later, of course, the *Sixties*—were cohesive enough to be called a group, but they did have qualities in common. They differed from poets such as Nemerov, products of the New Criticism, in that they wished to speak with a personal voice; and differed from the Beat and confessional poets in that they wished to write about something more than the surface of life. They wanted to discover "deep" images. Their poetry would represent the unconscious.

The poems of James Wright, Robert Bly, Donald Hall, John Haines, Galway Kinnell, William Stafford, David Ray, and others, were a continuation of the "modernist" experiments of Pound, the Imagists and the Surrealists. The *Fifties* poets imported models from Germany, Scandinavia, Spain and South America. There was even a Minnesotan way of writing a Chinese poem. As I describe it, this movement may not seem new, but actually it was, in the sense that it was continuing an experimental movement that was never fulfilled in America.

During the thirties and forties poetry in America and Britain turned its back on the modernism of 1910, the experimentalism of the young Pound, Stevens, Cummings and Williams. Due to the New Criticism, poetry in the United States became a formalistic imitation of metaphysical verse, or under the influence of Auden a retailing of journalistic ideas. Modernism in English stopped before it had barely started, and the age that in other countries saw such poets as Pablo Neruda develop to their full stature, in the United States produced poetry of a conventional kind. It would be interesting to account for this retraction of the spirit; I think it was caused by the Depression, in the imagination of poets as well as in economics, but I must leave this for someone else to explore. The poetry of *The Fifties* was a renewal of the aborted modernism of the generation of 1910. There is not a great difference between some of the poetry of James Wright and this translation by Pound, in *Cathay,* 1915:

> Ko-jin goes west from Kō-kaku-ro,
> The smoke-flowers are blurred over the river.
> His lone sail blots the far sky.
> And now I see only the river,
> > The long Kiang, reaching heaven.

Here is the naming of objects, then the imaginative leap from object to heaven, or to the interior world of the psyche, that is characteristic of Wright. In one of his recent poems Wright says:

> Close by a big river, I am alive in my own country,
> I am home again.
> Yes: I lived here, and here, and my name,
> That I carved young, with a girl's, is healed over, now.
> And lies sleeping beneath the inward sky
> Of a tree's skin . . .

A movement from the outward, objective world, toward the inner world of the psyche—this is practically Imagism as Pound described it. In an Imagist poem, Pound said, "one is trying to record the precise instant when a thing outward and objective transforms itself, or darts into a thing inward and subjective."

The *Fifties* poets were rooted in American landscapes, somewhat to the bewilderment of New York reviewers who could not believe that anyone took nature seriously. It was evident from the rise of poets such as these that American poetry would not be confined, as English poetry had been, by the opinions of a single literary capital. Minnesota and Seattle were as good places for poetry as New York and in some ways more stimulating.

In speaking of the *Fifties* poets I seem to have fallen into the cliché I have criticized—thinking of poets as a group. Every true poet is *essentially* different from other poets. Yet poets are not autonomous; they need other people and other people's ideas. It is true that a poet usually finds out about poetry by himself and begins his work in solitude, thinking that no one else is doing the same sort of thing. But then he discovers that other poets have been moving along the same line, for all have been influenced by the ideas of their time. For a while these people agree; they write letters to one another and meet and discuss ideas; they may publish a magazine, issue manifestos, and make anthologies. Then the group splits apart, each one going his own way. But their criticism of one another has had far-reaching consequences. So it was with Pound. But for the thinking he did in conjunction with T. E. Hulme, Ford Madox Ford, and Eliot, Pound would not have developed into a major poet. So it was with the "Oxford poets" of the thirties: Auden, Spender, MacNeice, and C. Day Lewis. Their poems were remarkably similar. They referred to the gasworks, and spies, and History; they spoke of the same heroes—Homer Lane, Marx, and Freud. And so it is today. I believe that Denise Levertov no longer considers herself a follower of Olson, Ginsberg wishes no longer to be called Beat, and James Dickey is now loth to be associated with Bly; but at crucial moments these poets shared certain ideas with other poets and the moments determined the kind of poetry they would go on to write.

KEEPING ABREAST, OR HOMAGE TO
PABLO NERUDA PERHAPS

> Yesterday I met Thomas.
> He was wearing a cloak and smoking marihuana,
> and in his hip pocket he carried a volume
> of Pablo Neruda.
> "What is this, Thomas?" I said.
> "Are you going to a masquerade?"
>
> "I have cast off my old ways," he answered,
> "and I advise you to do the same.
> It is all testicles nowadays and light,
> and a series of ecstatic exclamations."
> Whereupon he struck the guitar

which he produced from his briefcase,
and began to sing of various mountains
in Chile. The stars figured prominently
and there was talk of the full testicles of night.

"Thomas," I said, "is this the new poetry?"

"It is the new world," he replied.

This kind of answer always leaves me feeling foolish.

Alas, I am outmoded.
But that is always the way—you read Rilke
and think you're safe for a while,
and then comes along a Neruda.
What did I ever do to Pablo Neruda?
I cannot take to hanging out in cafés,
and my Spanish is bad.
I am incurably addicted to the old kinds of poems.

The carob trees are preparing a corrida,
and I am the bull.
Death death death death . . .
They are chanting for the death of the old poetry.
O why was I ever taught anything?
Star, bird, light, and the breasts of Peruvian virgins—
these are, it seems, what is wanted.
The curved blade hangs in the air—
my carcass is roped to the heels of the mules.
Tomás, Tomás—a nice boy from Amherst,
a nice Jewish boy . . . if you could become a surrealist,
maybe I could too.
                    Tell me I still have a hope!

DONALD HALL

Notes on Robert Bly and
Sleepers Joining Hands

This is not a "review," partly because transitions are fatuous; transitions and order translate "notes" into "review" or "article." And partly because I have no objectivity. This poet has been my friend for twenty-five years.

Bly is the most systematic poet in the United States. Gary Snyder is second. Both men are learned, eclectic priests. Both are born teachers, neither teaches at a college. Snyder is more accurate than Bly, in his learning; Bly is wilder in his weddings of the unweddable. Bly is more inclusive; Snyder only recently approaches the west, by way of cave paintings; Bly moves like a huge hummingbird from Jung flower to Zen flower, from the Buddha to the Great Mother. Snyder writes lines loving the motion and the feel of language. Bly seems mostly unaware of this pleasure. If Bly could write his poems in amino acids or bird calls, he would just as lief; the spirit matters to him, and not the shoulders of consonants.

Twenty years ago, before he had published poems to anyone's notice, Bly started to write a series of books of poems with titles like *The Road to Poverty and Death*. These books represented different stages of the soul's journey. At first, the books were rather thin. They have become fuller, over the years. Bly has increased his range, his openness; the style of his poems has loosened; he has written prose poems; he has learned a lot from his reading; he is able to write at length now—but is still writing the books he began to write decades ago.

Ohio Review 15, no. 1 (1973):89–93. Reprinted with permission.

The other poet of the soul's journey, since Roethke's death, is Galway Kinnell. And he is perhaps the most *un*systematic of poets.

One of the books that began to emerge was something that Bly referred to as "the country poems," in conversation. When a considerable group of country poems had been written, they appeared as a book called *Silence in the Snowy Fields*. The *Silence* poems are soft and frequently happy, even in their melancholy somehow secure. They are the less complicated, more primitive aspect of Bly's vision, and therefore appropriately the first to be published. They are psychically the earliest, approaching the uruboros.

When *The Light Around the Body* came out, people were offended. We don't want our poets to change.

But Bly hadn't changed at all.

If the readers had noticed the old J. P. Morgan poems in *New World Writing,* they would have seen the politics of the outer world judged by the standards of the inner world—and years before Vietnam. And if they had looked into magazines and anthologies, where Bly for years had published poems which he did not choose to include in *Silence,* they would have seen poems about the phallic violence of the patriarchs, and they would have seen the dislocations of surrealism.

Many of the frightening poems of *Light Around the Body* were older than many of the gentle poems of *Silence*. The Vietnam war did not change Bly's ideas. The Vietnam war was the horrifying embodiment of the "father of rocks," the "father of cheerfulness," which he had named years before.

A lot of bad political poetry has been written, poetry which proclaims the virtue of the poet in his convictions about wars in Asia.

Do you all agree? Please don't agree quite so quickly! Bad as these political poems have been, the criticism of political poetry has been worse. Literary and academic people are *terrified* whenever an artist expresses an opinion.

273

Bly's poems do not attest to Bly's virtue. (Some of Bly's political actions outside the writing of poems seem to me virtuous indeed, both courageous and useful. Naturally he has been ridiculed and sneered at by hacks and cowards, but that is no matter.) The point about Bly's political poems is clear or ought to be: the violence is Bly's own. Certainly he understands his own murderousness, and no man can protest war if he does not understand himself a murderer.

Bly's moral judgments about the war in Asia derive from his general system, visible even in *Silence,* and his moral judgment is not *ad hoc. Ad hoc* judgments evaporate under pressure. Bly's judgments would survive the flames and the stake.

Sleepers is the best of the three books, and is synthetic. It racapitulates the first two books and takes a further step. The further step *depends* on the ideas in the prose, and *occurs* in the long title poem that ends the book. Still, the ideas of the prose, like the accidents of history in the political poems, find room only in a mind that is already prepared for them. Bly had written "A Man Writes to a Part of Himself" a decade before he read Neumann. And though Neumann's ideas helped the long poem to evolve, parts of it are as old as anything he has ever printed. The poem was begun when he was in his twenties.

The first section includes more country poems—the privacy poems, the shack poems—with their wonderful moments of intuitive connection:

> When I woke, new snow had fallen.
> I am alone, yet someone else is with me,
> drinking coffee, looking out at the snow.
>
> ("Six Winter Privacy Poems," no. 6)

This intuition is basic to the despair elsewhere. Without the memory or knowledge of connection, how do we feel separation? "And how did this separation come about?"

"Water Under the Earth" and "Hair" began as portions of the long title poem, but after considerable struggle were removed to stand alone. Since the whole of Bly's work is one poem, the decision is less crucial than it would be for most poets.

Bly's connectedness with all things, his systematic and evolutionary empathy, never shows better than in some lines from "Water Under the Earth":

> I am only half-risen,
> I see how carefully I have covered my tracks as I wrote,
> how well I brushed over the past with my tail.
> I enter rooms full of photographs of the dead.
> My hair stands up
> as a badger crosses my path in the moonlight.

And this first section ends with the "Teeth Mother" poem, mistakenly considered a poem "about" Vietnam and therefore unread in the very act of being read. It is a poem of vast and general intelligence, a poem created out of the knowledge of *history* surely, but psychic history and geopolitical history made one as they must be made.

The prose passages, "I Came Out of the Mother Naked," are crucial to any understanding of Bly's ideas. Bly takes them as literal and historical: nobody should forget this reality. Myself, I remember the voices conversing with Yeats. "Shall I give up poetry and promulgate your doctrines?" "No! No! We come to give you metaphors for poetry!"

If it be understood, for heaven's sake, those "metaphors for poetry" have the reality of flesh, and the imprint of spirit.

Relative to metaphor, history is mere decoration.

"Sleepers Joining Hands" is the earliest and latest of Bly's work. It has taken this long for him to use material which leaves him so vulnerable:

> . . . I sent my brother away.
> I saw him turn and leave. It was a schoolyard.
> I gave him to the dark people passing.
> He learned to sleep alone on the high buttes.
> I heard he was near the Missouri, taken in by traveling Sioux. . . .

In this poem, Bly talks of the presence of the fathers in him who drive the shadow away, fathers of spiritual pride and arrogance. And he speaks of his own suffering, and the suffering of others:

I see the birds inside me,
with massive shoulders, like humpbacked Puritan ministers,
a headstrong beak ahead,
and wings supple as the stingray's,
ending in claws, lifting over the shadowy peaks.

Looking down, I see dark marks on my shirt.
My mother gave me that shirt, and hoped that her son would be the
    one man in the world
who would have a happy marriage,
but look at me now—
I have been divorced five hundred times,
six hundred times yesterday alone.

I hear the sound of hoofs . . . coming. . . . Now the men
move in, smashing and burning. The huts
of the Shadowy People are turned over, the wood
utensils broken, straw mats set on fire,
digging sticks jumped on, clay bowls
smashed with dropped stones. . . .

It is a great journey poem, the journey through the horrors of loneliness in New York City, through the joys of solitude, and the spiritual selfishness possible to solitude, and into the present life:

What I have written is not good enough.
Who does it help?
I am ashamed sitting on the edge of my bed.

I think that Bly has more to write, within the scope of this poem—though it does not matter exactly whether it occurs in expanding this poem or in further work. This poem is very beautiful, and the best of Bly's work. But parts of the journey are still unwritten, parts of the journey that move from the original loss and despair, and the later spiritual withdrawal, into the condition of the end of the poem:

All the sleepers in the world join hands.

We do not have the whole journey. We have a synopsis, almost. It will take the rest of a lifetime to make the metaphors that are the footsteps of this journey, which is the journey to a good death.

CYNTHIA MACDONALD

Instruction from Bly

The poet told me if I was serious
I must isolate myself for at least a year—
Not become a hermit, but leave
My family, job, friends—so I did. My sister
Agreed to take over as mother though not
As wife. I wonder if she will become that too;
I've always thought maybe she didn't marry
Because she wanted Howard herself. So I
Have moved here to North Dakota where
I work in a gas station, the only woman s.s.
Attendant in N.D. Nowhere could be more isolated
And no job could: whistles and "baby
Pump some of that to me" crack in the cold
Or melt in the summer.

try	try	try	
crycry	crycry	crycry	cry

I have been here seven months. Poetry should
Be flowing from my navel by now, if . . .
Out of the solitude, I expected I would erect
Something magnificent, the feminine analogue
Of Jeffers' tower. Maybe it would have gone
Into the ground instead of up.

s   k   y

high

Amputations (New York: Braziller, 1973), pp. 33–35. Reprinted with permission.

I have discovered I drink when I am solitary. I
Have discovered I can read page ninety-two of
Remembrance of Things Past twenty times in solitary
Without ever reading it. If I don't die of alcoholism,
I will of cholesterol: solitary cooking.

    fryfryfry   fryfry   fryfryfryfry   frydie

Rhyme is important, my way of keeping
A grip on things. I wonder if the poet meant
It would all happen after I left, or if he is a sadist
Who wants to send all those stupid enough to sit
At his feet to N.D. or S.D. or West Va.,
Hazing before possible joining. I wonder if Jean
Is in the double bed.

        tower
        power

I cannot think about the children, but I
Do all the time. "Women artists fail
Because they have babies." The last thing I wrote
Was "The Children at the Beach" and that was over
A month ago. I am alone so I have to have company so
I turn on TV; at home
I only turned it off.

     thumbtacks   processionals
           north
           red

It is time to go to work. First I need a drink. I consider
The Smirnoff bottle on the coffee table; a fly
Lands on it. And then it all happens: the life
Of that bottle flashes before me. Little by little,
Or quickly, it is used up; empty, as clear as it was
Full, it journeys to the dump; it rests upon the mounds of
Beautiful excess where what we are—

Sunflowers, grass, sand—
Is joined to what we make—
Cans, tires and it itself in every form of bottle.
I put on my s.s. coveralls, a saffron robe, knowing I have
found
What I was sent to find. The sky speaks to me; the sound
Of the cars on Highway 2 is a song. Soon I will see the
pumps,
Those curved rectangles shaped like the U.S. and smell the
gas,
Our incense. O country, O moon, O stars,
O american rhyme is yours is mine is ours.

PETER STITT

From "James Wright:
The Art of Poetry XIX"

JW: In *Saint Judas* I tried to face the fact that I am not a happy man by talent. Sometimes I have been very happy, but characteristically I'm a miserable son of a bitch. I tried to come to terms with that in the clearest and most ferociously perfect form that I could find and in all the traditional ways. That was partly a defensive action, because I hurt so much then. After I finished that book I had finished with poetry forever. I truly believed that I had said what I had to say as clearly and directly as I could, and that I had no more to do with this art.

PS: You've told me that before. What was wrong, and how did you get going again?

JW: At that time I had come, for personal reasons but also for artistic reasons, to something like a dead end. I was in despair at that time, and what usually has consoled me is words—I've always been able to turn to them. But suddenly, it seemed to me that the words themselves had gone dead, I mean dead in me, and I didn't know what to do. It was at that time that Robert Bly's magazine, which was then called *The Fifties,* appeared. I wrote him a long letter because his magazine contained a translation of a poem by Georg Trakl. Some years earlier, at the University of Vienna, I had read in German the poetry of Trakl and I didn't know what to do with it, though I recognized that somehow it had a depth of life in it that I needed. Trakl is a poet who writes in parallelisms, only he leaves out the intermediary, rationalistic explanations of the relation between one image and another. I would suppose that Trakl has had as much influence

Paris Review 62 (1975):48–50. Reprinted with permission.

on me as anybody else has had. But the interesting thing is that when I read Robert Bly's magazine, I wrote him a letter. It was sixteen pages long and single spaced, and all he said in reply was, "Come on out to the farm." I made my way out to that farm, and almost as soon as we met each other we started to work on our translation of Trakl.

You should see us working together on something. We get up in the morning and won't even look at each other. We pace back and forth. He'll turn without looking at me and say to his wife, Carol, "Yeah, he likes J. V. Cunningham." Then I get one up on him by quoting him a Cunningham poem. And we sit and stare at each other. We would say things that I would not repeat even for the *Paris Review*. And yet I'm a member of his family too. I'm Mary's godfather. They loved me and they saved my life. I don't mean just the life of my poetry, either. . . .

PS: Did he have the strong influence on your work of that time that is sometimes ascribed to him?

JW: Yes. He made it clear to me that the tradition of poetry which I had tried to master, and in which I'd come to a dead end, was not the only one. He reminded me that poetry is a possibility, that, although all poetry is formal, there are many forms, just as there are many forms of feeling.

PS: The book that followed, of course, is *The Branch Will Not Break*. How do these things show up there?

JW: At the center of that book is my rediscovery of the abounding delight of the body that I had forgotten about. Every Friday afternoon I used to go out to Bly's farm, and there were so many animals out there. There was Simon, who was an Airedale, but about the size of a Great Dane. There was David, the horse, my beautiful, beloved David, the swaybacked Palomino. Simon and David used to go out by Bly's barn. David would stand there looking out over the corn fields that lead onto the prairies of South Dakota, and Simon would sit down beside him, and they would stay there for hours. And sometimes, after I sat on the front porch and watched them, sometimes I went and sat down beside Simon. Neither Simon nor David looked at me, and I felt blessed. They allowed me to join them. They liked me. I can't get over it—they liked me. Simon didn't bite me. David didn't kick me; they just stayed there as they were. And I sat down on my fat ass and looked over the corn fields and the prairie with them. And there we were. One afternoon, a gopher came up out of a hole and looked at us. Simon didn't leap for him, David didn't kick him, and I didn't shoot him. There we were, all four of us together. All I was thinking was, I can be happy sometimes. And I'd forgotten that. And with those animals I remembered then. And that is what that book is about, the rediscovery. I didn't hate my body at all. I liked myself very much. Simon is lost. David, with what Robert called his beautiful and sensitive face, has gone to the knacker's. I wish I knew how to tell you. My son Marsh, the musician, is in love with animals.

PS: What effect do you feel your role as translator—the sort of work you did with Bly—has had on your own poetry?

JW: It's led me into some further possibilities of saying something that I think I wanted to say from the beginning. And that, unfortunately, being damned as I consider myself, I felt that I had to say or I would die. I think that most of the people who are alive in the world right now are very unhappy. I don't want people to be unhappy, and I'm sorry that they are. I wish there were something I could do to help. I'm coming to face the fact that there isn't much I can do to help. And I think I've been trying to say that ever since I've started to write books. That's what my books are about.

Two Poets Translating

The following conversation took place in the translation seminar recently conducted at Columbia University by Frank MacShane. The Swedish poet, Tomas Tranströmer, was visiting the United States and was joined on this occasion by one of his principal translators, the poet Robert Bly.

RB: I began translating in about 1958. I had a few good teachers at college, among them Archibald MacLeish. But none of them ever mentioned Neruda to me, or Vallejo, or any of the Scandinavian poets. I stumbled along for five or six years using English and American models for my own work, with no fruitful results. Then I went to Oslo in 1956, and I discovered Neruda and Norwegian and Swedish poets no one knew about. It was then I learned that if you're going to write, one of the most important things for you is to find someone who is in your part of the spectrum. The American psychic spectrum is much wider than the English spectrum—except for Blake—and I found myself helped most by poets in languages not English. That's when I decided to translate Neruda and the Scandinavian poets in order to get closer to them. I taught myself Spanish by looking up words in Neruda poems. If you look up the same word about twelve times you eventually remember it. I was a Norwegian-American and I wanted to learn Norwegian anyway.

Five or six steps are involved in translating a poem. The first job is to find out what the words mean. You can use a dictionary for that. It isn't so terribly important to know the original language perfectly. After all, a poem only has fifteen or twenty or fifty or a hundred words in it. You can surely find out what those words mean. What is much more important is that you know English.

Translation 4 (1977):47–58. Reprinted with permission.

The second step then is to set down a literal translation of the poem in what may be a flat and stupid way. At that point you have to decide whether you can feel the poem or not, that is, love it. This is an intuitive matter. Are the emotions of this poem within your spectrum of emotions? If not, forget it. Leave it alone. It's like a woman: if a woman doesn't move you, leave her alone. Someone else will come along and she will move that person.

In the third step you put away your literal version and feel the poem again in the original. Then you try to write down single lines, speaking in American this time, rather than in "English" or "translatorese." Most professors stop before they get to this stage. William Carlos Williams will help you here. He grasped clearly that we live between two separate languages—book language and American. American is a wild and fresh language: there is much energy in its tone and rhythms. So the third step is to take what you feel and put it into American spoken language. I believe you can be helped greatly in this step by reading contemporary poets who have a lively sense of the American language, which changes every fifteen or twenty years. It's no use reading Keats for this.

After that stage is over, it's wise—even essential—to show your version to someone who really knows the original language from birth. Then you can see how far you've veered. James Wright and I have always asked Hardie St. Martin to help us here. He would write us two typed pages on a single Neruda poem. You may have put intonations in that are not in the original. Your unconscious may have misperceived and so altered the image. I don't think you have any right to change images. Form may have to be abandoned, but not the integrity of the image. Now you have to take account of all these corrections and compass readings.

At the fifth stage you try to take account of the sound. The original has a lot of sound in it—flowing, powerful sound. If it didn't, it wouldn't be any good. The sound means the subconscious has joined in and helped produce the poem. What are you going to do if you find no sound in the translation? Often I've just given up right there. At other times I've gone back to the original, memorized it, and learned something from its sound. The American language offers you such tremendous possibilities in rephrasing that you may be able to bring some solidity into the sound. Tomas and I have a good time translating because he is sensitive to the sound, even in an English version.

TT: But it's a little hard to do with letters. It's much better to have the translator sitting beside you in the same house and if possible in the same surroundings where the poem takes place.

RB: Can you give an example of why that's important?

TT: Yes, I remember one from "Breathing Space July" which you translated:

The man who lies on his back under huge trees
is also up in them. He branches out into thousands of tiny branches.
He sways back and forth,
he sits in a catapult chair that hurtles forward in slow motion.

The man who stands down at the dock screws up his eyes against
     the water.
Ocean docks get older faster than men.
They have silver gray posts and boulders in their gut.
The dazzling light drives straight in.

The man who spends the whole day in an open boat
moving over the luminous bays
will fall asleep at last inside the shade of his blue lamp
as the islands crawl like huge moths over the globe.

Now in this poem you use the words "ocean docks," which I questioned because I was referring to a small dock for small boats. It's not a dock for steamers.

RB: The reason I used "ocean docks" is that with us, a lake dock simply has little sticks going down into the water. The line in Swedish described a dock with boulders in it. Your island is on the Baltic Sea and the dock is firm.

TT: In Sweden the winter is so severe and the ice presses on the piers or small boat docks, so we have to have big stones just to keep them in place. I was simply giving a description of a physical fact, but the phenomenon of docks with "boulders in their gut" is very strange. In the French translation, it even became a surrealist image, because the translator didn't realize that there are such docks!

So the best thing to do is to bring the translator to the pier or dock and say, "I'm thinking about that. What do you call it?" People have told me that one reason your translations are so good is that you have visited my place in Sweden. You know what you're talking about.

RB: It's weird the way the landscape gets into the poem in some occult way, and that's part of the poem too.

TT: This is a simple example because it deals with physical things, with facts. But when we come to the complex things that have to do with different societies and traditions, it is much more difficult. It is not merely a question of language; it has to do with the whole area around language, with the associations that come with each word.

RB: May I add to what I was saying about the physical environment of the poem? If the landscape of a poem is one which you don't feel or understand, it's probably better for you to leave it alone. For example, if there's a tremendous country feeling in a poem and you're a city person, you should avoid the poem. You can get every word right, yet the mood won't be right. There are certain electrical impulses and spirits and moods that belong only in the city or in the country.

Let's now take a look at some of Tomas's poems.

TT: Here is the poem in Swedish:

HEMÅT

Ett telefonsamtal rann ut i natten och glittrade på landsbygden och in
    förstäderna.
Efteråt sov jag oroligt i hotellsängen.
Jag liknade nålen i en kompass som orienteringslöparen bär genom
    skogen med bultande hjärta.

RB: I'll now read the first four versions I made of this poem:

HOMEWARD

A telephone conversation ran out in the night and glittered in the
   country towns and in the suburbs.
After I slept unpeacefully in the hotel bed.
I resembled the needle in a compass which the cross-country runner
   carries through the forest with beating heart.

HOMEWARD

A telephone call ran out into the night and shone there over the
   villages and the suburbs.
Afterwards I slept restlessly in the hotel bed.
I resembled the compass needle that the cross country runner carries
   on ahead with thumping heart through the woods.

HOMEWARD

A telephone call spread out into the night was shining here and there
   in the country fields and outskirts of cities.
After I hung up I slept restlessly in the hotel bed.
I was like the needle in the compass that the cross country runner
   with chest thumping carries through the fir forest.

And now here is the version I sent to Tomas:

HOMEWARD

A telephone call floated out into the darkness, and I felt it glittering
   here and there in the towns and at the edges of cities.
Then I slept restlessly in the hotel bed.
I was like the needle in the compass that the forest runner has along
   as he runs cross country with his chest thumping.

   You'll see that one of the words I had trouble with is "suburbs." It didn't seem to fit into the poem and I don't know why.

TT: Here is a typical difference between associations. In America, the word means the place where the middle and upper classes live. In the center of the city are the slums. But in Sweden it's quite different. The whole sociological drama is missing there: all it means is that the land is less built up, that there is more land around the houses. But the dictionary meaning of *Förstäderna* is simply "suburbs." But "suburbs" is wrong.

RB: You'll see that I changed the first verb several times— from "ran out" to "spread out" to "floated out," and I'm still not satisfied. At one point I asked him what the situation of the poem was and he wrote, "I'll give you the background. I'm away from home but in Sweden, probably in Värmland, and making a telephone call to Monica. It's about ten o'clock in the evening. It's a good telephone call and I suddenly feel how our communication is leaking out into the surroundings like a glittering river or something. It's not in the air, but more on the ground, so to say, like glittering ditches here and there. Or like a Milky Way stretched out in the landscape.

Student: What about "flowed"?

RB: Lovely! I didn't think of that. What do you think of that, Tomas?

TT: Well, the dictionary would absolutely agree.

RB: Good, I knew the "o" sound was right. But "flowed" is much better. Thank you very much. "The telephone conversation flowed out into the night." Now what about "glittered" as compared with "shined" or "was shining"?

Student: Tinsel glitters.

RB: I know what you mean; I worried about that, too. But if you have "gleam" there's a toothpaste called "Gleem."

Student: What about "shimmer"?

RB: That's a moving kind of thing, I'm afraid, like a girl's skirt which shimmers.

Student: What about "glisten"?

RB: I've thought a lot about the difference between "glisten" and "glitter."

Student: "Glisten" softens the Swedish word *glittrade,* which emphasizes the "t" sound.

Another Student: "Glitter" is dry, like gold.

TT: I think the telephone call was a sort of liquor, maybe only water, perhaps something stronger. But the word used should be something like "flows." It shouldn't be a dry glittering but a wet one.

RB: There's probably a word that we all know that means the light that's given off by a little stream when it's running at night in the moonlight, and we're not able to pick it up. That's why translation takes such a long time. Two weeks later you're walking down the street and the word comes to you.

TT: In the last two lines there are two other problems. Robert has used the words "cross country runner" in the last lines, but that is wrong. I was referring to a very popular sport in Scandinavia called orienteering. It's spread recently to England and Germany, and I think it will soon be known in the United States as well.

RB: At first I thought he was talking about cross-country skiing and I asked him if it was. He said no. But I'm afraid it's impossible to use a word like "orienteering." It just doesn't exist in the English language yet. A technical word or a dry word becomes a huge hole in the poem through which all the emotion drains out. One of the reasons for laboring toward spoken language is to keep the emotions in the poem fresh and not let them drain out. What shall we do about that?

TT: The other word that causes trouble in the last line is "heart."

RB: "Heart" is difficult or impossible to use most of the time. I kept coming across *corazón* again and again in Spanish poetry— but there it is also "courage." With us "heart" is weak and vague. It ruins most of the lines it inhabits.

TT: But here I'm referring to the word in its original sense— donk-donk-donk-donk. It's not a symbol. It's the heart itself.

RB: Well, a translation is never just. It's only a series of compromises. The reason I'm against "heart" is that this is a poem about an emotional situation between a man and a woman. And in a poem we don't like to be told everything. We like to guess certain things. So if I read, "with heart thumping," I say, Oh, oh, he didn't think I'd get it.

TT: But for a foreigner like me, "chest thumping" sounds a little ridiculous. It sounds like a sport: like having a world champion of chest thumping, or something like that.

RB: You may be right. Perhaps "heart" is the right word. I have the feeling you're using it not because it refers to love but in spite of that fact. All a translator can do is put the poem away and look at it later on. Two months later he might change his mind. How about saying, "which the orienteer runner carries through the quest with chest thumping"?

Let's now look at another one of Tomas's poems which he sent me even before he decided on a title for it.

Natten efter olyckan drömde jag om en koppärrig man
som gick och sjöng i gränderna.
Danton!
Inte den andre—Robespierre tar inte såna promenader.
Robespierre gör omsorgsfull toalett en timme
på morgonen, resten av dygnet agnar han at Folket.
I pamfletternas paradis, bland dygdens maskiner.
Danton
(eller den som bar hans mask)
stod som på styltor.
Jag såg hans ansikte underifrån:
som den ärriga månen, till hälften i ljus, till hälften i sorg.
Jag ville säga något.
En tyngd i bröstet: lodet
som får klockorna att gå,
visarna att vrida sig: år I, år II . . .
En frän doft som från sågspånen i tigerstallarna.

Och—som alltid i drömmen—ingen sol.
Men murarna lyste
i gränderna som krökte sig
ner mot vänt rummet, det krökta rummet,
väntrummet där vi alla . . .

CITOYENS

The night after the accident I dreamt about a pockmarked man
who walked along the alleys singing.
Danton!
Not the one—Robespierre took no walks like that,
he spent one hour each day
on his morning toilette, the rest he gave to The People.
In the heaven of broadsides, among the machines of goodness.
Danton
(or the one who wore his mask)
seemed to stand on stilts.
I saw his face from underneath:
like the pitted moon, half of it lit, half dark.
I wanted to say something.
A weight in my chest: the lead weight
that makes clocks go,
and the faces to turn: Year I, Year II . . .
A harsh odor as from sawdust in tigers' cages.
And—it was like that in the dream—no sun.
But the alley walls
were shining, as they curved away
down toward the waiting-room, the crooked room,
the waiting-room where we all . . .

There is one line in my version Tomas didn't approve of: "In the
heaven of broadsides, among the machines of goodness."

TT: Well, what are "broadsides"?

RB: They are a sort of political pamphlet. One of the best
printers in San Francisco, when he hears that a political figure is
coming there from the East, from Washington, prints up a

broadside attacking him, and then they hand out hundreds of copies of it.

TT: Is it an English word, too?

Frank MacShane: Yes, but there it means a single sheet.

TT: Well, in France during the revolution, they were always producing pamphlets, and that's what I meant.

RB: What kind of pamphlet?

TT: Marat and Robespierre were the chief pamphleteers—on all sorts of subjects, mainly political. You use the word "goodness," but the word I want is "virtue," because no one can say that Robespierre was *good,* but he was extremely virtuous. He was a man without faults. He had a model private life. He never took any bribes and he never had scandals with women. What he wanted was to create a society where everyone was full of virtue. At the same time, he did terrible things.

RB: Are the pamphlets then the machines?

TT: In a way. He had a very abstract sense of virtue, with no love in it. A love of mankind but a hatred of persons. Utopians are often like that. But I'm afraid I never heard of broadsides in this connection.

Student: If you want to use the word "pamphlet" and keep the same distance you mentioned, what about "a paradise of pamphlets?"

Student: The trouble is that doesn't give a sense of the Roman quality of the French Revolution. Virtue is a *Roman* quality, and paradise is out of tune with it.

RB: I like that observation. A great problem in translation is that you can't translate the poem unless you feel its setting and mood. You've just been talking of its historical environment; it's true that no one can translate this poem until he or she has a sense of what is going on inside the poem's psyche. I made my own interpretation from the facts Tomas gave me, but it is only an interpretation.

TT: Let me give you the background. I don't think it's absolutely necessary to give you the background, but on this occasion it would be fun. I have had two accidents in my life and have been saved from both. The first accident was an adventure, but the second was quite different. It was in 1970 and I had an old Saab which had just been inspected in a garage. Everything was said to be working perfectly, including the brakes. Then while I was driving along the highway, I found myself in a line of traffic, with everybody going rather fast. Suddenly the cars slowed down. I stepped on the pedal and it just went down to the floor. WHAM. I ran into the Mercedes in front of me. My poor little car ended up like an accordion. I was saved. I got out. All I had was a shirt, a pair of trousers, shoes, and a book about the French Revolution. That was all that survived.

Later I had to take the train home. It was a rather shaking experience. I had a dream that night, and it is just as I have described it here in the poem, so I didn't invent anything. Except perhaps the image that makes the old clocks go.

RB: Now I struggled along in this poem, with a weight on my chest, trying to find a way in which I could imagine it in my own life. If I could imagine it in my psychic situation I could tell what tone to give to the words. So last night, I said to a friend, "What are these walls?" He said, "Don't you see these alley walls? They are like the vagina curving down." I said, "You mean the waiting room?" He said," Yes, he's about to be born." I was astounded. I don't rule that out. Now what do you say, Tomas? You're stubborn; are you going back into womb instead of dying?

TT: The waiting room comes from my memory of a waiting room. A year before, my mother was dying and I spent a lot of time at the hospital. So the waiting room image was very close to me. It's a banal thing: I'm in the waiting room waiting for death and . . .

RB: And not for life.

TT: There's another thing that's involved here which I came across in a play called *Danton's Death*. After I wrote this poem, I went to the library and looked up the play. The strange thing is that he wrote about Danton's walks, and somewhere in the play Danton takes a very long walk. This is meant to show how careless he was even though he was in danger all the time. He should have been writing a pamphlet, but he walked around instead. And this was just before he was executed. Danton loved to walk in the streets and talk to ordinary people. He was not full of virtue like Robespierre.

RB: What have the tiger cages got to do with that? The "piercing odor from the sawdust in the tigers' cages"?

TT: When I was a child I used to visit the circus, and before the show began I used to go and look at the tigers. And there was this fantastic smell from the sawdust, all the piss from the cats.

RB: Why do you think it appeared in the dream at this point? Was there something very dangerous about the tigers?

TT: Yes, it was a very dangerous room there in the hospital.

RB: As if you might enter the waiting room and die there?

TT: It has to do with two things at least. First of all the accident. I had escaped death. Also, I'd been reading about the French Revolution. At this time, about 1970, there were also strong political pressures in Sweden for writers to become types like Robespierre. We were all supposed to be machines of virtue at that time. So everything was mixed together.

RB: Would you like to have for *krökta rummet* "crooked room" or "curved space"? As in Einstein? Either seems a possible translation of the Swedish.

TT: "The curved space" might be better than "room," then. In Swedish the word *rummet* means chamber and a room in the house, but it also means space.

RB: We've now looked at three poems. Are there any general questions?

Student: How much of the translation is done by mail?

RB: The best translations come from the time when I went over to see Tomas and we had three or four days together. Then he would come to Madison and we'd repeat the process.

Student: Do you ever try to guide him with a translation of your own?

TT: You know, I trust him very much as a poet, so I think he should take some liberties. He should try to make a good American poem out of mine. But I also have to hold him back sometimes. The important thing about a translation is that it should work in a new language.

But translation isn't exclusively a thing that goes on from one language to another. If you really come down to it, every reader makes his own translation of every poem he reads. Every reader has his own language, his own environment, his own imagination. So every reader has his own poem, so to speak. The text is the same but the poems are different.

RB: One thing that is so beautiful about translation is that you begin translating from your enthusiasm for the poem; and you want to bring the poem over. Then you work on it and you discover that you've received a terrific gift from that poem by getting so close to it. You get closer to the poems you translate than to any other poems except your own. You can learn a great deal from the poems you translate. To work for three days on one poem is a completely different experience, and richer, than reading in that time a whole book of translations. There's no comparison. We are fed by studying a single poem. What is lovely about the New Critics is that they made you read very carefully.

A translation is not a draining job: it's the most intense reading you'll ever do in your whole life. I believe a great deal in the intensification translation can do for anyone who works in poetry. Tomas does a great deal of translating, as do many European writers. But in our own country we do not have that habit. Frost, for example, translated no one. Lowell does good work, but he translates into Lowell. The nuances are gone. We want to know what Baudelaire is like. Lowell's instinct is wonderful in wanting to bring other poems over into our language, but somehow he violates the psychic energies of the original. I think he's a fine poet, but still within our framework. What I long for in translation is to feel the fragrance that surrounds a strange character like Mallarmé. I don't really know what Mallarmé is like, because we've never had a translator from the French who was willing to give himself to Mallarmé and who knew American well enough to bring the fragrance back. There are lots of people who are willing to translate French, but it's a different matter to sink slowly down into the weird mind of another poet and not be impatient and just go with him as far as you can.

HUGH KENNER

From "Three Poets"

A specially handsome book, first of all, with twenty pencil
drawings by Gendron Jensen, identified as "a forest eccentric."
They are twenty careful renderings of a snail shell, and if you flip
the pages you can see it turn over like Charlie Chaplin in his
sleep, but more massive.

Robert Bly's prose poems have a parallel hallucinatory quality. No more than you expect to see a shell turn over do you
expect:

> All seems calm, and yet somewhere inside I
> am not calm. We live in wooden buildings made of two-by-fours,
> making the landscape nervous for a hundred miles. And the Em-
> peror when he was sixty called for rhinoceros horn, for sky-blue
> phoenix eggs shaped from veined rock, dipped in rooster blood. . . .

It's the effect of two-by-fours on the landscape that makes us
accept the Emperor's whims.

"My beloved is to me as a cluster of camphor," we read in the
Song of Solomon (1:14) and the Ark, God told Noah (Genesis
6:14), was to be made "of gopherwood." The Ark was by some
accounts an allegory for the body, and that's all the explanation
you're going to get in these pages about what it's like to be alive
in a body; in it, yet through it mysteriously part of everything
else material.

One poem has horses leaping over fire, water, air; then "they
meet their fourth obstacle—flesh. . . . It is a Garden." It is indeed, with elephant trunks reaching lazily up tree branches, and

---

A review of *This Body Is Made of Camphor and Gopherwood, New York Times Book
Review,* January 1, 1978, p. 10. Copyright © 1978 by The New York Times
Company. Reprinted by permission.

gazelles that "hurry over the plain like blood corpuscles in a storm." The horses slow down, "confused among so many gentle animals."

That gives you a sense of it: Bly is attempting to write down what it's like to be alive, a state in which, he implies, not all readers find themselves all the time—certainly not all readers who lack the luck to live in rural Minnesota, where a voice isn't always trying to sell you something.

ALAN WILLIAMSON

From "Music to Your Ears"

Robert Bly stands for a more exuberant, surrealist, Jungian brand of antirationalism. For more than twenty years, he has argued its case in hyperbolic, occasionally self-parodying pronunciamentos; in (generally excellent) translations of irrationalist poets from other cultures; and in an initially oversimplified but increasingly careful, learned, dialectical exposition of Jung himself. As a poet, however, Mr. Bly has been limited by a relatively weak sense of the musical and connotative value of words; his poems often seem made of images and ideas alone. And he has a way of hectoring the reader (and quite possibly himself) into accepting his experience as visionary or profound—a tonality registered in his consistent exclamation points.

Mr. Bly's new book is culled from more than sixteen years of work, but restricted, as he tells us in his introduction, to poems that record a personal experience of "two presences" or forms of consciousness—one his own, the other a larger, "impersonal" one, shared with plants and animals. So conscious and extraliterary a criterion can lead to an overly intellectual and doctrinaire religiosity; and indeed, when Mr. Bly writes of farmyard animals,

> Asleep they are bark fallen from an old cottonwood.
> Yet we know their soul is gone, risen
> far into the upper air about the moon
>
> ("Night Farmyard")

A review of *This Tree Will Be Here for a Thousand Years, New York Times Book Review,* March 9, 1980, pp. 8–9; 14–15. Copyright © 1980 by The New York Times Company. Reprinted by permission.

we can only wish that what "we know" mystically had not interfered with the darker, frailer germ of poetry in the first line.

What does, on the other hand, seem new, heartfelt, and not altogether digested by the poet's theorizing is his insistence that the "second consciousness" presents itself to him as sadness— *lacrimae rerum*—though a sadness free of the irritating indignity of private depression. Mr. Bly resists a psychological explanation of this sadness; but his best poems connect it with the yearnings away from individuality felt in romantic love ("Women We Never See Again"), and with the anticipation of death, when we will, indeed, cease to distinguish ourselves from nature. I note all of the moving, though imperfect, "Prayer Service in an English Church":

> Looking at the open page of the psalm book,
> I see a ghostly knot floating in the paper!
>
> Circles within circles on the page, floating,
> showing that a branch once lived there!
>
> Looking at the knot long and long,
> I hear the priest call on the Saviour to come again.
>
> The old around me keep on singing . . .
> If the Saviour is a branch, how can he come again?
>
> And the last day . . .
> the whispers we will make from the darkening pillow . . .

"Long and long" might have been left to Whitman, "circles within circles" to Lowell. But no matter: the real stinger comes in the third line from the end, which does not mean that nature will save us; rather, that things don't happen twice, or, at best, that we are the living, ramifying tip of nature, a fact which may console but cannot allow us to "come again." Hence the humility of the final couplet: We must end in a blurred, whispery dissolution, not in the clarity of the Christian "last day." . . .

PETER STITT

From "Dark Volumes"

Robert Bly's new book, *The Man in the Black Coat Turns,* is the most somber he has written, though it is far from being either morbid or depressed. As usual with him, the surfaces of these poems crackle with energy, liveliness; we are attracted most by the crazy progression of the images, as in this passage of self-rebuke:

> How many failures we hide, talking. When I am too public,
> I am a wind-chime, ringing, to cheer up the black
> Angel Moroni, and feed him
> as he comes dancing, prancing, leaving turkey tracks in the mist.

The conflict in Robert Bly's work has always been between aloneness and community. He began with solitude, in the magnificently introspective poems of *Silence in the Snowy Fields.* Since then he has been very much a public poet—an antiwar activist, a performer on many campuses, the author of political verse. But in this book he returns to the world inside.

Mr. Bly has often complained that American poetry in general is too literal, too obvious. His own technique is based on the work of the surrealists and expressionists and embodies to an unusual degree Freud's early model of the conscious and unconscious levels of the mind. Mr. Bly's method is free association; the imagination is allowed to discover whatever images it deems appropriate to the poem, no matter the logical, literal demands of consciousness. He describes this process in a prose poem, "Eleven O'Clock at Night":

A review of *The Man in the Black Coat Turns, New York Times Book Review,* February 14, 1982, p. 15. Copyright © 1982 by The New York Times Company. Reprinted by permission.

Many times in poems I have escaped—from myself. I sit for hours and at last see a pinhole in the top of the pumpkin, and I slip out that pinhole, gone! The genie expands and is gone; no one can get him back in the bottle again; he is hovering over a car cemetery somewhere.

It is the images that carry meaning in a Bly poem, and because the images are arrived at spontaneously rather than logically, there is always a danger that the reader will not be able to follow the twists and turns of the poet's thought. Thus some of the poems here seem fragmented. But when the method works— which is most of the time—a surprising truth is reached. In this book, what is most surprising is a disjunction between the surfaces of the poems and their dark interiors. The speaker appears to desire the sense of closeness derived from family life, but in the pattern of his images he clearly longs for separation and solitude. These lines are typical:

the son stops calling home.
The mother puts down her rolling pin and makes no more bread.
And the wife looks at her husband one night at a party, and loves
     him no more . . .
. . . .
The father . . .
. . . turns away from his wife, and she sleeps alone.
                    ("Snowbanks North of the House")

Mr. Bly's radical attempts to incorporate free association into American poetry make him one of our few truly original contemporary poets. *The Man in the Black Coat Turns* is easily his richest, most complex book.

News from Robert Bly's Universe

The Man in the Black Coat Turns

Mountains, rivers, caves, and fields quicken us when we are in solitude. We then leap toward connections lost to our rational selves and see in ways that defy logic. This seeing, as Bly explains in *Leaping Poetry: An Idea with Poems and Translations* (1975), occurs when the newest of our three brains is activated. The first, the Reptile Brain, acts coldly to preserve us against dangers real or imagined. The Mammal Brain, constituting the cortex, creates our institutions, affections, and sexual fervors. The third, and least-used brain, one lying as a one-eighth inch thick layer over the Mammal Brain, is the New Brain, the neocortex; this generates "wildness" and produces the "leaping poetry" written by Lorca, Rilke, Neruda, Takahashi, and Vallejo.

When this New Brain is activated, our words evoke miracles. "Watery syllables" well up from mythic depths, from the Dordogne caves and the aboriginal South Sea islands where men lived "under the cloak / of an animal's sniffing." Ancient angers explode. In one of Bly's new poems, "Words Rising," howls once declaimed by ancient priests dressed in furs holding aloft luminous barley heads continue to rage. They give pain, and at the same time excite, generating verbal wildness; we are "bees" with language for our "honey." We express what was hitherto inexpressive, archetypal, residual, in our ancestor's brains, long before the invention of the wheel. Both celebrant (priest) and sufferer (aborigine and political victim) dwell within our words:

> Wicker baskets and hanged men
> come to us as stanzas and vowels.

Previously unpublished, 1982.

We see a million hands with dusty
palms turned up inside each verb,
lifted. There are eternal vows
held inside the word "Jericho."

Language as mystery reflects profound events unlimited by time
and space, generated in our New Brain. During meditation,
cortexual cells produce dance and ecstasy.

Obviously I simplify, and urge readers interested in the full
story to turn to Bly's provocative essays (in addition to "Leaping Poetry" see "I Came Out of the Mother Naked" in *Sleepers
Joining Hands,* 1973, and the prose sections of Bly's new Sierra
Club anthology, *News of the Universe*). I wish here to employ
some of his main distinctions as a way of perceiving his new
poems. His verse techniques match up with his theories. No
matter how good Bly was in the past—and he was good—this
new poetry is an advance of impressive dimensions. *The Man in
the Black Coat Turns* should prove one of the seminal works of
the eighties. Much of what I shall offer here are readings stimu-
lated by hints taken from Bly's poems. I risk, of course, by
trying to be too rational (male-conscious), damaging his subtle
fabrics.

Some readers complain that Bly's poems are almost completely devoid of living persons except for himself. *Clear the stage*
is Bly's hallmark. The creative occurs in isolation, in locales
apart that nurture the poet. Forest, pasture, clearing, the isolated
building, all suit him for meditation. His writing-shack is so
private that even his wife doesn't know where it is, and he has to
carry his own water with him in jars. He recalls Thoreau with
whom he has many similarities, and tangentially, Wordsworth.
He would not hesitate to eat that woodchuck raw, one feels, if it
would intensify his perceptions; and he would welcome the
stark fear induced in Wordsworth by that shadow looming suddenly over the water near Mt. Skiddaw. "Urge and urge and
urge," wrote Whitman; "Always the procreant urge of the
world."

Bly is unlike other contemporary nature poets who seldom
take themselves off very far from the boat landing or the fire
tower.[1] There's nothing genteel in him. His reclusiveness is in

itself a tough metaphor. He is no Sunday dabbler, taking nature trails through museum-forests which some kind ranger has marked for easy recognition. His places are invested with agents of psychic confrontation, images of fragile yet powerful association: mythic mothers and fathers bearing fangs; the male instincts to kill, waste, and subdue, as omnipresent in our psyches as ever, in conflict with our gentler, creative selves. Only in solitude is our mental subsoil properly activated, equal to these conflicts, stilling the nagging, demanding Father who speaks for order, reason, and obedience. You can't build a birdhouse or haul much manure sitting on your haunches in a forest, or in the lotos position beside a stream.

To achieve quiescence, Bly has tried various disciplines including Tibetan meditation. No matter the guides, he remains himself, quizzical, self-reliant, Frostian, choosing from an eclectic feast only what will enhance his work and spirit. There is no wastage.

We observe Bly on his own mind-stage set with minimal properties, peopled with those few souls acting out scenes as his vision invites them in. Like Whitman (about whom Bly has written a most valuable and perceptive essay)[2] he invites us to loaf with him and share his urges and leapings, which may drift to us with the ease of bird feathers afloat, or which may leap with the brilliance of an arcing trout, or the grace of a doe in a meadow. *Energy* and *largeness,* two of Whitman's favorite concepts, induce *ecstasy* and *insight* for Bly. To adapt one of Mary Baker Eddy's images, Bly is utterly at ease in those natural vestibules where the material sense of things disappears.

Before scrutinizing some of Bly's new poems, I should like to speculate briefly on Bly as a Surrealist. Despite the fact that he sees his work deriving, or inspired, by poets he calls Surrealist—Rilke, Vallejo, Lorca, and Neruda, among others—I don't find the term all that useful when applied to him. Most obviously, Surrealism refers to that movement in the arts initiated by André Breton, ca. 1924, attracting Aragon, Eluard, Desnos, Cocteau, Dali, and Tanguy, among other writers and artists. They sought juxtapositions of irrational images, often derived from easy associations. The result was at times a trivial melange of a superficial zaniness produced by an imagery of pyrotechnics rather than one emergent from a substratum of psychic fears and joys, from troubled areas of dream and archetypal energies. Bly's surrealism is of these deeper perceptions. No Tinker Bell waves her wand over a giggle of pastel oblivion ha-has. No snickering, skeleton-bone, Halloween belly-riffs here. Bly's images emerge from a neocortexual loam, with an unpredictability and dancing speed distressing to readers prizing the linear, the rational, the easily deciphered in their poems—readers with Mammal brains. Bly is a whirl of color in a field of cabbages.

"Visiting the Farallones" will clarify some of what I have been saying. In this new poem, Bly touches concerns that have occupied his energies for years—the pollution of the environment and the callous destruction of life on the planet. While his fervor has not changed, his approach has. He seems more content now to allow his rage a less programmatic, less didactic, breath. Imagery, rather than direct statements. He trusts us, his readers, more.

Clubbing seals to death initiates the poem, followed by allusions to the decimation of whales and tortoises. The latter are crammed into shipholds. Often in Bly's poems, present news triggers memories of past disasters. The plundering of the tortoises is most probably a leap back to the nineteenth century (a.k.a. "The Age of Darwin") when sailing ships loaded on tortoises for ballast and for food. There are more connections, as Bly leaps to the broader theme of decadent human cultures. The Roman empire rotted first in the remote provinces. The American frontier, symbolized by a wagon breaking to pieces on boulders, is gone, the landscape littered today with beer cans and polluted with smog and chemicals. "Darkness," Bly says, is *reality*—as is the soft feather he sees lying near him on some snow, leading his gaze to the carcass of a half-eaten rooster. For most of us, a half-devoured bird is revolting, no matter how rich its thematic evocations. But if we are to be enlightened, Bly believes, we must scrutinize the painful and the gross as well as the scenic and the palatable. "Crumbling" is the word he employs to interweave his seemingly disparate materials. Animal species have crumbled, as have empires, and once-vital frontiers.

Thus far, Bly has *seen* objects as they have appeared clearly on his stage. Now he produces a fresh image, one he does not literally see, and leaps to a contemporary scene emblematic of all crumblings. In an old folks' home life crumbles, wasted and brutalized. A sadistic society tucks these people out of sight, much as sailing ships stowed turtles. There's a perversion/inversion here of the life principle, of growth and ecstasy. The death-mother works in loathsome ways her wonders to perform.

In "Snowbanks North of the House," the mysterious man in black of the book's title starts up a hill, changes his mind, and returns to the bottom. Is he a minister? an undertaker? is he Bly's father? Is he Death? What would he have found on the hill? Once more, Bly generates thematic leaps by an initial meditation on something concrete—here it's a great snowdrift stopped about six feet from a house, a phenomenon I witnessed often when I was a boy in northern Wisconsin. In meeting the house, vectored air currents kept the snow back, almost as a punishment for the failures occurring within the house. If the sweeps had piled themselves tight against the building, that building would be insulated and warm. This house, though, contains failed marriages and memories of children who have departed and never write home, or who have died. A son dies. The bereaved parents never speak to one another again. The church too fails, as the wine loses its zest, and the minister "falls." These failures seem debris in some ocean of life, lifting and falling (failing) all night long. The saving image is the moon. It proceeds through clouds and stars, achieving a splendid isolation, where it glows undisturbed, a symbol for the self apart, striving for distance from human stress, for a lone sufficiency in moon-radiance.

The man in the black coat, who eschews the hilltop, appears to symbolize, like the snowdrifts, the poet in his sought out isolation. He seems an "advocate of darkness" (see "For My Son Noah, Ten Years Old"), an associate of the Earth death-mother who appears to ease our way through this mortal life. He also suggests what Bly terms "the masculine soul" or "Father consciousness." ("I Came Out of the Mother Naked"). In its "middle range," the masculine soul is "logic and fairness"; in its higher leapings it "hurries toward the spirit." Like the feminine consciousness, its counterpart and opposite, it is a "good," can't be eradicated, and is mysterious. It is a "veil," Bly says, drawn against the death so feared by the male spirit. The best we can hope for, Bly writes, is to join these two consciousnesses, so as to experience what lies beyond the veil. Bly's best images possess a koanlike quality of unresolved suggestiveness long after we have tried to decipher them—so also with the black-suited man, though I shall return to him at the close of this essay.

In another poem, Bly observes that "the walnut of his brain glows" when he is in solitude. The irradiation transfers energies from his other brains to the neocortex. Even when he is thus charged and alert, his insights are not all they might be; he has mere intimations of visionary possibilities, of deciphering the great secrets behind the Shelleyan veil. Even a genius like Albert Einstein reputedly burned only a small percentage of his neocortexual energies. By stimulating this third brain, Bly observes, he releases a genie who, alas, flies off to hover over some "car cemetery" and won't return to his bottle. We must accept the presence of such contradictions and our dimly realized visions. By accepting, we may be preparing for later insights of a hitherto unknown grandeur.

One of the best of Bly's efforts to reflect the glowings of that "walnut brain" appears in "The Dried Sturgeon," a prose poem found halfway through his book. Insight, ecstasy, growth, and death are the primary motifs. On an October walk along a riverbank, Bly sees a dried-out sturgeon which he examines with great care. A "speckled nose-bone" leads back to an eye socket, behind which is a "dark hole" where soft gills once grew. This hole is a sort of cave which the poet enters, confronting his darker, female self. A hunchback appears and is made whole by the "sweet dark," a virgin with magical black stones in her cloak. These seem elements in a fairy tale, evocative of the narrative inconsistencies children love. Our poet, himself flawed, enters his healing meditation via images of fish corpse, pine needle, sand, and hunchback. In that Persephone-underground, he experiences a thrill of proximity to Death, that *duende* experience he prizes in other poets. He is invigorated as he returns to objective light, to Father consciousness, symbolized by the sturgeon's scales which are "dry, swift, organized, tubular, straight and humorless as railway schedules, the big clamp of the boxcar, tapering into sleek womanly death." In a sense, he closes up the rich female concavities of the "dark hole." Reason dominates, and is symbolized by the straight line, by schedules, by speed—all antitheses for the female underworld. To this "womanly" region we return at our deaths, completing the circle that began on leaving our mother's womb to start our peregrinations to and through our father-selves.

Another striking presence of shadow/*duende* is in "Mourning Pablo Neruda," written in brief lines reminiscent of the Chilean poet's own. Bly is driving to his shack where he goes to think and write. Beside him on the seat is a sweating jar of water lying on its side. Glancing down, he observes that the jostling jar creates a wet shadow on the seat, a paradigm for Neruda's death, a shadowing itself of subtle, tragic effects. Bly drives through an area of granite quarries, filled with blocks soon to be shaped into gravestones. A leap: Our memories of the dead are watery traces within us, mere hints of the moisture still resident within granite. If we accept this diminution, we see that the dead have merely flowed "around us" to the Gulf Stream and out to the Eternal Ocean, a grand universal occasioned by the poet's reflections on the water in the jar.

Nowhere are Bly's techniques of moving from the concrete to the universal better realized than in "Finding an Old Ant Mansion," another prose poem. Again on retreat, asleep on a floor, he wakens when he dreams that a rattlesnake is biting him. He arises, dresses, and goes to a pasture. He senses the ground beneath his tennis shoes, their rubbery texture allowing *feel* in a way leather would not. He likes these "rolls and humps," and marvels at the elasticity. The earth "never lies flat," he says; it must accommodate a varied debris both falling down upon it (trees) and emerging from its depths (stones). He passes through a strip of hardwoods to another pasture, and finds a chunk of wood on the ground, strangely eaten in some sixteen layers by ants. He fetches the piece home and props it on his desk.

The cavities in the wood create doors into "cave-dark" places—Persephone redivivus. Leaps evoke memories: the shadows recall the "heavy brown of barn stalls" he knew as a boy, and other dark insights—a daughter understands her mother's silences. The ant-artifact is a universe all its own, a paradigm for our psyches, so antlike and male, in their obsessions. We scurry to execute our father's hopes and wishes for us: "infant ants awaken to old father-worked halls, uncle-loved boards, walls that hold the sighs of the pasture, the moos of confused cows . . . some motor cars from the road, held in the same wood, given shape by Osiris' love." According to designs taught us by our great benefactor and primal father image, himself son of Nut and Geb, the legendary Osiris who provided our ancestors with civilization and taught them agriculture, we shape our achievements.

The ant-riddled wood suggests primeval forces (it recalls, perhaps, in its unchewed state, the erect father) and provides residences, "apartments," for spirits to reside. The ants, thus, have wrought "a place for our destiny," that sweep of time within which "we too labor, and no one sees our labor." Uncannily, and with a delicate compassion, Bly retrieves the specific from the universal, returning the motif to himself. He recalls his own father whose labors he has symbolically discovered in this chunk of wood. What follows? Who will discover Bly's labors when he dies? His *wood* will lie somewhere in a pasture "not yet found by a walker." This poem moves me: the gentle voice, so mature and exploring, is the exfoliation of a man large in both physique and spirit. Bly's leap into that final image of our lives as wood pieces waiting for discovery resolves the poem profoundly in areas of the psyche hitherto untapped. To most observers, that ant-eaten, riddled hunk of dead fibers would deserve, if noticed at all, to be thrust aside by a boot.

Bly's gatherings of objects include many we normally feel squeamish about: a partially devoured bird, a dangling eyeball. A "sick" rose is as conducive to insight as a healthy rose. To see whole, Bly implies, we must encompass all of experience we can, the positive and the negative, the creative and the destructive. In "Kennedy's Inauguration," a Sister hands Bly the seed of a sweet-gum of witch hazel tree, a globular fruit with hornlike projections. When it ripened, it discharged its seed in an explosive burst, shooting it out several feet. The pod is as fertile, one feels, as Persephone's pomegranate. Now pinecone dry (an echo of the desiccated sturgeon), the pod is the size of a cow's eyeball. The *seeing* once possible there, like that in the eyeball, has "exploded out / through the eye-holes," leaving behind a husk of spikes and dark vacancies resembling hen beaks "widening in fear."

Bly next reviews his day. He went on errands twice, both times avoiding the funeral parlor. He held three "distant" conversations (by phone?). The gift of the seed followed. Now, as he starts to meditate, the cow's eye reminds him of a *Lorenzo* shot by a cannonball that left his eye dangling from his face, a horror. Like the seedpod, history itself explodes and is both germinative and sterile, humanizing and destructive. In this poem, though, it "seeds" the worst—mayhem and torture: a Papal candidate is murdered by an enemy. Belgian King Leopold's plantation overseer (ca. World War I) chops off the hands of an African youth and deposits them near his father, to punish the latter. Fascists destroy contraceptive clinics and carry the women off to breeding brothels. Our drugged sex-mistress, Marilyn Monroe, victim, one feels, of male sexual obsessions gone mad, lies dead on her bed. Young men are decimated in purposeless war, viz., the Vietnam conflict which Bly, as we know, protested vociferously and courageously. A Marine whose head and feet are shot off "cries" for a medic. We leap next to Kennedy's inauguration. The vigorous, youthful man stands in the cold, taking his oath of office. Nearby waits the old poet Robert Frost. One senses Bly's affection for both Kennedy and Frost, and his hope that the inauguration might produce a new national destiny. Hindsight, of course, tells us otherwise. The hen beaks in the seed persist in their screaming. The Reptile brain kills and wastes. A father ejects his seed from his loins, delaying his son's return to his primal mother. She, in imitation of Persephone, carries a round red fruit in her hand. Both figures draw us into magnetic fields; both must be departed from, abandoned, and returned to. The father, finally, despite an affection for him, may be the more difficult of the pair to please.

In a revealing moment in "The Prodigal Son," a son kneels on dried cobs in a swine pen and reflects on the hostile history with his father. He hears the latter's death-fearing plea to the doctor: "Don't let me die!" and recalls a particularly venomous altercation. As he was dragging his father over the floor, the father saw a crack in the boards and shouted for him to stop: "I only dragged my father that far!" Conflict seems the brutal norm between a father and a son. As the son resists the father, he pursues his own maleness and leaves his home. His departure vexes not only the father but also the mother—both feel deserted by him (cf. the parents in "Snowbanks North of the House"). Before he can accept his father as an equal, the son must sire his own children, learn to dance to his own music, honor his dreams, and write his poems.

In "The Ship's Captain Looking over the Rail," Bly observes that to tell a captain or a father that they are "good" is to say nothing; for these men conceal their true scars, limps, and blemishes from their underlings—sailors and children. In "Kneeling Down to Look into a Culvert," the final poem in the book, Bly merges his own father- and sonhoods. The culvert (as reason, rod, conduit) is a masculine image from which the female water is released into merry light. Bly imagines his children splashing in the brightness at the culvert's end, where they sense his presence, and where he performs a similar commemorative act for his own father.

"My Father's Wedding 1924" links Bly's father with that puzzling figure in the black coat. Once again a prosaic object, another chunk of wood, stripped of its bark, triggers leaps and recollections. What was Bly's father like, as a younger man? Was he a masked bird-father, Bhutanian, with giant teeth and a pig nose, dancing ritually on a bad leg? Was he really as assured as he seemed? No. He concealed a limp from his son. Only when he, Bly, fathered his own children, did he see that the father's limp hid his craving to be loved. Showing affection has not been a desirable masculine trait. Like the log which once held bark, Bly's father kept people at a distance, even members of his family. He covered his vulnerabilities with a gnarled, rough exterior. At his wedding, his *true* bride was not the woman of flesh and blood beside him; rather, she stood invisible between him and his bride interposing herself as a kind of Fata Morgana. This strange ceremony was performed by a man in a black coat, a preacher who lifted his "book" and called "for order."

Who is the preacher? I think that he serves as a father-spirit who marries us to that mythic mother, the Death-Mother, as she awaits us in those mysterious shadowy holes, death-spaces, burnished through eye sockets, wood, and culverts. The father in black appears when we wed ourselves to our deaths, which we seem to do when we allow our emotions, our feminine selves, full play, and accept our father, resolving our struggles with him. Thus, partially fulfilled, we are then able to proceed toward the Mother and our deaths with a minimal fear. Male and female spirits are in balance.

I don't pretend that my reading of the black figure as a kind of Robert Mitchum Bible-thumper who initiates our journey back to the womb is the only possible reading. The image remains open and intriguing. To read the figure merely as Death is, I think, facile. There remains a considerable mysterious light around his body. Finally, my efforts to sort meanings throughout have made me aware of how male-directed the critical act is; one must seek to illuminate elusive matters hidden in a poet's psyche, and to provide coherent interpretations. This all seems quite foreign to the neocortexual leaps of the spirit Bly extols. Nevertheless, in a poet as gifted as Bly, neocortexual quiverings do occur, even in his critics and interpreters, male and female, and do lead to that special congress which changes the critic's life.

NOTES

1. See my essays on Howard McCord and David Wagoner in *The Great American Bake-Off* (1979) and *Second Series* (1982), both Long Beach, Calif.: Scarecrow Press.

2. In *Walt Whitman: The Measure of His Song,* ed. Jim Perlman et al. (Minneapolis: Holy Cow! Press, 1981).

JOSEPH SHAKARCHI

An Interview with Robert Bly

(At the invitation of the Jung Center, Robert Bly was in Denver to give a lecture on the concept of "The Shadow," and to conduct a seminar entitled, "Fairy Tales for Married Couples and Lovers." The following interview took place during the two days preceding these events.)

JS: In 1972, according to Ekbert Faas, you said, "In the last eight or nine, ten years, the thinking I've learned most from has been Buddhist." Your writing has also shown the influence of Zen, Taoist, and ancient Chinese thinking. Does Eastern thought continue to influence your writing and thinking?

RB: Yes, there's no question that it does. In the West or, I should say, in popular Christianity, religious people are willing to accept either the body or the spirit as good, but not both. Clyde Reed told me that when he was at the Mount Athos monastery in Greece, two years ago, a curious incident happened. No females are allowed there—no female cats, no female mice, no female dogs, no women! They go to tremendous lengths on that, and Mount Athos is probably the oldest ascetic institution still working. He spent a couple of days there and one night found two old monks sitting on the mountainside. They all sat silently for a while in the shyness of unknown languages, and finally one of the monks spoke four words in English: "The body is bad." (*Laughter.*)

I find it amazing to meet, through reading, the cultures influenced by Taoism and Buddhism, in which monks don't say that sentence over and over again. If teachers or students feel that an ascetic stage is useful for a while, they say, "Why not?" But few

Massachusetts Review 23 (1982):226–43. Reprinted with permission.

Buddhists go along with this mad Tolstoyan Christian idea that the body is bad. Their "middle way" has been a big shock to me. I rejoice tremendously in Zen thought, and in the poems of Kabir and Mirabai made of an interweaving of body, mind, soul, and spirit, with sexual energy woven into spiritual energy.

Lately though, I've developed some suspicion of Eastern teachers. Gioia Timpanelli, the fairy storyteller, says that several of our dragons live in the stomach, others in the anus, others in the genital area, and that's where they have to be faced. I suspect that some contemporary Asian teachers want to bypass those dragons, and go directly to "The Princess," to the heart.

JS: It's significant that Jonah spent three days in the stomach of the whale.

RB: Ah! That's nice! The story about Jonah is moving. It surely suggests the need to go down into the dark. One doesn't go always towards the light. Jonah says that what we really need is "endarkenment."

JS: Jonah also has to spend three days there. It's not just an overnight stay. He has to really spend some time there.

RB: Yes, three days! As a student of myth, I'm a child of Joseph Campbell. Campbell describes the sun and moon energies as opposites. The moon is related to consciousness involved with the earth plane. On the earth, everything changes, and you must release the moment and let it go. The moon does this. The moon is full and it releases that; it becomes one-quarter full and it releases that and becomes dark. So Campbell says that moon-teaching teaches human beings not to hold to the present moment, but to let it go. Well, the moon also goes into the dark three days every month. Is there a connection? Very mysterious. . . . Jonah is probably a story from the time when men owned the moon.

JS: Usually we think of the moon as associated with women because of the menstrual cycle.

RB: Well, the moon eventually moved over to women, apparently. No one knows when, maybe 1500–2000 B.C. If men lost the moon, I suppose it means they got the sun, or took it. That taking may be connected with the invasion of Greece by male-oriented tribes from the North. And Apollo comes full of light, Apollo comes surrounded by gold.

JS: In the original Apollo myth, Apollo rises for only half the time, and submerges for half the time.

RB: That's beautiful. They never lost the connection with the dark. Apollo's throne is near the Python. So we're the only ones who have lost our connection with the old dark that was under Apollo, Jonah's dark.

The bull-calf, Joseph Campbell says, is connected with the moon. Its horns are the horns of the moon. And Moses said, "Do not fool around with that calf. Do not fool around with the moon." Wild stuff. All of this could be called material from our own moon-teaching past, which includes the Mesopotamian past, and the Palestinian past, as well as the Anglo-Saxon past in *Beowulf;* we gradually become aware of teachings about the dark that are hard to get from the Asians.

JS: Does this mean that you're moving away from Buddhism?

RB: I feel, though I can't prove it, that certain Buddhists know this darkness well. (*Shows photographs of Bhutan dancers in masks, resembling Kali, or the "Teeth-Mother."*) Buddhists know about the monsters in the stomach. They know about this, but in some way it is integrated with them, or the culture says it for them. So they are a little advanced for us. I feel that we have a lot of work to do on the dark ourselves. I'm a little hesitant about going forward so fast into Eastern things, as we did in the sixties.

JS: This reminds me of D. H. Lawrence's criticism of modern capitalist society as being centered on instant gratification of our desires. For example, when you're hungry, you go to McDonald's. You order a hamburger and it's right there. You don't have to do anything, and there's no time or work involved.

RB: That's got to be related. I remember suddenly a story of Reuven Gold's, the storyteller from Chicago.

One day a ritual slaughterer, when doing his work in this little Russian village, notices that an old Christian peasant watches and then shakes his head. This happens two or three times. The slaughterer gets bugged by this. And he says, "What can this mean? I've been to Warsaw, I've been to Krakow, I've had the best teachers, I know how to do ritual slaughter perfectly. I sharpen my knives every week. What could I be doing wrong?" So he watches carefully, and notices that the old peasant shakes his head precisely at the point when he's sharpening the knives. But he says, "What could I be doing wrong? The stone is ritually right. I use water, I lay the knife on the stone, I sharpen the knife. This old man knows nothing about it!" But he sharpens his knives the next week, and again the old man shakes his head.

Finally he says: "Listen, every time you watch, you shake your head. I'm sick of it. I follow the ritual just as I was taught it. What am I doing wrong?" The old man says, "The slaughterer who was here before you knew how to do it." (He gives his name, and it's the name of the man who later became the Baal Shem-Tov). "He was aware that these chickens wanted to live longer, every creature wants to live. And so it was his own tears that he used to sharpen the knives with."

JS: Getting back to Eastern writers, you've been doing translations of Rumi, Kabir, and Mirabai. Have you felt them influencing your own writing?

RB: Oh, yes, I think so, because one of the things about us is that we're very shy in the spiritual area. At least I am. In our culture, people have spiritual impulses and thoughts but they don't find them reflected in newspapers or television, and so they think they're the only ones that have them. It reminds me of the quotation from Heraclitus that Eliot placed at the beginning of *Four Quartets:* "We all have a certain mind in common, but everyone acts as if he had it alone." So Kabir teaches boldness in dealing with these matters, and that's been helpful.

JS: Have there been any particular works about Eastern thought and religion that have been especially influential?

RB: I like Watts's *Nature, Man and Woman.* And Blyth's haiku books. I began by studying Jacob Boehme—I mentioned him in *The Light Around the Body*—and Meister Eckhart. I like Blyth's

Zen in English Literature. He quotes a Chinese poem, and then he quotes some Robert Louis Stevenson, and says, "You see. Very close to each other." He will put Dickens right next to Basho. An absolutely mad book. But he is aware that certain spiritual buds that the Ch'an people bring into flower are present in bud form in writers like Stevenson—where we'd never expect to see it—in Dickens, in Hardy, in Thoreau. That is one of the books I value because it makes genuine links between our own culture and the Asian.

JS: It's interesting that you focus on books that link our cultures, because I was expecting you to mention books like the *Bhagavad Gita* or the *Tibetan Book of the Dead*.

RB: I have never found the *Bhagavad Gita* terrifically interesting, nor the *Book of the Dead*. To me they're too far along the road, too far along the path. You know what the witches say? "There's a silver thread, and you mustn't get too far separated, because if the silver thread breaks, you die." I feel that some of the Americans studying Tantric Buddhism, for example, are thinning out that silver thread a little too far. Just because the Tibetans have a *Book of the Dead* doesn't mean that we have to read it.

JS: Again, it's trying to make the jump too fast.

RB: Certain spiritual centers become a sort of Tibetan McDonald's. (*Laughter.*)

JS: One other question regarding religion. In the past, you've often been critical of Christianity, yet you've also referred to yourself as "a Middle-Western Lutheran." Can you reconcile those two? How do you feel towards Christianity now?

RB: Ah, you can't reconcile them. It's hopeless. I feel that Christianity has done a lot of damage to the spiritual psyche by remarks like that monk's "The body is bad." On the other hand, Christianity is the only carrier, after the destruction of the Scandinavian religions, of the transcendental world. So we have to say that Christianity *is* the way by which the transcendental world has come to us, at least the way it came to me as a Northern European. I wouldn't have read any Buddhism if

Christianity hadn't already carried it to me. The transcendental world flowed to us through Bible stories we heard as children. So, therefore, one's attitude toward it is very complicated.

Lately I've been thinking, "Who am I to say I'm a Sufi?" There's some kind of arrogance in saying, "Yes, I'm a Sufi," or "I'm a Buddhist." I think that Christianity is probably as good a religion as we deserve. So was Nixon as a president. (*Laughter.*) How is one to say that we are such a marvelous nation that we deserve a better president than Nixon? How are we to say that we're so marvelously spiritual that we deserve a better religion than Christianity? I can't say that anymore.

JS: See, I would react differently because I'm Jewish, and to me Christianity is a different religion than my own. But I find myself more drawn to Buddhism, by far, than to Christianity, and I see a lot of similarities between Judaism and Buddhism. I'm thinking of how some other poets who were Jewish, or who are Jewish, have also been drawn to Buddhism, like Leonard Cohen and Allen Ginsberg.

RB: That's true.

JS: I don't know if you want to talk about this, but didn't you study with the same spiritual leader, Trungpa, that Ginsberg follows?

RB: Yes, I got some of my first instruction in meditation from Trungpa while he was still in Scotland, before he came over here; he had a small meditation center in Scotland. He was thinking of moving to the United States and I told him he should meet Allen. A few years later, Allen, Gary Snyder, and I gave a benefit reading with Trungpa in Boulder. So I've had a long association with him, but I don't like the way the center has developed in Boulder.

JS: You just mentioned Gary Snyder, and you've often praised his work. Do you see any relationship between his work and your own?

RB: I feel a tremendous closeness myself. I don't know how he feels. He has the practicality of a farm person as he approaches literature. And then, of course, I feel that both of us go back to Thoreau and Emerson.

And I've always liked his poems—from the start, it was apparent that he was a marvelous poet. In 1958, I put an ad in *Poetry* magazine that said: "Announcing a new magazine called *The Fifties*." Phil Whalen, I think, sent me four or five poems of Snyder's from *Myths and Texts*. I'd never heard of Snyder at that time, but I immediately accepted them for the first issue. I printed Snyder and Ignatow, I think, in the first issue, neither of whom I'd ever heard of before. It was just crystal clear what a good poet he was when that stuff came in the mail. There are other ways I guess that we are linked, but those are a couple of them.

JS: Do you think Snyder's poetry has actually influenced yours?

RB: I'd just say that I feel tremendous encouragement from the fact of his poetry. It gives evidence that American and Eastern thought can be merged, and that clear physical images, ordinary in mood, can be a carrier for the spirit, and for the soul. So I'm sure there's been some influence in technical ways, but mainly I have felt tremendous encouragement, not from anything he's ever said to me, just from his example, and the clear, consistent way that he follows his own bent.

There are differences. He entered poetry apparently through Pound and Olson, who both emphasized laying down the perception clearly. I entered I guess through Yeats, the Spanish, and the South Americans. What we had in common was a love for Chinese poetry. In the early sixties there was a sort of Olson-influenced poetry conference at Berkeley, and I believe many speakers there, Snyder and Creeley among them, attacked the image as being in essence decorative. So on the matter of the image we were on opposite sides. Isn't that interesting? In the *Black Mountain Review,* second issue I think, Creeley ridiculed Dylan Thomas. Kenneth Rexroth resigned from the magazine on that point and wrote a blistering letter to Creeley. Rexroth tries to hold the ends together!

JS: Let me ask you about one concept that Snyder has often brought up. Traditionally, poets have been characterized as seers or visionaries, especially in ancient times. Snyder has said that he sees the poet's role in society as being that of the shaman—the tribal healer, or "medicine man." Do you see yourself along any of those lines at all?

RB: In *News of the Universe,* I remarked the most helpful addition to thought about poetry in the last thirty years has been the concept of the poet as a relative of the shaman. I think it's very helpful, and I like it better than the concept of the poet as a seer, or the poet as a carrier of moral values. I don't know how far as an "educated man" I am a shaman, or how far my poetry relates to all that, but I feel the health of it.

JS: Do you see your role in society any differently?

RB: I don't think I want to talk about that.

JS: I wanted to ask you about your recent use of the dulcimer, because that hearkens back to the old tradition of the poet as a troubadour. I'm thinking of the Provençal poets, and so on.

RB: It goes farther back, also, to *Beowulf.* Students of *Beowulf* believe they have reconstructed the harp typically used for Anglo-Saxon poetry; a picture of the reconstruction appears on the cover of Chickering's new translation of *Beowulf.* It's a small stringed instrument with a sounding box. I do feel myself in that tradition, at least, I should say, minimally. I am a beginner.

JS: Again, regarding Snyder and yourself, some people feel that you could both be criticized for something we were just referring to—namely being moralistic in your poetry. Whether it's didactic or instructive, there are often direct statements of political or philosophical thought in your poetry. I wanted to see what your reaction is to this sort of criticism.

RB: Who knows? They may be right. You can never say anybody's wrong. But if I were asked about it, I would say that I understand the poem to be a container of energy, and the more kinds of energy in the poem the better. Some poems have Taoist energy, which is more related to shamanism and wilderness. In the Confucian world, you give instruction in a poem; the poem lays out certain rules to help people live decently. Snyder does a lot of that. Some people connect such instruction with high school principals and stuff, but I don't. I consider it to be a good form of energy, a true form of energy, if the instruction is intelligent.

JS: Aside from poets, are there novelists or dramatists, or people in other arts—musicians, film makers—that you feel a great amount of kinship or respect for?

RB: (*Pause.*) I haven't thought about that much, so I can just mention some names in a dumb way. I often feel a kinship with painters. One of them is the Seattle painter, Morris Graves. And some of the abstract expressionists—Gorky, for example, and Helen Frankenthaler. I like Rothko's work for its struggle with the Teeth-Mother.

In music, I suppose the deepest feeling I have is for Ali Akbar Khan. I heard a concert of his the other night, and it was staggering. Saddik Hussein played the tablas. And I admire some of Keith Jarrett's work. In fact, I wrote a poem about Jarrett's *Koln Concert* a year or two ago. The contemporary American composers I don't know well, and that is awful.

JS: It's interesting that the two you mentioned are improvisational musicians, like Ravi Shankar, who Ali Akbar Khan has played together with.

RB: I know this is a loony idea, but improvisation in art has to be connected with the idea that the body is not all bad. If you think the body is bad, it means you have to hold it down by getting a symphonic score and making sure that nobody leaves it. But Ravi Shankar and Ali Akbar Khan trust their bodies; they trust the impulses coming from the body. In the middle of the evening, they trust it. Ali Akbar Khan gets harsh and wild, and teeth start appearing all over his instrument. (*Makes barking noises. Laughter.*) He is trusting his body at those moments.

JS: Doesn't that also show real trust for their minds? They're not afraid of letting what's in their minds come out.

RB: Aha! I like that. That's absolutely true.

JS: I notice you haven't mentioned any writers of drama or fiction; they're literary forms that most people think of as closer to poetry.

RB: I think the trouble with drama is that there isn't enough of this in it (*shows photo of Bhutan dog-dancers*). You can't get the profoundly negative energies on stage without a mask, and drama isn't using masks now. I love Ionesco, but I love drama like this (*refers to photo*) even more, and I don't see dramatists doing that. I may be wrong. I like Salinger and Bellow at times, but I don't see Bellow moving towards that either. I see him moving in another direction, towards heavily mental material, if we could make such a distinction.

JS: In the past, you've criticized the state of American poetry, compared to European and Latin American poetry. Do you think, now, that American poetry over the last ten or twenty years has been showing any signs of growth?

RB: Oh, I do think American poetry is strong. We both could name ten or twelve strong poets working right now. But I think it's stuck. I don't know how, but I think it has something to do with Whitman. I have tried to think lately of ways in which Whitman's inheritance has been limiting. For example, Whitman does not spend much time praising the work of art, as a work of art. He is tremendously interested in the flow of feeling and in process. But I don't feel that Americans—or I at least— got a very clear grasp from him of what a work of art is. I compared him in a recent essay to Pushkin; I think the Russians got a very clear idea of what a work of art is from Pushkin. Perhaps that is why in some ways Pasternak is more intense than our free-verse writers, though I can't really defend that. Goethe made the remark that there are three elements in a work of art: content is the easiest to understand, meaning is more difficult, and form is most difficult of all. I feel that our inheritance from Whitman includes the first two, but not the last. . . .

JS: I was wondering if you have any sort of systematic philosophical outlook on such problems as the relationship between mind and body, between reality and the imagination, or on materialism versus idealism, and so on.

RB: No, I believe in five or six different systems: the astrological system, the Jungian system, the Catholic, the leftist system, the Gurdjieff system, and the Bronze Age system Joseph Campbell is now teaching. Reality is so complicated that one needs about six more!

JS: Do you see yourself as combining, or synthesizing those different ideas?

RB: No! I'm not sure that fruitful thought should emphasize systhesis. I believe thought involves following certain impulses of the teacher farther. If you set yourself the task of synthesizing thought, you may spend the rest of your life doing that, and the moment before you finish, you notice you've left something out!

JS: At different times you've stressed different things, like "mother consciousness," "twofold consciousness," Buddhism, Jungian theory, fairy tales, etc. Do you have any unifying principle that connects these different strands of thought?

RB: I don't know, and I don't intend to look for it. (*Laughter.*) There are many truths, and they're lying scattered around. Every once in a while, you notice another one lying on the ground.

JS: Who have you felt most influenced by in terms of Jungian thought?

RB: In evolving Jungian thought, I feel the most helpful writers are Marie-Louise von Franz—*Problems of the Feminine in Fairy Tales, Shadow and Evil in Fairy Tales*—and James Hillman. Both of them belong to the second generation. Thinking continues in the Jungian groups, among many analysts; *Quadrant* often prints marvelous articles.

JS: On the topic of Jungian thought in relation to your poetry, do you see Surrealism as an attempt to capture elements of the unconscious and bring them up into the conscious mind?

RB: Yes, I do. Of course it's possible that surrealism is very much a city phenomenon—it began in Paris—and it doesn't respect the consciousness of nature. I touched on that in *News of the Universe.* Surrealism tries to bring material from the unconscious directly up into the conscious, bypassing somehow the world of nature. Perhaps it fragments nature, and deals with it in fragments. But I feel that Dürer or Bosch love the consciousness of nature itself. In their painting a sort of triangle begins to appear, made of the painter's conscious mind, nature, and the unconscious, and the energy agrees to move in that circuit or circle. That's a new thought for me.

JS: Let's go then to "twofold consciousness"—that being the direction I'd guess you'd say you're moving in.

RB: I think that the scientists, especially nuclear physicists, are coming out of a long period of single consciousness, which is the way Blake phrased it—save us, he said, from "single vision and Newton's sleep." They have come to recognize that when a scientist undertakes an experiment with subatomic particles, he is dealing with two powers: the power of the subatomic particle, and the power of the observer. Are those two consciousnesses? He has to take account of both of those, because the presence of the observer apparently affects the movement of the subatomic particles.

Something important is contained here, difficult to grasp. It won't do to describe the world in the way that surrealists do, leaving out the consciousness of nature. I may be wrong on this, but I sense something disturbing has appeared, though I'm not sure my analogies are right.

JS: So you see twofold consciousness as going beyond surrealism?

RB: Yes.

JS: In *This Body Is Made of Camphor and Gopherwood,* you put a lot of stress on seeing the body in a positive way. This seems to lead into the twofold consciousness in *This Tree Will Be Here for a Thousand Years,* where the stress is on nature. It seems that you're saying that once we're in touch with our own bodies, then we can get in touch with other physical bodies and objects.

RB: Yes. Thinking of those two books, you must remember that only the last three or four poems in *This Tree Will Be Here for a Thousand Years* are contemporary with *This Body Is Made of Camphor and Gopherwood,* and the other poems are much older. The first poem in it goes back to a year after *Silence in the Snowy Fields.* So I wouldn't think too much about chronological sequence there. In chronology, *This Tree Will Be Here for a Thousand Years* really follows *Silence in the Snowy Fields,* except for a few recent poems.

JS: Snyder does the same sort of thing, perhaps holding onto a poem for a number of years until it will fit into a particular volume. Do you do that deliberately with your volumes, in order for each one to have its own unity? Do you first plan a volume, and then write poems to go in it? Or do you look at the poems you have written, and then plan a volume?

RB: It's more like the latter. I realized I was still writing a few poems every year in the style of *Silence in the Snowy Fields,* and I decided not to stuff those into other books, but to just wait. And if I had enough to make a book, I'd do it. If not, I'd just never publish them.

JS: To elaborate on the idea of twofold consciousness, which you wrote about in *News of the Universe* and in *This Tree Will Be Here for a Thousand Years,* when you talk about animals, plants, and subatomic particles having consciousness, do they have the same kind of consciousness that humans do? Or the same consciousness as each other?

RB: I talked about that a little in *News of the Universe.* If one adopts the metaphor of the spectrum, with infrared at one end and ultraviolet at the other, one can then imagine the whole range as consciousness, rather than color. We are used to the consciousness that is verbal, but there may be consciousness that is not verbal. There are certain stones that seem to be able to hold memories of human events, and there are people who can pick up stones and hold them, and then the memory returns to the person. That's very strange.

JS: In *Silence in the Snowy Fields* and in *This Tree Will Be Here for a Thousand Years,* you use elements we think of as nonliving, like "snow" and "darkness," in such a way that they appear to have consciousness. I was wondering if, for you, this has any similarity to the way Gary Snyder and Ted Hughes use elements of nature in a mythic sense. While they use animals—Snyder uses Coyote, and Hughes uses Crow—are you using "snow" and "darkness" in the same way?

RB: I think it's possible. Myth brings up a mystery that the rational mind doesn't really faze. It is a serious mystery. Suppose a person feels that in a certain part of the forest he or she feels a hostile or evil energy. Just for fun, let's call it Kali energy. The question that myth brings up is, "Is this energy a human energy that's merely bounced off the place, or is there actually a being in the universe called Kali?" Metaphor doesn't commit itself, but myth does. Myth says that Kali does exist and that she is out there. That's a big step—to go from forest as something that reflects some dark part of ourselves (that's a metaphorical use of it), to forest as something out there with its own consciousness.

Gestalt psychology teaches that a witch in your dream always represents a "dark side of your self." But what if that isn't true, or isn't the only truth? The Indians seem to feel that there may have been a being out in the woods, called Bear, that would come and sleep with girls. That's really pretty unacceptable to the modern mind.

JS: In the introduction to *This Tree Will Be Here for a Thousand Years,* you talk about the "grief" of nature. At the same time, in some of the poems in that volume, you express feelings of great joy arising from nature. In one poem, "A Dream of an Afternoon with a Woman I Did Not Know"—although this isn't a nature poem—after you describe a dream, you end with the line, "I loved that afternoon, and the rest of my life." How do you see the relationship between grief and joy there?

RB: I'm not sure there is so much grief in that poem, although perhaps there is some. The ancient tragic view would be that grief and joy are close to each other, but neither is close to happiness. Happiness is a function of the ego; in the first half of life, the ego longs for happiness, and when it doesn't get it, it falls into depression. Happiness and depression make a pair; and later in life, grief and joy seem to make a pair. If that poem has joy in it, it is because it belongs to a long slow development. The sequence really begins with a poem in *Silence in the Snowy Fields* called "A Man Writes to a Part of Himself." In that poem, the feminine is a long ways from me—in fact, in a primitive valley.

JS: We were talking about the moon belonging to the woman, because of her menstrual cycle, but Campbell mentions that the moon originally belonged to the man. I was thinking that maybe men have a similar cycle that just isn't as clearly apparent, maybe even a physical or instinctive cycle.

RB: I think so. It affects the psyche.

JS: Some critics, including Faas and Michael Atkinson, have used the term "journey" in reference to your poetry. Some of your books of poetry, in particular *Sleepers Joining Hands* and *This Body Is Made of Camphor and Gopherwood,* seem to describe a journey or odyssey in which there's a quest for spiritual and psychological growth, or for higher consciousness and "wholeness." Would you say that this is an accurate view?

RB: Certainly. I seem to think naturally in journeys and stages. To me this is ordinary common sense. One notices that fairy stories often lay out stages of growth. It has only been after the Christian victory that European man has forgotten these stages; and that is partly because Christianity deals with instantaneous conversion, as if the work had been done *by another.* But in ancient life, growth was thought of as slow, very slow, involving "stages" and a "journey."

I noticed stages clearly in Rainer Maria Rilke. He thought about the stages of growth; that's one reason he's been so important to me. He probably came out of Goethe, who developed in reaction to the eighteenth century. The eighteenth century felt that there was a static truth, and your job was to apprehend it. When Freud arrived, it became apparent that all that stability was nonsense. Or perhaps the First World War made it clear. But, now, I don't really enjoy poetry unless I can sense in it some awareness of a journey.

JS: Does this journey correspond to the Jungian idea of "individuation"?

RB: Yes, with interesting differences! The word "individuation" implies that the aim of the journey is to become more individual. Who can say if that is the aim? It is as if the ego had chosen that word.

JS: Part of the journey that you've written a lot about is the awareness of "mother consciousness" and the integration of this consciousness. You focused on this in *Sleepers Joining Hands*. Do you feel that mother consciousness is now growing in our society? Do you see any evidence of it in contemporary poetry?

RB: We'd need several hours to be fair to this question! Unfairly, we could say that in the sixties we saw the positive side of mother consciousness, and now we're going to see the negative side. If we look at mother consciousness not on its divine side, but on its earth side, increasing mother consciousness means that women are becoming more possessive of young boys, more wild and violent in their anti-abortion attitudes, more intolerant in general. Armies continue the discipline that mothers begin. A lot of women support militarism now; Margaret Thatcher shows how that's done in the "ruling circles." A dark side of mother consciousness is possessiveness, holding on to sons, while rejecting daughters. With sons, it acts to interfere with or block the effort of older men to pull the younger men on into spirit. The Industrial Revolution has damaged, by pulling the man out of the house, the old community of men. The old men are not able to "initiate" the young men as old men did in ancient times. Reagan's administration shows already a great decline in the positive side of mother consciousness; plans to help schoolchildren, the poor and old, or people being tortured have already been dropped.

JS: You've been doing a lot of seminars on fairy tales for couples and lovers, on the relevance of fairy tales to relationships. Is this also related to mother consciousness and the masculine/feminine split?

RB: I consider fairy tales to be the oldest literature left in Europe, maybe ten to twenty thousand years old. They differ from much literature we have had in the last two thousand years in that they don't put much emphasis on the social milieu. Balzac and Tolstoy are masters of the social milieu, the thousand details of the social environment. Fairy stories talk about the possibilities for development in the genes, and how these possibilities slowly unfold in fortunate circumstances—not in all circumstances. The possibility of "separates" developing into "wholes," male and female developing into a more unified being—these possibilities lie deep inside fairy stories. Those concerns are more within the area of poetry than of fiction. Explaining human personality through the influence of the social is simply not where fairy stories are at all. Most novelists belong either to the right or left. Fairy stories are deeply non-Marxist, deeply nonliberal, and deeply nonconservative. (*Laughter*.)

JS: Speaking in political terms, you've been characterized in the past as a sort of radical, or *enfant terrible* of American poetry, but those terms seem to refer to your thematic content, while your poetic style has not been characterized as radical. Is this a deliberate choice on your part? Is there a specific reason for keeping your poetics nonradical, but more clear?

RB: I have said that American poetry is too old-fashioned, in that it leans toward Renaissance English solutions of poetical problems. If then someone believes that American poetry should be close to English poetry, they consider me a terrible radical. If someone senses that I like English poetry, but long for a new opening, then they say, "Oh, he's right down the line. He's moderate."

Often in the United States, being radical in poetics means not studying anything. Writing poetry well now means a lot of study; to find a way out we need to go back before the Renaissance. I've been sensing lately that there are certain parts of *Beowulf* that are deeper psychologically than anything I've found in psychology. . . . Pound and Eliot were interested in exploring new ways, but they were right-wing politically. And I'm not right-wing politically. It is very odd that with us the major pioneers have been right-wing, while in South America the major pioneers have been left-wing. I really don't understand it at all.

JS: You've talked about form and content being sometimes in conflict with one another; maybe that's part of it. You were saying earlier that you saw Pound as having destroyed form and, if I remember correctly, you said, "Once you've destroyed form, what have you got left?"

RB: Eliot and Pound experienced the shock of the First World War. Thinkers at that time surmised that the huge European cultural forms were so lacking in what Jung called the "shadow," that the shadow simply arose and smashed the whole civilization. Eliot and Pound felt it their duty then to smash the smaller forms which contained also a parallel exclusion of the shadow. That's why the first draft of *The Waste Land* included a parody of eighteenth-century poetry.

But we are past that time now. No one alive feels physically that anger at forms. So to follow their poetics is silly. People are not feeling it; Poundians are just doing it by rote. We're in a different era. What are we feeling physically? Enough destruction of European forms has taken place now; in fact, they're almost all destroyed. But human beings cannot live with destroyed forms, unless they live the way that rats do. The job we have as writers is very different from the job Pound and Eliot had. One needs positive energy and a fresh view to move beyond their world. I know you think a lot of Gary Snyder's work, and we sense that he is not continually looking at the ruins and exulting and saying, "Isn't it wonderful. Everything is ruined." Instead he tries to see some way out of the valley.

JS: Snyder, though, is someone who is singular for his prosodic invention: very inventive use of line breaks, of appearance of lines on the page, of punctuation, spelling.

RB: I'm not sure that is a contradiction; he wants to establish a believable style, in which truths could be said. He does have a great suspicion of European culture in general, and finds the American Indian culture more healthy; perhaps his suspicion is a hangover from the Eliot generation.

JS: One question about politics. The political climate is a lot different than the 1960s. There may be a few similarities, but what we used to think of as "the movement" seems to have pretty much either disintegrated, fragmented, or broken down, or else has been absorbed by the establishment. Do you have any views on the reasons for this happening?

RB: Well, I think we're back in a normal state now, in which the right-wing is basically in control, and everything is conservative. I think some seeds of the sixties will come back, but in general what it proved to me is that if you have a population composed mainly of mother-dominated boys, and mother-rejected girls, the political movement that you make will be ineffective, and will disappear within four or five years. It's a very depressing conclusion, but that's the way it seems to me. . . .

JS: Any idea of what's next?

RB: (*Plays dulcimer.*) I never answer questions about the future!

Bibliography

My sources for the selected bibliography which follows include *Poetry East*, no. 4/5 (Spring–Summer 1981), edited by Richard Jones and Kate Daniels (published in 1981 by Beacon Press as *Of Solitude and Silence: Writings on Robert Bly*); "On Robert Bly and His Poems: A Selected Bibliography" by Samuel H. McMillan, published in the *Tennessee Poetry Journal 2*, no. 2 (Spring 1969); and *Moving Inward: A Study of Robert Bly's Poetry* by Ingegard Friberg (1977). I would like to thank Richard Gambrell for a copy of his annotated bibliography; the Watershed Foundation for their catalogue of commercially available cassette tapes; and the Goldfarb Library of Brandeis University for its research facilities. I would also like to thank Robert Bly for his time, his suggestions, and his help. *Note:* An asterisk indicates that the work is included in this volume.

I. By Robert Bly

POETRY

Silence in the Snowy Fields. Middletown, Conn.: Wesleyan University Press, 1962; London: Cape, 1967.
The Light Around the Body. New York: Harper & Row, 1967; London: Rapp & Whiting, 1968.
Chrysanthemums. Menomonie, Wis.: Ox Head Press, 1967.
Ducks. Menomonie, Wis.: Ox Head Press, 1967.
The Morning Glory: Another Thing That Will Never Be My Friend. Twelve Prose Poems. San Francisco: Kayak Books, 1969; rev. ed. 1970.
The Teeth-Mother Naked At Last. San Francisco: City Lights Books, 1970; Millwood, N.Y.: Kraus Reprint Company, 1973.
Christmas Eve Service at Midnight at St. Michael's. Rushden, Northamptonshire, U.K.: Sceptre Press, 1972.
Water Under the Earth. Rushden, Northamptonshire, U.K.: Sceptre Press, 1972.

The Dead Seal Near McClure's Beach. Denver: Straight Creek Journal, 1972.
Jumping Out of Bed. Barre, Mass.: Barre, 1973.
Sleepers Joining Hands. New York: Harper & Row, 1973.
The Hockey Poem. Duluth, Minn.: Knife River Press, 1974.
Old Man Rubbing His Eyes. Greensboro, N.C.: Unicorn Press, 1975.
Point Reyes Poems. Half Moon Bay, Calif.: Mudra, 1974.
The Morning Glory. New York: Harper & Row, 1975.
The Loon. Marshall, Minn.: Ox Head Press, 1977.
This Body Is Made of Camphor and Gopherwood. New York: Harper & Row, 1977.
Visiting Emily Dickinson's Grave. Madison, Wis.: Red Ozier Press, 1979.
This Tree Will Be Here for a Thousand Years. New York: Harper & Row, 1979.
What the Fox Agreed to Do. Athens, Ohio: Croissant & Company, 1979. Pamphlet.
Finding an Old Ant Mansion. Knotting, Bedford, U.K.: Martin Booth, 1981.
The Man in the Black Coat Turns. New York: The Dial Press, 1981.

TRANSLATIONS

Hans Hvass. *Reptiles and Amphibians of the World*. New York: Grosset & Dunlap, 1960.
Georg Trakl. *Twenty Poems of Georg Trakl*. Trans. James Wright and Robert Bly. Madison, Minn.: The Sixties Press, 1961.
Selma Lagerlöf. *The Story of Gösta Berling*. New York: New American Library, 1962.
Cesar Vallejo. *Twenty Poems of Cesar Vallejo*. Trans. Robert Bly, James Wright, and John Knoepfle. Madison, Minn.: The Sixties Press, 1962.
Tomas Tranströmer. *Three Poems*. Trans. Robert Bly, Eric Sellin, and Thomas Buckman. Lawrence, Kans.: T. Williams, 1966.
Knut Hamsun. *Hunger*. New York: Farrar, Straus, 1967; London: Duckworth, 1974.
Gunnar Ekelöf. *I Do Best Alone at Night*. Trans. Robert Bly and Christina Paulston. Washington, D.C.: Charioteer Press, 1968.
Gunnar Ekelöf. *Late Arrival on Earth: Selected Poems of Gunnar Ekelöf*. Trans. Robert Bly and Christina Paulston. London: Rapp & Carroll, 1967.

Yvan Goll. *Selected Poems*. Trans. Robert Bly and others. San Francisco: Kayak Books, 1968.

Pablo Neruda. *Twenty Poems of Pablo Neruda*. Trans. James Wright and Robert Bly. Madison, Minn.: The Sixties Press, 1968; London: Rapp & Whiting, 1968.

Juan Ramón Jiménez. *Forty Poems of Juan Ramón Jiménez*. Madison, Minn.: The Seventies Press, 1970.

Tomas Tranströmer. *Twenty Poems by Tomas Tranströmer*. Madison, Minn.: The Seventies Press, 1970.

Pablo Neruda and Cesar Vallejo. *Neruda and Vallejo: Selected Poems*. Trans. Robert Bly, John Knoepfle, and James Wright. Boston: Beacon Press, 1971.

Kabir. *The Fish in the Sea Is Not Thirsty: Versions of Kabir*. Northwood Narrows, N.H.: Lillabulero Press, 1971; Calcutta: A Writers Workshop Publication, 1972.

Tomas Tranströmer. *Night Vision*. Northwood Narrows, N.H.: Lillabulero Press, 1971; London: London Magazine Editions, 1972.

Rainer Maria Rilke. *Ten Sonnets to Orpheus*. San Francisco: Zephyrus Image, 1972.

Miguel Hernandez and Blas De Otero. *Selected Poems*. Trans. Timothy Baland, Robert Bly, Hardie St. Martin, and James Wright. Boston: Beacon Press, 1972.

Basho. *Basho*. San Francisco: Mudra, 1972.

Federico García Lorca and Juan Ramón Jiménez. *Lorca and Jimenez: Selected Poems*. Boston: Beacon Press, 1973.

Tomas Tranströmer. *Elegy, Some October Notes*. Rushden, Northamptonshire, U.S.: Sceptre Press, 1973.

Kabir. *Grass from Two Years*. Denver: Ally Press, 1975.

Kabir. *Twenty-Eight Poems*. New York: Siddha Yoga Dham, 1975.

Harry Martinson, Gunnar Ekelöf, and Tomas Tranströmer. *Friends, You Drank Some Darkness*. Boston: Beacon Press, 1975.

Kabir. *The Darkness of Night*. Ruffsdale, Pa.: Rook Press, 1976. Broadside.

Kabir. *Try to Live to See This: Versions of Kabir*. Denver: Ally Press, 1976; Rushden, Northamptonshire, U.K.: Sceptre Press, 1976.

Vicente Aleixandre. *Twenty Poems of Vicente Aleixandre*. Madison, Minn.: The Seventies Press, 1977.

Rolf Jacobsen. *Twenty Poems of Rolf Jacobsen*. Madison, Minn.: The Seventies Press, 1977.

Kabir. *The Kabir Book: Forty-Four of the Ecstatic Poems of Kabir*. Boston: Beacon Press, 1977.

Rainer Maria Rilke. *The Voices*. Denver: Ally Press, 1977; London: Sceptre Press, 1977.

Antonio Machado. *I Never Wanted Fame: Ten Poems and Proverbs*. St. Paul, Minn.: Ally Press, 1979.

Tomas Tranströmer. *Truth Barriers*. San Francisco: Sierra Club Books, 1980.

Mirabai. *Mirabai Versions*. New York: Red Ozier Press, 1980.

Rainer Maria Rilke. *October Day and Other Poems*. N.p., Calif.: Calloipea Press, 1981.

Rainer Maria Rilke. *Selected Poems of Rainer Maria Rilke*. New York: Harper & Row, 1981.

Mawlānā Jalāl al-Dīn Rūmī. *Night & Sleep*. With Coleman Barks. Cambridge, Mass.: Yellow Moon Press, 1981.

ANTHOLOGIES AND ESSAYS

The Lion's Tail and Eyes: Poems Written Out of Laziness and Silence. Madison, Minn.: The Sixties Press, 1962. Includes poetry by Robert Bly, James Wright, and William Duffy.

A Poetry Reading Against the Vietnam War. Edited by Robert Bly and David Ray. Madison, Minn.: American Writers Against the Vietnam War, The Sixties Press, 1966.

The Sea and the Honeycomb: A Book of Tiny Poems. Edited by Robert Bly. Madison, Minn.: The Sixties Press, 1966; Boston: Beacon Press, 1971.

Forty Poems Touching on Recent American History. Edited by Robert Bly. Madison, Minn.: The Sixties Press, 1966; Boston: Beacon Press, 1970.

Leaping Poetry: An Idea with Poems and Translations. Edited by Robert Bly. Boston: Beacon Press, 1975.

David Ignatow: Selected Poems. Edited by Robert Bly. Middletown, Conn.: Wesleyan University Press, 1975.

News of the Universe: Poems of Twofold Consciousness. Edited by Robert Bly. San Francisco: Sierra Club Books, 1980.

The Fifties #1, #2, #3. Edited by Robert Bly and William Duffy. Geneva, N.Y.: Hobart and William Smith Colleges Press, 1981.

The Sixties #4, #5, #6. Edited by Robert Bly and William Duffy. Geneva, N.Y.: Hobart and William Smith Colleges Press, 1982.

The Eight Stages of Translation. Boston: Rowan Tree Press, 1983.

"Five Decades of Modern American Poetry." *The Fifties* 1 (1958):36–39.

"On English and American Poetry." *The Fifties* 2 (1959):45–47.

"Some Thoughts on Lorca and René Char." *The Fifties* 3 (1959):7–9.

"On Current Poetry in America." *The Sixties* 4 (1960):28–29.

"Some Notes on French Poetry." *The Sixties* 5 (1961):66–70.

"Prose Versus Poetry." *Choice* 2 (1962):65–80.

"A Wrong Turning in American Poetry." *Choice* 3 (1963):33–47.

"The Surprise of Neruda." *The Sixties* 7 (1964):18–19.

"Concerning the Little Magazines: Something Like a Symposium." *Carleton Miscellany* 2 (1966):20–22.

"The Dead World and the Live World." *The Sixties* 8 (1966):2–7.

"Robert Lowell's *For the Union Dead*." *The Sixties* 8 (1966):93–96.

"The First Ten Issues of *Kayak*." *Kayak* 12 (1967):45–49.

"Looking for Dragon Smoke." *Stand* 9, no. 1 (1967):102.

"The Collapse of James Dickey." *The Sixties* 9 (1967):70–79.

"Leaping Up into Political Poetry." *London Magazine* 7 (1967):82–87.

"On Pablo Neruda." *Nation*, March 25, 1968, pp. 414–18.

"Some Notes on Donald Hall." *Field*, no. 2 (1970):57–61.

"American Poetry: On the Way to the Hermetic." *Books Abroad* (now *World Literature Today*) 46 (Winter 1972):17–24.

"Developing the Underneath." *American Poetry Review* 2 (March/April 1973):44–45.

"The Network and the Community." *American Poetry Review* 3 (January/February 1974):19–21.

"Reflections on the Origins of Poetic Form." *Field*, no. 10 (1974):31–35.

"The Writer's Sense of Place." *South Dakota Review* 13, no. 3 (1975):73–75.

"A Note on James Wright." *Ironwood* 10 (1977):64.

"Tranströmer and the Memory." *Ironwood* 13 (1979):84–87.

"The Stages of an Artist's Life." *Georgia Review* 34 (1980):105–9.

"Recognizing the Image as a Form of Intelligence." *Field*, no. 24 (1981):17–27.

"What Whitman Did Not Give Us." In *Walt Whitman: The Measure of His Song*, ed. Jim Perlman et al. Minneapolis: Holy Cow! Press, 1981, pp. 321–34.

"Form That Is Neither In nor Out." *Poetry East*, no. 4/5 (1981):29–34.

"The Witch, the Swan, and the Middle Class." *Plainsong* 3, no. 2 (1981):18–33.

ROBERT BLY ON TAPE

Robert Bly. Reading at the YMHA New York Poetry Center. Washington, D.C.: The Poets' Audio Center, The Watershed Foundation, 1966.
Robert Bly. Contemporary American Poets Series. Washington, D.C.: The Poets' Audio Center, The Watershed Foundation, 1972.
For the Stomach: Selected Poems. Black Box #3. Washington, D.C.: The Poets' Audio Center, The Watershed Foundation, 1974.
Crisis in American Poetry. Seattle, Wash.: Omega Institute West, 1980.
Poems and Stories. Seattle, Wash.: Omega Institute West, 1980.

II. About Robert Bly

BOOKS

Bly, Robert. *Talking All Morning*. Ann Arbor: University of Michigan Press, 1980.
Friberg, Ingegard. *Moving Inward: A Study of Robert Bly's Poetry*. Gotenborg: Acta Universitatis Gothoburgensis, 1977.
Jones, Richard and Kate Daniels, eds. *Of Solitude and Silence: Writings on Robert Bly*. Boston: Beacon Press, 1981.
Nelson, Howard. *Robert Bly: An Introduction to the Poetry*. New York: Columbia University Press, 1984.

ARTICLES AND CHAPTERS IN BOOKS

Alexander, Franklyn. "Robert Bly." *Great Lakes Review: A Journal of Midwest Culture* 3 (1976):66–69.
Altieri, C. F. "Varieties of Immanentist Experience: Robert Bly, Charles Olson, and Frank O'Hara." In *Enlarging the Temple*. Lewisburg, Pa.: Bucknell University Press, 1979), pp. 78–93.*
Atkinson, Michael. "Sleepers Joining Hands: Shadow and Self." *Iowa Review* 7 (Winter 1976):135–53.
Brooks, Cleanth. "Poetry Since *The Waste Land*." *Southern Review* 1 (1965):498–99.
Collins, Douglas. "To the Editor:" *Lillabulero* 4 (1967):60–61.
Dacey, Philip. "The Reverend Robert E. Bly, Pastor, Church of the Blessed Unity." In *A Book of Rereadings,* ed. Greg Kuzma. Lincoln, Nebr.: Best Cellar Press, 1979, pp. 1–7.

Davis, William Virgil. "Hair in a Baboon's Ear: The Politics of Robert Bly's Early Poetry." *Carleton Miscellany* 18 (1979–80):74–84.

Dickey, James. *Spinning the Crystal Ball*. Washington, D.C.: Library of Congress, 1967, pp. 8–10. Pamphlet.*

Faas, Eckbert. "Robert Bly." *Boundary 2* 4 (1976):707–25.*

Garrett, George. "Against the Grain: Poets Writing Today." In *American Poetry*, ed. Irvin Ehrenpreis. New York: St. Martin's Press, 1965), pp. 221–39.

Gitzen, Julian. "Floating on Solitude: The Poetry of Robert Bly." *Modern Poetry Studies* 7 (1976):231–40.

Hall, Donald. Introduction. *Contemporary American Poetry*. Baltimore: Penguin Books, 1962; 1969.*

Harris, Victoria. " 'Walking Where the Plows Have Been Turning': Robert Bly and Female Consciousness." *Poetry East,* no. 4/5 (1981):123–38.*

––––––. "Landscape of Affirmation: Two Early Poems of Robert Bly." *Plainsong* 3, no. 2 (1981):37–40.

Heyen, William. "Inward to the World: The Poetry of Robert Bly." *The Far Point* 3 (1969):42–50.*

Hoffman, Frederick, J. "Contemporary American Poetry." In *Patterns of Commitment in American Literature,* ed. M. La France. Toronto: University of Toronto Press, 1967, pp. 193–207.

Howard, Richard. "Robert Bly." In *Alone With America*. New York: Atheneum, 1969; rev. ed., 1980, pp. 57–67.*

Janssens, G. A. M. "The Present State of American Poetry: Robert Bly and James Wright." *English Studies* 51 (1970):112–37.

Kinnell, Galway. "Poetry, Personality and Death." *Field,* no. 4 (1971):56–60.

Komie, Lowell. "Ecstasy and Poetry in Chicago: A Middle-Aged Lawyer Goes to his First Poetry Reading." *Harper's,* March 1978, pp. 129–31.

Lacey, Paul A. "The Live World." In *The Inner War: Forms and Themes in Recent American Poetry*. Philadelphia: Fortress Press, 1972.

Lammon, Marty. "Something Hard to Get Rid of—An Interview with Robert Bly." *Ploughshares* 8, no. 1 (March 1982):11–23.

Lensing, G. S. and R. Moran. *Four Poets and the Emotive Imagination: Robert Bly, James Wright, Louis Simpson, and William Stafford*. Baton Rouge: Louisiana State University Press, 1976, pp. 71–85.

Libby, Anthony. "Fire and Light: Four Poets to the End and Beyond." *Iowa Review* 4 (Spring 1973):111–26.

––––––. "Robert Bly Alive in Darkness." *Iowa Review* 3 (Summer 1972):78–91.*

_____. "Roethke—Water Father." *American Literature* 46 (November 1974):267–88.

_____. "Dreaming of Animals." *Plainsong* 3, no. 2 (1981):47–54.

McPherson, Sandra. "You Can Say That Again (Or Can You?)." *Iowa Review* 3 (Summer 1972):70–75.

Martin, Peter. "Robert Bly: Poet on the Road Home." *The Straight Creek Journal,* October 24, 1972, pp. 10–16.

Matthews, William. "Thinking About Robert Bly." *Tennessee Poetry Journal* 2, no. 2 (1969):49–57.*

Mersmann, James F. "Robert Bly: Watering the Rocks." In *Out of the Vietnam Vortex: A Study of Poets and Poetry Against the War.* Lawrence, Kans.: University Press of Kansas, 1974), pp. 113–57.*

Mills, Ralph J. " 'The Body With the Lamp Lit Inside': Robert Bly's New Poems." *Northeast,* series 3 (Winter 1966–67):37–47.

_____. " 'Of Energy Compacted and Whirling': Robert Bly's Recent Prose Poems." *New Mexico Humanities Review* 4, no. 2 (1981):29–49.*

Molesworth, Charles. "Contemporary Poetry and the Metaphors for the Poem." *Georgia Review* 32 (Summer 1978):3i9–31.

_____. "Domestication of the Sublime: Bly's Latest Poems." *Ohio Review* 19, no. 3 (1978):56–66.

_____. " 'Rejoice in the Gathering Dark': The Poetry of Robert Bly." In *The Fierce Embrace: A Study of Contemporary American Poetry.* Columbia, Mo.: University of Missouri Press, 1979, pp. 112–38.*

Mooney, Stephen. "On Bly's Poetry." *Tennessee Poetry Journal* 2, no. 2 (1969):16–18.

Nelson, Howard. "Welcoming Shadows: Robert Bly's Recent Poetry." *Hollins Critic* 12 (1975):1–15.

Novak, Robert. "What I Have Written Is Not Good Enough: The Poetry of Robert Bly." *Windless Orchard* 18 (1974):30–34.

Oates, Joyce Carol. "When They All Are Sleeping." *Modern Poetry Studies* 4 (1973):341–44.

Quinn, Fran. "An Essay in Five Disconnected Sections on the Great Mother Conferences." *Plainsong* 3, no. 2 (1981):43–46.

Rexroth, Kenneth. "The New American Poets." *Harper's,* June 1965, pp. 65–71.

Shakarchi, Joseph. "An Interview with Robert Bly." *Massachusetts Review* 23 (1982):226–43.*

Simpson, Louis. *North of Jamaica.* New York: Harper & Row, 1972, pp. 208–16; 239–42.*

Stepanchev, Stephen. "The Subjective Image." In *American Poetry Since*

1945: A Critical Survey. New York: Harper & Row, 1965, pp. 185–87.

Stitt, Peter. "James Wright: The Art of Poetry XIX." *Paris Review* 62 (1975):48–50.*

———. "James Wright and Robert Bly." *Hawaii Review* 2 (1973):89–94.

Thomas, Ben. "Bly and Tradition: Lighted by Fire from Within." *Tennessee Poetry Journal* 1, no. 2 (1968):19–22.

Thurley, George. "Devices Among Words: Kinnell, Bly, Simic." In *The American Moment.* London: Edward Arnold, 1977, pp. 210–28.

Tranströmer, Tomas. "Two Poets Translating." *Translation* 4 (1977):47–58.*

———. "Letters to Bly." *Ironwood* 13 (1979):94–101.

Ventura, Michael. "Robert Bly—The Poet Who Moves His Arms a Lot." *L. A. Weekly,* February 12–18, 1982, pp. 6–9; 89.

Williams, Miller. "Intuition, Spontaneity, Organic Wholeness and the Redemptive Wilderness: Some (Old) Currents in Contemporary Poetry." *The Smith,* no. 18 (1975):141–51.

Williamson, Alan. "Language Against Itself: The Middle Generation of Contemporary Poets." In *American Poetry Since 1960: Some Critical Perspectives,* ed. Robert Shaw. Chester Springs, Pa.: Dufour, 1974, pp. 55–67.

Zweig, Paul. "The American Outsider." *Nation,* November 14, 1966, pp. 517–19.

REVIEWS

"Alienation and Acclaim." *Times Literary Supplement,* November 14, 1968, p. 1285. Review of *Twenty Poems of Pablo Neruda.*

Brownjohn, Alan. "Pre-Beat." *New Statesman,* August 2, 1968, p. 146. Review of *The Light Around the Body.*

Carroll, Paul. "On Bly's Kabir." *American Poetry Review* 8 (January/February 1979):30–31.

Carruth, Hayden. "Poets on the Fringe: *This Tree Will Be Here for a Thousand Years.*" *Harper's,* January 1980, p. 79.

Case, L. L. "Robert Bly and David Ray, eds.: *A Poetry Reading Against the Vietnam War.*" *El Corno Emplumado* 23 (1967):148–50.

Cavich, David. "The Poet as Victim and Victimizer." *New York Times Book Review,* February 18, 1973, pp. 2–3. Review of *Sleepers Joining Hands.*

"Chained to the Parish Pump." *Times Literary Supplement,* March 16, 1967, p. 220. Review of *Silence in the Snowy Fields.*

Cotter, James F. "Poetry Reading." *Hudson Review* 31 (1978):214–15. Review of *This Body Is Made of Camphor and Gopherwood.*

Dacey, Philip. "This Book Is Made of Turkey Soup and Star Music." *Parnassus: Poetry in Review* 7 (1978):34–45.

Davis, William V. "Defining the Age." *Moons and Lion Tailes* 2 (1977):85–89. Review of *The Morning Glory.*

Davison, Peter. "New Poetry: The Generation of the Twenties." *Atlantic Monthly,* February 1968, pp. 141–42. Review of *Light.*

Fowlie, Wallace. "Not Bards So Much as Catalyzers." *New York Times Book Review,* March 12, 1963, p. 36. Review of *Silence.*

Friedman, Norman. "The Wesleyan Poets—III: The Experimental Poets." *Chicago Review* 19 (1967):52–73. Review of *Silence.**

Gifford, Henry. "The Master of Pain." *Poetry* 105 (December 1964):196–97. Review of *Twenty Poems of Cesar Vallejo.*

Gitlin, Todd. "The Return of Political Poetry." *Commonweal,* July 23, 1971, pp. 375–80. Review of *Forty Poems Touching on Recent American History.*

Goldman, Michael. "Joyful in the Dark." *New York Times Book Review,* February 18, 1968, pp. 10; 12. Review of *Light.*

Guest, Barbara. "Shared Landscapes." *Chelsea* 16 (1965):150–52. Review of *Silence.*

Gunn, Thom. "Poems and Books of Poems." *Yale Review* 53 (1963):142. Review of *Silence.*

Hall, Donald. "Notes on Robert Bly and *Sleepers Joining Hands.*" *Ohio Review* 15, no. 1 (1973):89–93.*

Hammer, Louis Z. "Moths in the Light." *Kayak* 14 (1968):63–67. Review of *Light.*

Helms, Alan. "Two Poets." *Partisan Review* 44 (1977):284–88. Review of *Sleepers.*

Holmes, Theodore. "Wit, Nature and the Human Concern." *Poetry* 100 (August 1962):319–24. Review of *Twenty Poems of Georg Trakl.*

Howard, Richard. "Poetry Chronicle." *Poetry* 102 (June 1963):182–92. Review of *Silence.*

Hughes, D. J. "The Demands of Poetry." *Nation,* January 1963, pp. 17–18. Review of *Silence.*

Kenner, Hugh. "Three Poets." *New York Times Book Review,* January 1, 1978, p. 10. Review of *This Body.**

Leibowitz, Herbert. "Questions of Reality." *Hudson Review* 21 (August 1968):553–57. Review of *Light.*

Logan, John. "Poetry Shelf." *Critic* 21 (January 1963):84–85. Review of *Silence*.

Lyne, Sandford. "Review: *News of the Universe* and *Talking All Morning*." *Poetry East* 3 (1980):80–83.

Mazzocco, Robert. "Jeremiads at Half-Mast." *New York Review of Books,* June 20, 1968, pp. 22–25. Review of *Light*.*

Mills, Ralph J. "Five Anthologies." *Poetry* 109 (February 1967):345–50. Review of *A Poetry Reading Against the Vietnam War*.

Molesworth, Charles. Review of *This Body. Georgia Review* 32 (Fall 1978):683–88.

Mueller, Lisel. "Five Poets." *Shenandoah* 19 (1968):65–72. Review of *Light*.

Palmer, Penelope. "Review of *Twenty Poems of Pablo Neruda*." *Agenda* 6, no. 3 (1968):124–28.

Punter, David. "Robert Bly: Gone Fishing for the Sign." *Modern Poetry Studies* 10 (1981):241–45. Review of *Talking All Morning*.

Ray, David. "Robert Bly." *Epoch* 12 (Winter 1963):186–88. Review of *Silence*.

Root, William Pitt. "Comment." *Poetry* 123 (October 1973):34–56. Review of *The Sea and the Honeycomb* and *Twenty Poems of Tomas Tranströmer*.

Simon, John. "More Brass Than Enduring." *Hudson Review* 15 (1962):455–68. Review of *Georg Trakl*.

Simpson, Louis. "New Books of Poems." *Harper's,* August 1968, pp. 73–77. Review of *Light*.

Stitt, Peter. Review of *This Tree. Georgia Review* 34 (Fall 1980):663–66.
——— . "Dark Volumes." *New York Times Book Review,* February 14, 1982, p. 15. Review of *The Man in the Black Coat Turns*.*

Taylor, W. E. "The Chief." *Poetry, Florida And . . .* 1 (1968):12–16. Review of *Light*.

Wesling, Donald. "The Recent Work of Donald Hall and Robert Bly." *Michigan Quarterly Review* 1 (Winter 1981):144–54. Review of *This Tree* and *Talking All Morning*.

Williamson, Alan. "Music to Your Ears." *New York Times Book Review,* March 9, 1980, pp. 8–9; 14–15. Review of *This Tree*.*

POETS ON POETRY   Donald Hall, General Editor

Poets on Poetry collects critical books by contemporary poets,
gathering together the articles, interviews, and book reviews
by which they have articulated the poetics of a new generation.

Goatfoot Milktongue Twinbird
Donald Hall

Walking Down the Stairs
Galway Kinnell

Writing the Australian Crawl
William Stafford

Trying to Explain
Donald Davie

To Make a Prairie
Maxine Kumin

Toward a New Poetry
Diane Wakoski

Talking All Morning
Robert Bly

Pot Shots at Poetry
Robert Francis

Open Between Us
David Ignatow

The Old Poetries and the New
Richard Kostelanetz

A Company of Poets
Louis Simpson

Don't Ask
Philip Levine

Living Off the Country
John Haines

Parti-Colored Blocks for a Quilt
Marge Piercy

The Weather for Poetry
Donald Hall

Collected Prose
James Wright

Old Snow Just Melting
Marvin Bell

Writing Like a Woman
Alicia Ostriker

A Ballet for the Ear
John Logan

Effluences from the Sacred Caves
Hayden Carruth

Collected Prose
Robert Hayden

Platonic Scripts
Donald Justice